Starwalker Press

MYTHOLOGY OF THE PRENATAL LIFE

This book first appeared in 1960 as a privately published monograph. It is a companion volume and sequel to *The Nature of the Self*, written in 1959 and re-published in 2012 by Starwalker Press. These two books represent the crowning achievement of the author, Francis J. Mott, a prolific writer whose work was far ahead of its time. During the 1970s, he corresponded with the influential and innovative psychiatrist R. D. Laing, who in turn studied and annotated a copy of *Mythology of the Prenatal Life*. Here, this unique material is published for the first time, in facsimile handwriting, so the reader can follow the thoughts and associations of R. D. Laing himself as he read through the text.

Francis J. Mott was born in England in 1901; in spite of ill-health as a child and little formal schooling, he showed a precocious intelligence which led him eventually to study the work of many controversial and innovative thinkers, some of whom he met in person. The list includes Otto Rank and Nandor Fodor, former protégés of Sigmund Freud, and among the first people to write about prenatal experience in a psychological and spiritual context. Francis J. Mott spent time in the USA and Canada, where he found the principal audience for his developing ideas concerning a universal pattern of creation in the natural world, which included human experience. He lectured, conducted group psychology and individual dream analysis, wrote and published several books. As a platform for this work, he founded a group which came to be known as 'The Society of Life'. He served in the Canadian Air Force in World War II, until his discharge in 1945 when he returned to England. In 1933 he married Gwendolen Mayhew, his support in every way until his death in 1980; they had two children.

Francis J. Mott was intellectually vigorous, pursuing with passion his research and publishing his writings until the last year of his life.

In writing *The Nature of the Self,* Francis J. Mott draws on extensive case material, particularly dreams, to unravel the mysteries of the world of pre- and perinatal experience, and to demonstrate how the residue of this realm is reflected in our post-natal life, in symptoms of various kinds – physical, emotional and mental. He also demonstrated how these intrauterine dynamics inform familiar symbolic and mythological themes. *Mythology of the Prenatal Life* takes this exploration further with extensive detail, etymology and anthropological references concerning well-known mythic motifs. Anyone interested in the development of human consciousness is sure to find Mott's work to be truly revelatory. Artists, poets, healers, psychoanalysts, mythology enthusiasts, anthropologists and students of symbolism will discover here a rich and completely new understanding of the inner dimensions of human experience.

BY THE SAME AUTHOR

BOOKS
The Crisis of Opinion

The Meaning of the Zodiac

Biosynthesis

The Nature of the Self (Starwalker Press, 2012)

The Universal Design of Birth

The Universal Design of the Oedipus Complex

The Universal Design of Creation

Play Therapy and Infantile Paralysis

The Myth of a Chosen People

Doorknobia

Black Hand Over Europe (translation from French, original written by Henry Pozzi)

PLAYS
The Haunted Woman

The Little Robe (a version of *Oedipus Rex* written in the light of this book)

The Greater Power (radio play)

PUBLISHED PAPERS
Oedipus and Beyond

Drama and the Evocation of Unconscious Images

A Pulmonary Conception Fantasy

The Concept of a Prenutritional Libido

Prehuman Stages of the Libido

The Libido as a Cloak of Intrauterine Affect

Mother Goose and the Gastrointestinal Tract

    The Psychoanalytic Review

    The Journal of Clinical Psychopathology

    The Psychiatric Quarterly

Copyright © Francis J. Mott 1960, 2013.
Annotations reproduced by kind permission of the Estate of R. D. Laing.
All rights reserved in all editions.

With the exception of brief quotations for review purposes,
no part of this book may be reproduced, shared, recorded,
stored or transmitted in any medium or form whatsoever
without prior written permission from the copyright owner.
1st edition 1960: monograph published by
The Integration Publishing Company, UK.
2nd edition 2013: revised edition, annotations by R. D. Laing,
Starwalker Press, London.

ISBN: 978-0-9558231-8-3

STARWALKER PRESS
BCM Starwalker
London WC1N 3XX
Email: enquiries@starwalkerpress.com
www.starwalkerpress.com

Printed by Lightning Source (UK, USA and Australia)
Editor: Melanie Reinhart
Cover and page design: Tamara Stamenkovic
Back cover quote: R. D. Laing, letter to Barrie Reynolds, June 1977.
Glasgow University Library Special Collections, MS Laing L336/19
Engraving: Robert Fludd, *Utrius Cosmi (1617)*
Image: Linda Hall Library of Science, Engineering & Technology
Bibliographic research, editing, proof-reading: Salena Oppenheimer
Scan transcription: Loraine Mayers

Note: The material in this book is for education, research and
reference only. No part of it is intended to substitute for appropriate
professional treatment of medical, psychological or other conditions.

STARWALKER PRESS

Books for the healing journey

MYTHOLOGY OF THE PRENATAL LIFE

Francis J. Mott

CONTENTS

Publisher's Foreword, 9
Acknowledgements, 11
Chapter One: The Myth of the Shining One, 13
Chapter Two: The Mother and the Maiden, 90
Chapter Three: The Golden Bough, 106
Chapter Four: The Traveler and the River, 126
    The Twelve Labours of Hercules
    The Fight with the Nemean Lion, 134
    The Fight with the Lernean Hydra, 135
    The Struggle with the Kerneian Stag, 136
    The Erymanthian Boar, 137
    The Cleaning of the Stables of Augeias, 138
    The Killing of the Stymphalian Birds, 138
    The Capture of the Cretan Bull, 139
    The Capture of the Mares of Diomedes, 142
    The Capture of the Amazonian Girdle, 143
    The Capture of the Oxen of Geryones, 144
    The Recovery of the Golden Apples of the Hesperides, 145
    The Capture of Kerberos, 147
Chapter Five: The Significance of Salt, 156
    1. Mind, knowledge, wisdom and learning, 157
    2. Establishment of covenants, 158
    3. Money and wealth, 159
    4. Emblem of the immortal spirit, 159
    5. Movement and journey, 160
    6. Health and medicinal, 160
    7. Sexual desire and fecundity, 161
    8. Etymology, 162
    9. Rank, protocol and procedure, 163
Chapter Six: The Testimony of Thebes, 171
Appendices
    i. Notes on the Symbolic Representation of the Placenta and the Umbilical Cord by Primitive and Ancient Peoples, 190
    ii. The Uterine Symbolism of the Zodiac, 195
    iii. Original Foreword and Introduction (1960), unedited, 205
    iv. Jacob's Ladder: a summary of the author's main ideas, 210
Bibliography, 230
Permissions, 232
Notes, 235

PUBLISHER'S FOREWORD

Mythology of the Prenatal Life is the companion volume and sequel to *The Nature of the Self*, which is extensively referenced in the present volume, with page numbers noted in the text in square brackets. Familiarity with the material presented in *The Nature of the Self* will greatly enhance the reader's understanding and enjoyment of *Mythology of the Prenatal Life*, but for convenience, the author's main ideas are summarized in Appendix IV, in an edited version of his essay *Jacob's Ladder*.

Francis J. Mott's original foreword is included in full and unedited, in Appendix III. Here, he describes how, through his work analyzing dreams, he reached an understanding of the mind's nature which was nowhere to be found in the writings of Freud, Jung and other modern psychologists. This is as true today as it was then. For the mystery which was revealed to Mott concerns the hidden dynamics of the prenatal life, and how these are in turn repeated and reflected in postnatal life. In addition, this same 'Universal Design', as he called it, can be seen at various different levels of existence, from the sub-atomic, through the cellular, and also in the cosmic – from the microcosm to the macrocosm. He says, '… I was able to build up a sort of mosaic picture of the evolution of the individual mind'. These themes are explored extensively in *The Nature of the Self*.

Mott soon began to observe suggestive coincidences between this 'mosaic picture' and certain symbolic elements present in mythology, and he offers in *Mythology of the Prenatal Life* his elaboration of these themes, drawing extensively on the mythology of different cultures, anthropological material and biblical references. Mott was convinced that the symbolic content of dreams and myths tells the same story, namely the story of the evolution of the individual human mind as rooted in, but also transcending, the biological journey of gestation and birth, and onwards. The dream offers memory-fragments of that process, buried deep in the individual. The myth reflects those same memories, but given cultural and collective forms as they are projected into the social arena in order to give expression to the feelings which struggle in each individual mind. As well as a deeper understanding of personal and individual psychological processes, the understanding of Mott's work offers a deepened appreciation of the arts of story-telling, image-making, dance and drama as expressed through the great variety of different national and cultural forms, down the ages.

Mott came to realize that what he had discovered was relevant to all mankind, both now and in its ancient history, as the generative root of mythology may be found in the internal evidence of the personal and subjective feelings. He says, 'Further, where historical reasons for the coalescence of gods and heroes are lacking, or where new associations or the acquisition of new attributes affront their historical origins, the basis upon which such developments were made can be revealed by understanding the dreamlike associative processes of the mind'.

Once the 'generative root of mythology' is seen, the incoherence of apparently disparate archetypal stories which involve the gods and goddesses of different cultures becomes transformed into an appreciation of the underlying unity of all life. In this book, the depth and breadth of Mott's understanding offers the reader an inspirational and revelatory journey through intriguing territory, well-known and unfamiliar at the same time.

ACKNOWLEDGEMENTS

This edition of *Mythology of the Prenatal Life* has been in preparation since about 1984, when the late Brian Wade of 'Changes' bookshop, London, gave us a rare copy of the original monograph of this text, long before 'Starwalker Press' existed. Since then, many people have contributed to the process of making this revised edition available. In particular, grateful thanks is extended to the individuals mentioned below, with apologies to anyone who may have been omitted.

Richard Mowbray of the 'Open Centre', London, Maggie Hyde and Dr. Geoffrey Cornelius of the 'Company of Astrologers', all offered encouragement in numerous ways, including lending precious copies of Francis J. Mott's other works; Betty Hughes provided experiential demonstration of Mott's perspectives in the therapeutic context; Loraine Mayers converted the original monograph to editable text; Pamela Blair conducted research in the Glasgow University Library Special Collections; the estate of R. D. Laing gave permission to include his annotations; Dr. Dorian Gieseler Greenbaum was on hand just at the right moment with a most interesting etymological contribution; Sophia Smith offered her unflagging enthusiasm and engaged in numerous helpful conversations with the editor.

Tamara Stamenkovic designed two thematically matched covers, emphasizing the book's relationship with its 'root text', *The Nature of the Self*; she also transformed photo-scans of R. D. Laing's faint pencil handwriting into printable images. Salena Oppenheimer was involved throughout, in so many ways: researching unsourced quotes, co-editing the text and proof-reading. Her fine understanding of the material enabled her to offer numerous intelligent and valuable suggestions.

Finally, without the generosity and interest of the copyright holders, this book could not have evolved as it did. They agreed to the inclusion of the R. D. Laing annotations, and showed unfailing patience with the vagaries of a major revision. It is our hope that in publishing this edition, a long-held wish of Francis J. Mott will have been realized. In the original foreword, he wrote:

> *I look forward to the day when the demand for this work*
> *may be such as to warrant*
> *a full scale revision for its reproduction in print.*

CHAPTER ONE

The Myth of the Shining One

Scattered fragmentarily through human dreams, represented in the most diverse and superficially unlikely symbols, there lies the same testimony, which in the great myths is made sharp and clear. The most basic item of this testimony is that the unborn baby feels himself to be a shining nuclear focus lying within the sphere of the womb [9-17]. He feels that his skin is a coat of shining power [13] and that he is the veritable king of creation [83]. Yet he also feels that he occupies the magic cave of the womb with a mysterious twin, the placenta, who is at the same time lover and waste-pot, bloodsucker and restorer [18-42]. Into this mysterious twin he seems to plunge himself to be slain and renewed [27-28], and at the same time he feels that he pierces that twin with energy and is pierced by it in return [27]. All this is a superimposition of a cosmic configuration upon the flesh and blood of the uterine organism [16]. Dreams tell us what the cosmos impressed upon our flesh and blood, and myths do likewise. The uterine impression is the most basic, the most tremendous, and the one most emphatically presented in the myths. This great theme appears again and again in a myriad of symbolic forms, as illustrated by the instances which follow, which are by no means exhaustive. There is a vast work of synthesis yet to be done.

The first item which I shall adduce is the hymn to Zeus Diktaios, for knowledge of which I am indebted to the late Jane Harrison and her book *Themis: A Study of the Social Origins of Greek Religion*. Zeus, the Father God of the ancient Greeks, was fabled to have been born on the island of Crete. Upon a Cretan mountain named Dikte there is a cave where Zeus was by legend born. On the eastern coast of Crete, near the ancient town of Palaikastro, there was a temple dedicated to Zeus Diktaios, or the Zeus born on Dikte. Near the ruins of this ancient temple, the relics of a stele were found, and upon this stele were found parts of the hymn to the god. I shall first reproduce as much of the hymn as remains to us, and then seek to analyze it in terms of the statements at the head of this chapter, showing that Zeus was the Shining One, namely the unborn child bearing the impress of cosmic radiance. The hymn is the universal story of the feeling-drama which develops between the fetus and the placenta, which in turn becomes the instrument of the evocation of the soul from the cosmos [42]. Here are the translated relics of the Hymn to Zeus Diktaios:

> *Io, Kouros most Great, I give thee hail, Kronian, Lord of all that is wet and gleaming, thou art come at the head of thy Daimones. To Dikte for the Year, Oh, march, and rejoice in the dance and song, that we make to thee with harps and pipes mingled together, and sing as we come to a stand at thy well-fenced altar. For here the shielded Nurturers took thee, a child immortal, from Rhea, and with noise of beating feet hid thee away.*
>
> (Lacuna ...)
>
> *And the Horai began to be fruitful year by year and Dike to possess mankind, and all wild living things were held about by wealth-loving Peace. To us also leap for full jars, and leap for fleecy flocks, and leap for fields of fruit, and for hives to bring increase. Leap for our Cities, and leap for our sea-borne ships, and leap for our young citizens and for goodly Themis.*[1]

To find Zeus, the Father, hailed as 'Lord of all that is wet and gleaming' inevitably awakens the interest of one who, like myself, knows that the fetal skin feeling is constantly symbolized in dreams by light or fire [257-260]. It will be seen in the following pages that Zeus is not only 'Lord of the lightning' or 'Lord of the bright sky', but that his allied symbolism makes him patently a prime representative of the fetal skin feeling and its sense of 'shine'.

> *The supreme deity of the ancient Greeks, during their historical period at least, was Zeus. His name, referable to a root that means 'to shine', may be rendered 'the Bright One'.*[2]

Jane Harrison admits that the phrase 'wet and gleaming' may be an imperfect rendering of the hymn: 'Almighty Gleam', she says, would be simple and good. This may be so, and for our present purpose 'Almighty Gleam' is enough, though it is true that 'wetness' is often allied with 'shine' in symbols derived from modern dreams, perhaps owing to the fact that the fetal skin feeling is evoked in the waters of the amnion. Hence my tentative assumption that this Diktean Zeus is the representation of the fetal skin feeling, and what follows will not contradict it. Jane Harrison writes:

> *The opening words of the hymn are enough to startle the seven mythological sleepers ...*

because they presume to address Zeus as '*Kouros* most Great', which could be translated as the 'greatest of grown-up youths'. She continues:

> *To our unaccustomed ears the title sounds strange and barely reverent. 'Father,' and still more 'Mother,' and even 'Babe' are to us holy words, but a full-grown youth has to us no connotation of sanctity ... (The word) 'Kouros' connotes no relationship with a parent, it is simply 'young man just come to maturity'.*[3]

To invoke the Father as 'the greatest of young men just come to maturity' must seem odd to anyone who does not realize that the fetal skin feeling (the 'Almighty Gleam'!) is in fact the essence of the most primary maleness and of father feeling [175]. Once we understand this, we can see that the invocation to Zeus Diktaios is an effort to invoke in the depths of the self the nuclear power of the cosmos as evoked by the fetal skin. The 'Lord of Gleam' is the essence of that maleness so adequately expressed by the feelings and behavior of a young man just come to maturity. It is the essence of the fetal skin feeling.

The fetus generates the sense of nuclear skin feeling by sympathetic resonance with the cosmos. This feeling is the essence of what will be known to the child after birth as 'maleness'. It is the feeling also of light, of fire or, if you will, of 'gleam'. This Diktean Zeus, whose worship evokes these titles of primal maleness, gleaming and universal fatherhood is none other than the representative (the projection!) of the fetal skin feeling and its cosmic memories. The men and women who sang this hymn were not 'primitives'. Their origins already had a long history, obscured by the mixing of many tribal bloods. Their conscious minds had lost the direct sense of the fetal skin feeling and its cosmic elements, but they had not yet arrived at the stage where they would try, by high philosophic abstraction, to gain an intellectual sense of God. All they could do was to grope back through their feelings to the memory of the fetal skin feeling – to the primal sense of 'The Gleaming One' who was all male (*kouros*) – and through this to intuit the sense of the universal Father, the cosmic Nucleus, whose imprint the fetal self has taken on [83].

Where the fetal feelings are represented, there will also be found the representation of the placenta. The hymn 'brings its singers to the fenced altar' of the god, and there we find at once the symbols of the placenta. Even in modern dreams the altar frequently, if not invariably, symbolizes the placenta. This is perhaps not surprising, since the altar is essentially a place of blood and of sacrifice. In ancient times, indeed, it was little else. In modern times, in spite of the spotless altar cloths and rituals of vicarious sacrifice, it still remains the 'place of blood'. In the Christian church, the altar is the primary focus of the symbolic sacrifice during which the wine is drunk – the trans-substantiated blood of the God. The altar rail still stands for the well-fenced state of this holy place. This fence, this rail, is the line which may not be passed, for beyond it lies the realm of mystery where the Shining One (the 'Lord of Gleam') is drawn perpetually to destruction, ready to be born again into newness of life [32].

In the hymn, the reference to the altar thus serves to confirm the fetal nature of Zeus Diktaios, and supplies the placental element. And what the hymn tells us about the altar doubly confirms the truth of the context being explored here, for it states that it was here at this very altar that Zeus, as an immortal child, was stolen away by 'shielded Nurturers', with 'noise of beating feet.' A brief glance into Greek myth and religion will reveal what this strange statement means. The myth of the birth of Zeus asserted that he was hidden by armed men at the request of his mother, Rhea. The reason for this was reputed to be his father's tendency to eat his own children as soon as they were born.

This already could be significant in uterine terms, for we have seen that the flow of blood back into the fetal body from the placenta awakens the sense not only of rebirth, but also of eating – the two things being linked together in such a way as to be capable of creating the postnatal and irrational feeling of having devoured one's own self [29]. But the myth of Zeus's birth and his hiding away is not something peculiar to this divine child. It is simply a variant of what is evidently a general myth of divine birth. Another variant is told of Zeus's own son, Dionysus, who himself was a 'gleaming' or 'fiery' creature, having been born out of the flame by which Zeus consumed his mother. Not indeed at his birth, but when he was yet an infant, Dionysus was lured from his mother and stolen away, being torn limb from limb. We may see another variant of this in the legend of the birth of Jesus who, threatened by the wicked Herod, was taken down into Egypt, a land which again and again plays the role of destroyer, feeder and restorer in the ancient myths, especially those of the Hebrews. Some variants of the myth represent the infant Dionysus as brought to life again, but this is not universally so. Jane Harrison writes:

> We hear more for example of the sufferings of Dionysos than of his rebirth; the death of the child in such myths as those of Atreus and Thyestes, Demeter and Demophon obscures the element of Resurrection. But there can be little doubt that originally the New Birth and Resurrection lay behind. Lucian in his account of the strange solecisms committed by dancers says that he remembers how a man who was supposed to be 'dancing the Birth of Zeus and the Child-Eating of Kronos actually danced by mistake the calamities of Thyestes, deceived by their similarity.[4]

The original myth evidently told of a divine child who was stolen away, devoured or torn into pieces and then resurrected. This passage is interesting also because it records an actual instance of an ancient man ignorantly confusing symbolic material which he had inherited from his primitive forebears, but which he no longer understood.

The existence of an ideal or primal myth underlying these variations is no mere supposition, for there are powerful indications that the same essential myth belongs not only to ancient Greece but to all mankind. We shall see it also in the myths of ancient Egypt and in the stories of the Old Testament, as well as in the rites of primitive people. Jane Harrison, being unaware of the universal uterine basis of the myth, tries to explain the killing and resurrection of the divine child (and hence the reference to it in the hymn to Zeus Diktaios) as a primitive initiation rite. While it also is, this is not the *source* of the myth. Of its universal primitive character, Harrison writes:

> Everywhere, in Africa, in America, in Australia, in the South Pacific Islands, we come upon what is practically the same sequence of ceremonies. When a boy is initiated, that is when he passes from childhood to adolescence, this pantomime, this terrifying, pretended killing of the child, this painting him with clay and bringing him back to life again as a young man, is everywhere enacted. Till the boy

has died and come to life again, till he has utterly 'put away childish things' he cannot be a full member of the tribe.[5]

We can very well understand why this drama of death and rebirth should be the center of the initiation rites of primitive man. For we can see that the putting aside and forgetting of an old life in order to take up a new one is precisely what the unborn feelings have done over and over again with every beat of the umbilical blood [27]. These insights permit us to understand what was in the feelings of the worshippers of Palaikastro when they stood before Zeus's 'well-fenced altar' and sang:

> For here the shielded Nurturers took thee, a child immortal, from Rhea, and with noise of beating feet hid thee away.

These people had been reared in the atmosphere of this myth as we of the Western world have been reared in the atmosphere of the Bible. They knew without telling the mystery of the stealing and dismembering of the divine child, as we know about Moses and the bulrushes. When, therefore, we find them standing before the altar (the representation of the placenta) invoking the Lord of Gleaming and recounting the story of his loss (and implied resurrection), we can hardly be in any doubt as to what they are doing. They are, in fact, not only apparently engaging in 'worship' as a modern Christian usually employs the term, but are also acting in concert to evoke within the feelings the uterine memories, in which may be sensed at least dimly the cosmic impression which those memories carry. The figures of the 'shielded Nurturers' make excellent representations of the actions of the placenta. They are armed Nurturers who steal away the child and, by implication, destroy him. The placenta, we know, is felt not only as the monster which draws away the fetal nuclear feeling (the divine child) to destruction, but it also nurtures and, in nurturing, seems to pierce as an armed adversary [21]. The phrase 'with noise of beating feet' is also significant, since it is through the umbilical arterial beat that the fetal nuclear feeling is drawn away by the placenta, and these arteries are directly linked with the legs and feet [105]. I shall shortly demonstrate that this sense of the beating feet in relationship to the placental activity is not confined to the hymn under consideration.

I think it bears repetition that the hymn is not intended solely as an act of praise. It is evidently rather the instrument of a collective effort to evoke the primal feelings, behind which the 'worshippers' may sense the lost vision of the cosmos, which all men possess when *in utero*. As presented in the hymn, Zeus appears in the light of an amalgam – an amalgam, one might say, of the instrument with its music. The 'instrument' is the uterine organism, which works through the perpetual destruction and restoration of the nuclear (male) feeling or *kouros*. The 'music' is the universal pattern of creation with which the uterine organism is in resonance [79]. Thus it is that through the fetal elements of Zeus Diktaios there shines the 'Almighty Gleam' of the Universal Nucleus whom men call Father.

The middle portion of the hymn is lost, with the broken piece of stone upon which it was written, but when the story is picked up on the next engraved relic, the hymn continues with the same uterine theme. Indeed, we find that it adds to the narrative elements which can be demonstrated as markedly umbilical. It sings of the *Horai* being fruitful, and of Dike possessing mankind, and these can be shown to represent the umbilical flow. The *Horai*, originally represented as two in number, eventually became three, like the *Charites* of Dionysus, to which they are comparable. This at once reminds us of the persistence of the number three in all that concerns the umbilical cord, as demonstrated again and again in the following pages. Jane Harrison tells us that the earliest *Horai* were represented as dancing around an 'old fertility pillar', while a relief at Budapest shows one of the *Horai* holding a coiled snake. The dance of the *Horai* was a symbolical expression for the rhythmic passage of time, which has plausible umbilical undertones, since the umbilical beat is related to the first human sense of sequence and rhythm. The *Horai* also danced to the playing of Apollo, a fact which appears most significant when we see, as presently we shall, that Apollo is himself but a variant of the Shining One. The Hora of spring, apt symbol of the umbilical vein, was said to accompany Persephone in her annual ascent from the underworld, an event which I shall later show to have the most profound umbilical symbolism. The *Horai* also were said to adorn Aphrodite as she rose from the sea and to make a garland for Pandora – both of which goddesses we shall later see in a markedly placental light. I will not linger here to demonstrate the undoubtedly umbilical nature of the *Horai*, but the reader will find much retrospective evidence in the text which follows.

The hymn refers to the activity of Dike, who may also be seen to have markedly umbilical characteristics. Sometimes represented as one of the three *Horai*, Dike seems to signify not only the sense of *pattern* but also of *reversal*. Harrison sums up her nature in the following words:

> *Dike we have seen is the way of life of each natural thing, each plant, each animal, each man. It is also the way, the usage, the regular course of that great animal the Universe, the way that is made manifest in the Seasons, in the life and death of vegetation; and when it comes to be seen that these depend on the heavenly bodies, Dike is manifest in the changes of the rising and setting of constellations, in the waxing and waning of the Moon and in the daily and yearly courses of the Sun. In one passage at least, in the Medea of Euripides Dike stands for the course, even the circular course of the whole cosmos. In the general reversal of all things 'upward go the streams of the living rivers, Dike and all things are turned about'.*[6]

Dike thus stands for the rhythmic circular process shared by all things, and for the constant reversal of direction. The ancient Greeks seemed to have realized that this is a universal process – the way of life of that great animal, the universe. But they linked it directly with the umbilical feelings through the image of the *Horai*, who collectively symbolize the three tubes of the umbilical blood, in which there takes place the 'dance of life' in relationship to the 'fertility pillar'. Dike is so closely linked with this circulatory dance and its periodic reversals that she inevitably becomes part of them – even confused with them! She becomes one of the *Horai*. Just as in the figure of Zeus, the fetal skin feeling is amalgamated with the cosmic nuclear sense of maleness and fatherhood, so in the figures of the *Horai* and Dike the umbilical beat is amalgamated with the cosmic sense of circulation and reversal.

Thus we can understand why the hymn, after invoking the Lord of Gleaming and its recollection of the death and resurrection of the divine child, should pass naturally to sing of the *Horai* and of Dike. Similarly, we may understand why at the conclusion of the hymn, the god is called to leap for fruitfulness and newness of life. The whole nature of life is a leaping and a pulsing. The dancing of the 'shielded Nurturers' around the infant Zeus, the beating of their feet as they bore him away, the dancing of the *Horai* around the 'fertility pillar' – all these are representations of the beat of the blood in the umbilical cord. This blood not only bears the fetal nuclear feeling to 'death and rebirth', but in that cyclic process relates the feelings at their very roots to the cosmos. No doubt this leaping refers also to the movements of the fetus in the womb, through which in part the fetal skin feeling may be generated, but the hymn may also be regarded as invoking the dancing *Horai* to leap, and thus aiming to evoke the umbilical beat. It is this leaping and beating which indeed bears away the Old and brings to birth the New. This is the cosmic rhythm (sensed in the umbilical beat), which brings to man 'full jars', 'fleecy flocks' and 'fields of fruit.' The seasons bring the external manifestation of the cycle of death and rebirth which before birth was experienced in the umbilical circulation. The beating feet of the dancing *Horai*, as they perform the 'Dance of the Hours',[7] is at root the same beating of feet with which the divine child was carried away to be torn to pieces. Both are the symbolic expression of the umbilical arterial pulse, associated with the beat of the pulse in the fetal legs [105].

The association of beating feet with the death of a god is not confined to the hymn to Zeus Diktaios. We find it obscurely represented in the story of the Garden of Gethsemane, where another divine Son was, as it were, stolen away to be slain and resurrected. The Bible tells us that at the culmination of the Passover ceremony, Jesus gave his disciples a cup of wine, which he identified with his own blood.[8] In the Gospel of St. John, Jesus speaks the words, 'I am the true vine', a statement which is congruent with the wine-blood symbolism, since in both Hebrew and Greek the word for 'vine' has a strong relationship with the sense of coiling, which in ancient thought was often linked to the umbilical arterial helix [23-25].

The very Passover feast itself has strong uterine associations, and it is a fact that the Hebrew word for the Passover is related not only to hopping or to skipping, but also to lameness. The word comes from *pacach*, and it seems interesting that the word is related to that which describes Joseph's famous 'Coat of Many Colors', the fetal symbolism of which I shall presently show. Behind the meaning of the Passover lies the universal sense that the little 'lame' creature of the womb suffers the passage through the umbilical cord and is therein destroyed and renewed. The fetus is not only physically depleted in its feet, but the feet are felt as specially related to the placenta, the legs being umbilical arteries [105], for which reason the human legs and feet are haunted by old umbilical feelings, and hence the symbolism of lameness is an excellent symbol for awakening these old memories in the feelings – see the myth of Oedipus.

This is the true meaning of the 'Paschal Lamb' who is sacrificed that life may be renewed: a symbol which revives in all minds the forgotten but spiritually vital events of the umbilical cord. During these events of the last Passover, on the way to the garden of Gethsemane, Jesus warned Peter that he would three times deny his Master. Here we get an undoubted splitting of the symbolism, a device often met with in myths and in dreams, whereby alone the peculiar events in the feelings can be expressed in the very different sphere of external things and events. The triple denial is entirely in keeping with the umbilical nature of the story, and is simply a mythological manner of evoking in the feelings the threefold pattern of the umbilical cord [25]. As for the warning of the denial, this accords very well with the fact that in the umbilical cord the fetal nuclear self seems to be drawn away from the fetal body, and that it is sensed as being the father, who enters the mother (placenta) and there is destroyed and transformed into the son [189]. This umbilical experience lives on in the feelings and eventually takes on a form which responds to the idea of the denial or rejection of the father by the son and vice versa. That it should be Peter who is guilty of this denial is comprehensible when we reflect that Peter is the Rock, namely the nuclear and solid sense – hence male, hence father. It is this nuclear feeling which is involved with the splitting or 'denial' in the umbilical circulation.

The Gospel of St. John refers to the passage of the sad little cortège over the brook called Cedron. This brook is referred to elsewhere in the Bible as Kidron, a name said to derive from the Hebrew word *qadar*, which means 'dark colored' and, by implication, 'mourning'. Smith's book, *A Dictionary of the Bible,* asserts that Kidron is not a brook but a torrent, and adds the following information:

> *The distinguishing peculiarity of the Kidron valley – that in respect to which it is most frequently mentioned in the Old Testament – is the impurity which appears to have been ascribed to it.*

It was here, the Dictionary continues, that *King Asa demolished and burnt the obscene phallic idol of his mother;* here the wicked Athaliah was hurried to execution; and it *then becomes the regular receptacle for the impurities and abominations of the idol-worship ...*[9] Here, then, we have a torrent which is related etymologically to the sense of loss and mourning, which in turn is related historically with destruction, death and the deposit of impurities. It was, in fact, reputed to have been the common cemetery of the city. What better symbol could we have for the flow of blood in the umbilical arteries, wherein the fetal nuclear feeling is subjected to destruction, and thus is the source in us of our primary sense of woe, loss, death, impurity and destruction? The passage of Christ across the dreaded torrent is the symbol of the passage of the Shining One, the cosmic nuclear feeling, down the umbilical arteries to destruction in the placenta [28-29]. The title 'Christ' is from the Greek *pla*, meaning 'to rub with oil'. It is the Greek version of the Hebrew title Mashiyach, which derives from *mashach* = 'to rub with oil'. In Hebrew the word for oil is *shemen*, which comes from *shaman* = 'to shine', demonstrating that at root the title 'Christ' equates with the 'The Shining One'.

In the light of these associations, it is not surprising to find that Gethsemane and what happened there are redolent with placental associations. The very name of the place is derived from two Hebrew words *gath* and *shemen*, the former meaning 'a wine press' and deriving, it is suggested, from *nagan*, 'to thrum' or 'to play on a stringed instrument.' Quite apart from any etymological association, it is traditional that the treaders in the wine press were inspired to keep their feet going by means of suitable music. Thus we can see *gath*, the wine press, in terms not only of rhythm and of beating feet, but also in terms of the 'spilling of the blood of the grape'. This last is by no means a mere superficial assumption, for the Divine One whose drama was laid in Gethsemane declared that the juice of the grape was his own blood. We are reminded here of the hymn to the Diktean Zeus, where the worshippers cry with harps and pipes mingled together, and of the child who was borne away to the noise of beating feet. The beating of the feet of the *Kouretes* who stole the divine child, and the beating of the feet that 'trod the blood of the grape' both yield an identical image to the feelings.

The second half of the name 'Gethsemane' adds yet further illumination, for it derives from the Hebrew word *shemen*, which means 'grease' or 'oil'. Thus the wine press becomes also the 'oil press' where the oil or 'shine' is pressed out. Thus we come upon an association of ideas which links very readily with the process as described in *The Nature of the Self*, for it is in the beat of the feet and legs that the fetus sends its 'shine' into the placenta for destruction [30-41]. Yet it is this same umbilical beat which yields to the fetus refreshed blood and nuclear power [28-29], even as the beat of the feet in the press yields the refreshing wine. Thus the name 'Gethsemane' may be seen to be a fitting one for that place (the placenta) where the Shining One went over the dark, impure and deadly torrent of Kidron. It may be noted here that the Hebrew word for an olive, the source of oil to the Mediterranean peoples of that day, is *zayith*, a word which has close etymological links with brightness and light.

The events which took place in Gethsemane fit the present context and serve to support what is written above. Thus we are told that Jesus prayed three times, just as he already had fated Peter to deny him three times, and as he prayed there fell from him a sweat that was 'like great drops of blood'. Here we have another sign of the ubiquitous umbilical three, associated now with a direct representation of a bloody excretion. The Gospels tell us that when the last prayer was said, Judas came with an armed band to seize Christ and take him away. In this armed band we see a direct reflection of that band of 'shielded Nurturers' who bore away the infant Zeus. The figure of Judas, moreover, offers placental and umbilical associations. One of these associations lies in the fact that Judas carried the money bag. Money and gold generally have very strong fecal associations, as every depth psychologist knows, and silver is frequently a symbol for urine. A very powerful link is offered by the Bible itself between Judas's evil money and the bowel excretions:

> *Now this man purchased a field with the rewards of iniquity; and falling headlong, he burst asunder in the midst, and all his bowels gushed out.*[10]

Moreover, the money bag which Judas held was also the 'feeding bag' for the little group.[11] This link between the money bag and the opposed ideas of eating and excreting has a strong placental undertone since, for the fetus, the placenta is actually the excretory pot and the feeding pot in one [29-30].

The field in which Judas's bowels gushed out yields still further associations of a placental order, for we are elsewhere told that it was a 'potter's field' and was used to bury strangers, and that it was named 'the field of blood'. This field was bought with the thirty pieces of silver, and one version states that it was not Judas but the chief priests who bought the field. The thirty pieces of silver make very apt symbols for the three umbilical vessels, and are indeed so used in modern times by a wide variety of people in their dreams and associations, albeit in a completely unconscious manner. And when we find this 'umbilical money' linked closely with pottery, gushing bowels, dead people and a field of blood, we realize how well the whole picture symbolizes the relationship of the umbilical flow to excretion, death and that 'field of blood' which we moderns call the placenta.

Indeed, we are told that this field was called Aceldama, which name derives from two Hebrew roots, namely *chalaq* and *dam*. The word *chalaq* means 'to be smooth' and also 'to apportion or separate'. The word *dam* means 'blood'. The two words taken together could suggest something akin to the idea of a smooth field of blood where separation takes place – appropriate when applied to the placenta. All this symbolism points to Judas as an excellent symbol of the umbilical arteries and the placenta. To recapitulate: the placenta is the 'money bag' (that is, excretory pot) and also the 'feeding bag'. Additionally, it is the instrument of the betrayal and death of the Shining One. It is the place of excretion.

There is one element in the story of Judas, present in all four Gospels, which supports the idea that Judas is the representative of the placenta and the cord. This is the fact that the act of betrayal is directly related to the act of 'eating together' by Jesus and Judas. Three of the Gospels state that Jesus identifies his betrayer because they eat from the same dish. The fourth (Luke) implies it in the light of the other three. I quote these incidents below because of their undoubted impact upon the mind.

> *He that dippeth his hand with me in the dish, the same shall betray me (Matthew 26:23).*
>
> *One of you which eateth with me shall betray me ... It is one of the twelve that dippeth with me in the dish (Mark 14:18-20).*

Behold, the hand of him that betrayeth me is with me on the table (Luke 22:21).

He it is, to whom I shall give a sop, when I have dipped it (John 13:26).

Certainly the fetus and the placenta may be said to 'eat together', in the sense that the fetus 'feeds' the placenta with blood, and the placenta in turn 'feeds' the fetus. This interpretation is in no sense a wishful use of symbolism, since precisely the same dynamic may be seen in the story of Adam and Eve, where the serpent (symbol of the umbilical arteries) causes the placental Eve to eat, whereafter she gives the same food to the fetal Adam.

Eve — Adam

Eating and betrayal are a familiar theme in the Bible. We can see that as Eve betrayed Adam in connection with the act of eating, so also Judas betrayed Jesus. So also did Jacob betray Esau in association with the giving of food. Indeed, when the act of feeding together appears, this uterine significance may be suspected, in both myths and dreams. The feeding of Jesus and Judas from the same dish is of this order: Jesus is the Shining One who is betrayed to destruction by the placental feeding.

Yet another aspect of Judas serves to identify him, if a little less concretely, with the umbilical arteries and, above all, with the placenta – his name 'Iscariot'. Smith says that the name has received many interpretations, and mentions one which can be seen to have distinct placental possibilities, namely that it derives from the Hebrew word *ascara*, meaning 'suffocation' or 'strangling'. The fetus may sense throughout its later life a distinct oxygen shortage, while some medical writers assert that a powerful factor in determining the time of birth is precisely the relatively sudden diminution of the placental supply of oxygen.

Thus the fetal feelings towards the placenta as a perpetual destroyer may be overlaid and emphasized by these ultimate feelings that the placenta also is the cause of the horrors of birth. In this respect, therefore, as a suffocator, Judas would be correctly named. And this suggestion is strongly confirmed by the fact that the monstrous devourer who seduced and ate young men at the gates of Thebes (and who therefore showed marked placental

Judas

sphinx

Lamia

characteristics) was named the 'sphinx', which is to say 'the strangler'. We shall see later a good deal of evidence showing that the Theban sphinx, in common with all Lamia, is a symbol of the placenta.

This interpretation of the Gospel narrative is not wantonly offered in any sense as a denigration of the Bible. While I cannot accept the orthodox Christian view of the Gospels, I believe that they mean much more to one who understands even a little of their real significance. The Gospels present to our conscious and unconscious minds the most complete symbolism of the uterine feelings and their postnatal accommodation of any writings known to me, and this is further amplified when the postnatal phenomena of mental development are considered in this light. We need not concern ourselves here with the historical processes whereby a Hebrew Messiah assumed the symbolic overlay of the mind's evolution. But to one who glimpses the meaning of that symbolism, redolent with the atmosphere of Greek myth and rite, the Gospels appear as a great work of human art. Their intent is to hold before our feelings the symbolic representations of the hidden events of the uterine and infancy life, while keeping the conscious mind uplifted in an atmosphere of spiritual purity. But the hidden tale is one of blood and excretion, of betrayal and loss, for it was in these feelings between the fetus and the placenta that the rhythm was set up that 'tuned in the cosmic impress.' The Gospels artfully seek to offer to the conscious and the unconscious parts of the mind a skillful blend of the divine and the earthly, whereby they may be brought into some sort of synthesis in the self.

The Gospels present to our conscious and unconscious minds

What the Gospels seek to achieve is the same end that all true myths aspire to, and it is also in such a light that we may understand the feelings and desires of those who stood before the altar at Palaikastro crying:

28   *Mythology of the Prenatal Life*

For here the shielded Nurturers took thee, a child immortal, from Rhea, and with noise of beating feet hid thee away.[12]

Precisely the same meaning is to be found in other parts of the Bible. Perhaps the most impressive of all the myths of the Old Testament is that which tells the story of Joseph, his betrayal, his descent into Egypt and his apotheosis. My attention was early drawn to Joseph because of the very evident relationship between his mysterious coat and the dawning of an overweening egotism that ended in his rejection. The strong emotional tie which this coat cemented between father and son was also important, for I had become aware of the fact that the fetal skin feeling is in some strange way the instrument of identity between the fetus and his own father [185].

Although in our English Bible the famous coat which Joseph receives from his father is known as a 'Coat of Many Colors', this is evidently not the correct translation at all. In the Hebrew version the word used to describe the nature of the coat is *pac*, which appears to mean 'many breadths' or even 'many widths', a description aptly translated by the makers of the Douay Bible who used the phrase 'a coat of many pieces'. This description coincides with the idea that the fetal skin feeling is often represented in dreams as a covering of small regular pieces [247], though whether this is deliberate or accidental is too much to assert. Certainly the idea of a 'Coat of Many Colors' links with the representation of the fetal skin feeling as a cloak of light or color [13]. However, there is another possible meaning of the Hebrew word *pac* in this connection, since it is closely related with the Hebrew word *pacach*, which means 'to hop', 'to skip over' and 'to become lame' as well as 'to pass over'. As already mentioned, this might be a dim reflection of an old representation of Joseph's coat as the coat of the 'little limping man' (the fetus) who goes through the perpetual 'Passover' of the umbilical flow.

The fetal skin feeling, being the agent of the cosmic nuclear power, is inevitably the physical instrument of the ego [9-10]. This throws considerable light on the tale that Joseph, as soon as he received the 'Coat of Many Colors', dreamed two highly egocentric dreams. In the first dream Joseph's sheaf stood upright and those of his brothers encircled it and made obeisance to it. In the second dream the very Sun, Moon and eleven stars made obeisance to Joseph, a clever imagery which establishes the boy not only as the focus of the family, but also of the very universe. It links the fetal skin feeling not only outwardly to the external world, but also inwardly to the cosmos. It is a way of saying that the fetal skin feeling is nuclear and through that quality, 'perceives the cosmos'. The egotism shown by Joseph links him indirectly with another version of the Shining One, namely Lucifer. The name of this bright angel is Heylel in Hebrew meaning 'the morning star', derived from the primitive root *halal*, which has the significance not only of shining but also of boasting. That Lucifer is another version of the Shining One, representative of the fetal skin feeling, seems fairly certain and the link between his luminous nature and boasting makes a plausible parallel with the boasting of Joseph after he had received the mysterious coat.

The fate of the 'Coat of Many Colors' is entirely consistent with the uterine context. The brothers seized Joseph at Dothan, stripped the coat from him and threw him into a waterless pit. After having sold him as a slave, they killed a kid and dipped the coat in its blood. Having done this, they returned the torn and bloody garment to their father, who lamented the loss of his son in the following telling words:

> It is my son's coat; an evil beast hath devoured him; Joseph is without doubt rent in pieces.[13]

The fetal skin feeling does indeed come again and again to its destruction in the 'pit' and that 'bath of blood' which we call the placenta. The coat, soaked in the blood of a kid, is properly restored to the father, for the nuclear nature of the father is the source of the fetal skin feeling [193]. As already mentioned, the theme of the 'destruction of the hero' is familiar to the student of mythology for this is the fate of many a hero, from Dionysus to Osiris. Moreover, it always appears in a context which yields the presence of the placenta as the devouring and bloodsucking monster. It seems, therefore, hardly accidental that when we examine the etymology of the lament of Jacob for his son, we find that his description of

30   *Mythology of the Prenatal Life*

the slayer, namely the phrase 'evil beast', has a strangely placental undertone. In Hebrew the word for evil is *ra*, which comes from *rata* meaning 'to spoil by breaking into pieces'. The word for beast is *chay*, which comes from *chayah*, a word, which in outline is not too unlike the word *chavah*, meaning 'a life giver' which is, in fact, the origin of the name we call Eve. It surely must appear more than accidental that the 'evil beast' which Jacob thought had rent his son in pieces, should be described in Hebrew words which provide so many symbolic links with the placenta. For Eve is the placental life-giver, and we know that she is also the betrayer of the fetal Adam.

To this point, we have noted a number of things which confirm that Joseph and his 'Coat of Many Colors' are symbols of the fetus and his nuclear skin feeling. The myth proceeds to amplify this confirmation in some detail. We note first of all that Joseph was preserved alive only through the representations of Reuben, for the others would have killed him. This appears significant when we recall that the name 'Reuben' is derived from the roots *ra-ah*, 'to see', and *ben*, 'a son'. This etymological link with the act of sight and hence with the eyes, makes Reuben himself a candidate for the symbolic role of the Shining One. There is a strong etymological link in Hebrew between the eyes and the skin, since the word for skin has exactly the same outline as a word which means 'to wake' in the sense of 'opening the eyes'. Although this link between Reuben and the fetal skin feeling is quite indirect, it is supported by the fact that he is described by his father in the most plausibly fetal terms. The old man declares himself to Reuben thus:

> Reuben, thou art my firstborn, my might, and the beginning of my strength, the excellency of dignity, and the excellency of power: unstable as water, thou shalt not excel; because thou wentest up to thy father's bed; then defilest thou it: he went up to my couch.[14]

This declaration is almost entirely meaningless in terms of ordinary external relationships, but if we interpret it in terms of the fetal life and feeling, then it reveals considerable meaning. If Reuben is the symbol of the nuclear, male feeling of the fetal skin [175], then indeed he may be described as the source of strength, dignity and power, since he is in that context the very core and stuff of the human ego. Similarly, in that context he could be described as being 'unstable as water' and one who, like Proteus, could assume any shape. The truth of this can be realized only when we understand how simple is the uterine feeling complex, and yet into what diversity of character and personality it later develops. That Reuben should be called incestuous we can also understand in the light of the umbilical feelings, since we know that the nuclear feelings of the fetus seems to enter the mother (that is, the placenta) in the form of father, and to be reborn of her as son [186]. In the light of this analysis, Reuben and Joseph may be seen as the result of a doubling of the symbol, and the intervention of Reuben to save the life of Joseph becomes comprehensible as a symbolic device for showing that the nuclear fetal skin feeling survives the placental experience merely by being its own indestructible self.

The arrival of Joseph in Egypt is the sign for another doubling of the symbol of the Shining One, for there immediately appears in the narrative the captain Potiphar, whose name means 'belonging to the Sun'. Potiphar bought Joseph as his slave, but the narrative leaves us in no doubt as to the essential identity of the two figures, for Potiphar quickly turned everything he had over to Joseph's care. Potiphar's wife sought to seduce her servant, but he fled from her, leaving his garment in her hand. If Potiphar and Joseph are in essence one and the same, both being representatives of the Shining One (symbols of the fetal skin feeling), then Potiphar's wife represents the placenta, and her tearing away of the Shining One's garment during a sexual encounter is a further representation of the loss of the fetal skin feeling through the action of the placenta. This part of the story is thus a replay of the loss of the 'Coat of Many Colors'. That Joseph and Potiphar are one and the same, and that Potiphar's wife is therefore Joseph's wife, is supported by the fact that Joseph eventually married the daughter of Poti-pherah. Potiphar and Poti-pherah are essentially the same name: both 'belong to the Sun', and are therefore palpable representatives of the Shining One. The wife of the one and the daughter of the other both therefore make excellent representatives of the placenta, and a suitable wife for Joseph. The placental nature of Joseph's wife is further supported by her name, Asenath, which has certain etymological links with the word for a storehouse or granary. The placenta may certainly be regarded as not only a wife but as a feeding place. Moreover, this symbolism links Joseph's wife directly with Egypt itself, which figures overwhelmingly in the myth in terms of food. Egypt, Potiphar's wife and Asenath may thus be seen as a triple symbolism of the placenta: through them in various ways Joseph is both reduced and also restored again.

This umbilical and placental symbolism is clearly evident in the story of Joseph's sojourn in that prison to which he was consigned by the lie of Potiphar's wife. There he lives with the Pharaoh's butler and his baker, making a trio with resultant umbilical undertones. Significantly, all three have to do with eating and drinking. The baker is manifestly a preparer of food, and the word used for the butler is in Hebrew *mashqeh,* which comes from the root *shaqah,* meaning 'to quaff' and 'to irrigate'. As for Joseph, he is potentially the greatest feeder of all, since it is through him that Egypt is to be made a granary. The butler reveals his umbilical nature in the following dream:

> *In my dream, behold, a vine was before me; and in the vine were three branches; and it was as though it budded, and her blossoms shot forth; and the clusters thereof brought forth ripe grapes: and Pharaoh's cup was in my hand: and I took the grapes, and pressed them into Pharaoh's cup, and I gave the cup into Pharaoh's hand.*[15]

When we remember that Pharaoh's title was 'Son of the Sun', and that therefore he himself was the symbol of the Shining One, the butler who gives him a drink from a triple vine must seem to us highly umbilical-placental. But the baker also dreams in terms of triplicities:

> *I had three white baskets on my head: and in the uppermost basket there was of all manner of bakemeats for Pharaoh; and the birds did eat them out of the basket upon my head.*[16]

Here again there are three instruments of feeding, but now they are divided into one versus two, one being uppermost. And as the umbilical cord gives death and life in its two-way flow, so in the myth the baker dies upon a tree and his flesh is eaten by the birds, but the butler is restored to his place.

Now Pharaoh dreams two disturbing dreams:

He stood by the river. And, behold, there came up out of the river seven well-favored kine and fat-fleshed; and they fed in a meadow. And, behold, seven other kine came up after them out of the river, ill-favored and lean-fleshed; and stood by the other kine upon the brink of the river. And the ill-favored and lean-fleshed kine did eat up the seven well favored and fat kine. So Pharaoh awoke. And he slept and dreamed the second time: and, behold, seven ears of corn came up upon one stalk, rank and good. And, behold, seven thin ears and blasted with the east wind sprung up after them. And the seven thin ears devoured the seven rank and full ears.[17]

The river in Pharaoh's dream represents the umbilical cord, the seven kine (cattle) and the seven ears of corn standing for the sevenfold periodic cycle sensed by the fetus in the umbilical circulation [37-39]. It is worth noting that the Hebrew word for seven is *shib-ah*, which derives from the root *shaba*, signifying completion, so that the very word is an apt description of a completed cycle. No doubt the river in the Pharaoh's dream was the Nile, and the myth of Osiris shows that for the ancient Egyptians that river had strong umbilical associations. Also, as we shall later see in more detail, there was a link between the physical Nile and that mysterious heavenly river named Okeanos, which supplies a link between the umbilical and the cosmic rhythms. Pharaoh's dream appears to be a symbolic statement that the sevenfold rhythm of 'umbilical eating' forms a process that links man to the cosmos. This cosmic link is put into the mouth of Joseph, who insists the dream is a message from God.

God hath showed Pharaoh what he is about to do (Genesis 41:25).

What God is about to do he sheweth unto Pharaoh (Genesis 41:28).

God will shortly bring it to pass (Genesis 41:32).

The myth requires that Pharaoh's dream be regarded as prophetic in the simple historical sense and, perhaps surprisingly, many writers also adduce this dream and Joseph's interpretation as historical evidence of ancient dream interpretation. However, inclusion of the prenatal perspective reveals that the myth is telling us that God makes direct contact with the Son of the Sun, namely the fetal nuclear feeling. And what God reveals is precisely the sevenfold rhythm of Creation, which we know the fetus feels in terms of 'feeding' at his navel. Seen in this light, the seven lean years and the seven fat years are simply a mythological device for stating that in the act of feeding at the navel the fetus gains the sense of the sevenfold rhythm of the cosmos, to which the antithesis of the fat and lean

Pharaoh — chorionic embryonic chief

Joseph — embryonic servant

vine — the trophoblast

the grapes — wine from the endometrial blood

the vine-press — chorionic blood transformers

the river — the syncitiotrophoblast
the circular continuum around the chorion

the first 7 chorionic days — the seven good years
the next 7 chorionic days — the seven lean years

until blood starts to circulate

years adds the element of reversal [38-40]. Joseph's interpretation of the dream of 'the Son of the Sun' is actually the interpretation of his own nuclear feeling, for he himself is the Shining One, the wearer of the fetal 'Coat of Many Colors', and it is he who is restored again and again through the 'right interpretation' of the dream. We have already seen that Joseph and Potiphar are one and the same: so also are Joseph and Pharaoh. And as Joseph fell from grace in Potiphar's house, so now he is restored to grace by being given full command of all Pharaoh's domain through his understanding of the umbilical visions of the butler and the baker and their master. Egypt, through Joseph, now becomes the universal granary – universal symbol of the placenta.

The umbilical motif is carried on by the myth, in terms of the back and forth journeying of Joseph's family in search of food. As the umbilical blood journeys back and forth 'in search of food', so now do the sons of Israel. Upon their first journey, Joseph recognized them and puts them in prison for three days. Holding Simeon as hostage, he sent the others away laden with food, but in the mouth of each corn sack he caused their money to be put, and he demanded of them that Benjamin be brought to him in Egypt. Through these devices the brothers were drawn back again to the place of food, this time taking with them not only the money for new food, but also the money which Joseph had placed in their sacks. In this way the idea of circulation is conveyed: the money is brought in and returned and brought in again. In this way also the sense of feeding and excretion are linked, for money and feces are closely linked together in the human feelings. To this must be added the desperate sense of loss caused by the holding of Simeon and the demand for the presence of Benjamin.

Again, for the second time, Joseph sent his brothers away laden with corn and again he had their money put into their sacks' mouths. Moreover, into the mouth of Benjamin's sack was put Joseph's silver drinking cup. Joseph let them go a little way and then sent men in pursuit to arrest them, accuse them of stealing from him, and bring them back to him once again. But before he sent them off yet a third time, he made himself known to them and bade them bring down his old father to Egypt. In these simple family terms of famine and feeding, divorce and restoration, the cyclic relationship between the fetus and the placenta are once more represented. And the relationship of this back and forth journey to the cosmic process is beautifully symbolized in terms of a poignant reassurance given by God to old Jacob, that in the depths of Egypt, God would be with the old man and restore him again:

> *And God spake unto Israel in the visions of the night, and said, 'Jacob, Jacob'. And he said, 'Here am I'. And he said, 'I am God, the God of thy father: fear not to go down into Egypt; for I will there make of thee a great nation: I will go down with thee into Egypt; and I will also surely bring thee up again' ...*[18]

In these stirring words we read the triumphant assurance that God's creative powers are linked to the back and forth flow of the umbilical blood. The Creator's nature flows into man as he goes along the dreadful way to destruction and ever is restored again. It is in the cycle of the umbilical flow that man's soul is created – that man receives the impress of God. But to gain this impress man must submit to the 'descent into Egypt' over and over again, confident that God will restore him. All this imagery has one aim: to provide the conscious human mind with a means of sensing the forgotten experiences at its roots, and to provide man with a means of playing out vicariously the great fear at the root of his soul. Nor is this merely a narrowly understood means of psycho-therapeutics. Rather, it is a means of enabling man to free the rhythm in his mind, so that he is not afraid to experience the cycles of loss and restoration, and in consequence, he is not afraid to see God. When the scribes and the Pharisees asked Jesus for a sign of his authority, he replied in effect that God had no sign to offer save this cycle of loss and restoration:

> *An evil and adulterous generation seeketh after a sign; and there shall no sign be given to it, but the sign of the prophet Jonas; for as Jonas was three days and three nights in the whale's belly; so shall the Son of man be three days and three nights in the heart of the earth.*[19]

Christian dogma inevitably and naturally asserts that this refers to the burial and resurrection of the historical Jesus. But the reference to Jonas and his sojourn in the whale's belly carries us to realms both older and wider. Superficially, we may note the reappearance of the 'umbilical three', but the evidence of the myth of Jonah and the fish goes far deeper.

to feel the rhythm of ones heart and soul

loss and restoration
recovery

blastocyst { Jonas — whales belly — chorion
{ Son of man } { heart of the earth }
3 days 3 nights

burial and resurrection
swallowing and regurgitation
exhaustion — renewal
give and take
exchange
outward and inward

the implantation { scrounging, crucifixion, death, burial, resurrection }

To begin with, the name Jonah, which in the New Testament is given as Jonas, is the same word as *yownah*, meaning 'a dove'. Strong asserts that the Hebrew word is apparently related to the *warmth of their mating*,[20] – and the relationship to heat and fire generally is argued by Ernest Jones in the following passage:

> *The dove was also associated with fire. When the Kapota [the dove] touches fire, Yama, whose messenger he is, is honoured; in a Buddhist legend Agni, the God of Fire, assumes the shape of a dove when he is being pursued by Indra in the shape of a hawk (the Sanskrit name of which, by the way, is Kapotari, the enemy of doves). In the 'scoppio del carro' festival at Florence the holy fire is renewed every Easter*

> *Eve, and at the moment of celebrating High Mass a stuffed bird, representing a dove (called the dove of the Pazzi), is released from a pillar of fire-works in front of the altar, flies along a wire down the nave, and ignites the fire-works on the festive car that is waiting outside the door. Maury quotes as a reason why the Holy Ghost appears sometimes in the form of fire, and sometimes in that of a dove, the circumstance that in the Orient the dove was the emblem of generation and of animal heat. The association with heat is retained in Christian art, where the Holy Dove is always depicted surrounded by rays of light or flames of fire.[21]*

The swallowing of Jonah by the great fish may therefore be read as the swallowing of the divine fire by the monster – a symbolic representation of the destruction of the nuclear fetal feeling by the placenta. The fact that Jonah spent *three* days in the belly of the fish can be seen as an umbilical reference. This swallowing of the fire by the great fish will recur in more oblique form in another Bible myth: when the Philistines finally captured Samson (whose name in Hebrew derives from the root *shemesh*, 'to be brilliant', 'the Sun') they gave thanks to their God Dagon. Now, the name Dagon is derived from *dag*, which is the Hebrew word for 'fish'. There are signs here of some general myth of the swallowing of the fiery or brilliant energy or person by a great fish. This is undoubtedly a myth of the destruction of the nuclear Shining One by the placenta, and we have not far to seek to find its most primitive source. For there is no more primitive or widespread myth than that of the Sun-Hero who is daily swallowed by the Sea Monster at night, and as relentlessly regurgitated the next morning upon the Eastern shore.

Anthropologists have usually treated this myth as if it were a mere representation of the physical facts of the diurnal movements of the Sun. However, it can be demonstrated that this myth is a projection of the mind's uterine origins upon the celestial phenomena, for the basic myth contains indubitable uterine elements which could have no possible significance in a mere representation of primitive solar astronomy. Leo Frobenius gathered together numerous variants of this solar mythology, and constructed from them a basic myth which I now propose to outline, and in which the uterine elements are immediately evident:

A hero is swallowed by a sea monster in the West.

The monster swims to the East with the hero inside.

The hero kindles a fire in the monster's belly.

He cuts off a piece of the monster's heart and eats it.

The monster glides onto the Eastern shore.

The hero cuts open the monster's body and slips out.

He finds that he has lost all his hair in the heat of the belly.

Frequently the hero also frees those previously swallowed by the monster.[22]

If this were merely a solar myth it would be enough to represent the Western swallowing, the night journey and the Eastern regurgitation. But the complicating elements are not at all solar – they are uterine. The hero is the Sun, the symbol *par excellence* of the Shining One. The monster who swallows the hero is the placenta. The cutting of the heart probably symbolizes the fact that the nuclear feeling is evoked partly by the action currents of the heart. But it is also evoked by the lanugo hairs on the fetal skin, whose loss is also paralleled by the loss of hair in the monster.[23] The kindling of the fire in the monster's belly signifies that in the placenta, the Shining One still is intact in his fiery nature. We should not be misled by the birth symbolism which is fairly evident in my summary of Frobenius, and which might incline the reader to suppose that the myth deals merely with the memories of birth and some dim memory of having earlier been in the maternal body. The fact is, as I have shown [31-32], that *the perpetual feelings of the umbilical experience are summed up in one great shock at birth, so that the two are often confused.*

Frobenius saw that this myth dealt with some mysterious feeling of the relationship of the son and his father to the mother, but without knowledge of the umbilical feeling-complex he could not explain it. Yet his comments have immediate relevance to the material under consideration. Jung quoted him thus:

Perhaps in connection with the blood-red sunrise, the idea occurs that here a birth takes place, the birth of a young son; the question then arises inevitably, whence comes the paternity? How has the woman become pregnant? And since this woman symbolizes the same idea as the fish, which means the sea ... the curious primitive answer is that this sea has previously swallowed the old Sun. Consequently the resulting myth is, that the woman (sea) has formerly devoured the Sun and now brings a new Sun into the world, and thus she has become pregnant.[24]

The explanation offered by Frobenius is curiously complicated, for why should the primitive mind elaborate the daily cycle of the Sun in terms which have no evident relationship to it? It is the habit of our Western observers to think of all primitive ideas about nature as if they were a product of mere lack of understanding, whereas in fact they are self-evidently the outcome of an enormous inner feeling which imposes itself upon external fact. In the case we are now surveying, it is clear that the elaboration of the external facts of nature is not the product of stupidity, but of a most ingenious projection of the inner experience of the umbilical cycle upon the outer, solar one. For as I have shown in *The Nature of the Self*, the fetus feels that he is the Shining One, both Father and Son, and that he constantly enters the Mother (placental monster) wherefrom he emerges again and again [84, 187]. Here is the root of the Oedipus complex projected upon the solar cycle [187-189], inasmuch that the Old Sun (Father) enters the Monster (placenta-Mother) and is reborn as the new Sun (Son) every morning.

The Christian dogma of the Virgin Birth is evidently of the same general order as the primitive myth examined above. All such mythology derives from the inner experiences of man, and can appear afresh in any number of divergent forms and does so in unsuspected form every night in millions of dreams. This fact of the unity underlying all myths and dreams provides the natural basis for any number of syncretisms, and no one representation may claim priority. The notion of the Virgin Birth has its origins here, manifestly a device for calming the anxiety of Oedipal terrors which ferment in the core of the self. Christian dogma holds that the Father and the Son are one, and we can perfectly understand this in the light of our new understanding of the fetal skin feeling. The Father enters the Virgin through the mediation of the Holy Ghost. Ernest Jones writes of this:

> *A belief, often forgotten nowadays, but preserved in the legends and traditions of the Catholic Church, is that the conception of Jesus in the Virgin Mary was brought about by the introduction into her ear of the breath of the Holy Ghost. I do not know if this is now held as an official tenet of the Church, but in past ages it was not only depicted*

by numerous religious artists, but also maintained by many of the Fathers and by at least one of the Popes, namely Felix.[25]

In early Christian art the Holy Ghost was frequently represented by a dove. Jones refers to several paintings in which the dove was depicted as almost entering the Virgin's ear. He mentions also an old panel, which once stood in the Cathedral of Saint-Leu, and which depicted the Holy Ghost as a dove, from the beak of which projected a ray of light upon the Virgin's ear. Down this luminous pathway a tiny infant was descending, holding a little cross and evidently destined to enter the Virgin's ear. In such terms, we may see that ancient thought regarded the dove not only as a fiery or shining creature, but as the instrument whereby the Father could penetrate into the Virgin to bring forth the Son. The English word 'dove' actually derives from a root which means 'to dive'. All these associations serve to create the impression of the dove as a fiery and shining creature, able to 'dive into the female hollow'. This evidence supports the interpretation that Jonah was another version of this penetrant force, which in his story could dive into the belly of the great fish. Both sets of imagery reflect the same basic myth created by the projection of the umbilical feelings. The myth of Jonah represents these feelings in terms of a swallowing and regurgitation by a great fish. Christian myth represents them in terms of the entry of the Father, through the agency of the Holy Ghost, into the Virgin, as a result of which that Son was born who was in fact the Father, and who would go through a violent death before resurrection and reunion with the Father. In the words of Matthew:

> For as Jonah was three days and three nights in the whale's belly; so shall the Son of man be three days and three nights in the heart of the earth.[26]

Another Bible myth which reveals a similar content is that of Noah and his ark. The story of the Noachic Flood contains manifestly uterine elements which appear to have been superimposed upon the tradition of some ancient physical inundation. The name 'Noah' is Noach in Hebrew, and is derived from the root *nuwach*, meaning 'to rest', so that the name means something akin to 'The Resting One'. This is a possible reference to the fetus, albeit indirect. However, there is a word in Hebrew which may be transliterated as *nuwr* (pronounced 'noor'), which has the meaning of 'shine' or 'fire', and which could conceivably be the original source of the name 'Noah'. The passing of centuries, the lack of vowel points in the original Hebrew writing, the considerable similarity between certain Hebrew characters, the possibility of errors in protracted oral transmission – all these things make it highly possible that Noah originally meant 'The Shining One'. Certainly this conclusion tends to be supported by the etymology of the names of his three sons, Ham, Shem and Japheth.

The name Ham in Hebrew is Cham, and it derives from the root *chamam*, meaning 'to be hot.' or 'to enflame.' The word 'Shem' appears to signify something akin to 'a conspicuous position', and to be related to *shameh*, which means 'lofty' and 'the sky'. Not only does this have a suggestion of the 'bright sky' and of the Sun, but it is not far removed from the root *shaman*, meaning 'to shine'. Strong asserts that the name 'Japheth' is from *pathah*, meaning 'to open', but that there is also a word *yiph-ah*, which means 'brightness'. Thus, apart from their representation of the *umbilical three*, the names of the *three* sons give adjectival support to their father's shining nature. The ark is to be *three-storied*, and is to be built of gopher wood. The word 'gopher' appears only once in the entire Bible: Webster's dictionary refers to it as the unidentified wood used in the building of the ark. In the Hebrew a closely related outline *gephen*, which means 'a vine', in the sense of twining. Here is certainly a strong umbilical symbolism. Also, note that God commanded Noah to take into the ark 'clean beasts' by sevens, a significant fact when we know that the word for 'clean' used in the Hebrew text is *tahowr*, derived from *taher*, 'to be bright'.

After the Flood Noah sent out a raven, which 'went to and fro'.[27]

The significance of this little event is revealed when we learn that the Hebrew word for 'raven' derives from the root *arab*, and that this root is identical in outline to a word which means 'to braid'. Braided hair is used frequently both in dreams and in myths as a symbol of the umbilical cord, so that the idea of braiding, when conjoined with the idea of going back and forth, has a markedly umbilical flavor. It is in connection with the 'umbilicization' of the neck [232] and the top of the head [238] that such symbolism mainly occurs in mythology.

To return to the myth of Noah, a dove was sent out from the Ark but it came back and was held for seven days. Again it was sent out, and again it returned, and again it was held in the ark for seven days. Knowing the relation of the dove to the nuclear male energy, and the special relationship of the sevenfold beat to the umbilical cycle, this conjunction of the back and forth flight of the dove with sevenfold periods must appear to us as highly suggestive, to say the very least, when given the general context in which it all appears. God then made a rainbow appear in the sky as the token of his covenant. Now, the Hebrew word for a covenant is *beriyth*, and it means simply 'a cutting', and is traditionally related to the ceremony of passing between pieces of flesh. This 'cutting' may refer to the cutting of the umbilical cord, which was the instrument of 'passing between' (back and forth!) those 'two pieces of flesh' which *in utero* are the fetus and the placenta. In other words, the covenant is the link between the original inseparables, namely the fetus and the placenta: it is the restoration of 'the thing that was cut', namely the umbilical cord. Géza Róheim, who always gets near to the point without ever touching it, has this to say of the covenant:

> *The infant starts life in the dual unity situation. This means a state of things in which infant and mother form a whole and yet at the same time the two elements of a unity ... a covenant as a basic form of society is the dual unity restored.*[28]

The basis of the dual unity between the infant and the mother is the umbilical cord. This is the 'thing that is cut', and I believe that this is the reason why fundamentally the Hebrew word for a covenant means 'a cutting'. While this meaning may have been entirely lost, this does not in the least mean that the so-called unconscious does not fully understand it. The words and ideas of the conscious mind are relatively thin, but what truly strikes at the heart is the memory of the umbilical cord, the thing that was cut but restored in the feelings by the covenant. Further, Róheim unwittingly gives very powerful indications that the rainbow is a primitive symbol of the umbilical cord, thus making plain to us why the primitive Hebrews should have felt the rainbow as a covenant of God. He writes:

> *The snake owes its role in Australian belief mainly to two qualities. On the one hand snakes stand erect, and thus represent the phallos in erection; but they also swallow beings, and thus typify fantasies and anxieties connected with vagina and uterus. This ambisexual symbolism of the snake is associated with the rainbow. In the Wikmunkan tribe Taipan the rainbow serpent is a very great medicine*

man who cures sick people; he controls the heart and blood of man, and he is a great doctor. He possesses a big red stone knife at the end of a string, and when angry he throws it to strike a tree, which causes lightning, and then drags it back over the ground, making a rumbling noise. His totem place is the source of men's blood supply.[29]

The ambivalence which Róheim attributes solely to the feelings of the penis and vagina really has its source in the umbilical cord, as I have demonstrated [179]. The snake, which stands erect and strikes, but which also swallows creatures, corresponds far more closely with the umbilical cord than with the penis, though it is perfectly comprehensible that the feelings associated with the one should overlay the other [193]. The cord is felt to be a snake that thrusts and sucks. Of course, Róheim shares the common Freudian tendency to make everything sexual, assuming that the omnipresence of sexual symbols means only what it seems to say on the surface. But in fact these sexual symbols represent in the main the primary relationship between fetus and placenta through the cord.

Róheim's description of the Australian view of the rainbow clearly reveals the umbilical content. We can easily understand, for instance, why Taipan the rainbow serpent should be a very great medicine man: it is for the same reason that Asklepios (whose theriomorphic representation was the snake) was a great healer, namely that both are representations of the umbilical cord. Taipan controls the heart and the blood of man, a statement which may be readily interpreted in terms of the close relationship between the umbilical cord and the heart and blood of the fetus. The great knife which Taipan wields at the end of a string makes a crude but telling symbol of the aggressive out-thrusting sense evoked in the umbilical arteries. The association of the knife with the lightning makes an excellent symbol of the subtle electrical elements in the umbilical circulation and may be related to the double-headed stone axe which the ancient Greeks associated with lightning. The most telling item in the above Australian material, however, is the statement that Taipan, the rainbow serpent, has his totem place at the source of man's blood supply. This offers a telling representation of the fact that in a certain direct and immediate sense the umbilical 'serpent' is actually the source of man's blood supply. Examination of the sacred objects (*tjurungas*) of these primitive Australians, as illustrated in the same Róheim text, will reveal that many resemble crude representations of a cross-section of the umbilical cord. This umbilical interpretation of the rainbow serpent is supported by another passage from Róheim's book:

> *The Milky Way is really a mother and her son, stuck together forever in the act of copulation ... The Milky Way and rainbow serpent is an ambisexual composite being, derived from the primal scene ... 'Stuck in the Milky Way' means eternal coitus and union with mother.*[30]

I cannot pretend to guess by what association of feelings the Milky Way has come to be an Australian representation of the uterine organism, which may in fact be described with a certain half-truth as 'a mother and son together in eternal coitus'.[31] But the association of the manifestly umbilical rainbow serpent with this incestuous picture reflects a projection of the uterine memories upon the cosmos. By appearing in such a context, moreover, the rainbow serpent offers us a double assurance as to his umbilical significance. And so I return to my assertion that the appearance of the rainbow to Noah links him as fetal symbol to his inevitable counterpart, namely the umbilical cord and, by implication, the placenta. Moreover, I repeat that this immediately makes it clear why the Hebrew word for a covenant should derive directly from the idea of 'cutting'. The original covenant is the umbilical cord, not merely because it was the primary tie that each of us knew, but also because through the pattern of its beat and flow we each senses our still more primary link – namely to the Creator.

The myth of Noah ends on a note entirely relevant to what is written above. The first practical work Noah did upon leaving the ark was to plant a vineyard, with the result that he got drunk and lay naked in his tent, so that his sons saw his nakedness. There could hardly be a more convincing ending to this uterine myth. For indeed the fetus may be said to 'plant a vine', the umbilical cord, and 'to drink of its wine'. Indeed he may be said to lie 'uncovered within his tent', a passage which becomes even more suggestive when we know that the word for tent is *ohel*, from the root *ahal*, 'to shine'. Moreover, it is true that each one of us, in the uterine 'tent' has sensed a direct experience of our father's most intimate 'nakedness', because we felt an identity with the father in terms of the umbilical thrust into the placenta as mother [178-179].

A very complex representation of the umbilical feelings is to be found in the mythology of Osiris. The fetal nature of Osiris is portrayed by the fact that legend asserted him to have copulated with Isis, his female twin, even while both were still unborn. I have shown that this motif of incest is integral with the umbilical feelings [179]. The rite performed by Pharaoh at the Sed festival of ancient Egypt points in the same direction. In this rite the Pharaoh, or his priestly representative or substitute, lay down in the skin of a sacrificed animal and assumed the characteristic posture of a human fetus in the womb. When he emerged from this skin he was declared reborn in the following words:

Pharaoh has renewed his births.[32]

Although less certain, another indication of the fetal nature of Osiris may be seen in the fact that some have alleged his name to mean 'the many-eyed one', a title which would link him at once to the sense of the fetal skin as an 'all-seeing eye' or primal sense organ [9-11]. Inevitably the mythologist, when he hears of an eye-covered skin, thinks at once of Argus Panoptes, a very clear symbol of the fetus. Osiris has often been considered as a Sun god, but Frazer denies the propriety of this assertion. Yet it is clear that he who is the symbol of the fetus and his 'cloak of fire' [257-260] may present any one of several characteristics which relate to that symbol and may by natural association acquire one or more of the others. Thus, for example, the god with the eye-covered skin would become also the God of the Sun. Thus although Frazer may well be correct that Osiris was not 'properly' a Sun God (whatever that may precisely mean) he has become one. At any rate, the legends of Osiris show clearly that he was a symbol of the fetal hero, his cloak of fire and his umbilical adventures.

To begin with, Osiris was a great traveler who taught mankind in the course of his travels. This attribute is characteristic of the fetal hero, to be understood in the constant sense of traveling associated with the fetus in relationship to the umbilical cord [39-41] and also in terms of that mysterious 'teaching' which goes on in the course of its circulation [48-50]. This great and benign God won the admiration and gratitude of mankind, but his very prowess aroused jealousy which in turn led to that betrayal and dismemberment which are the common lot of the fetal hero.

Mythology of the Prenatal Life 47

At the very summit of his triumph, Osiris was trapped by the wicked Set, sealed into a coffer and thrown into the Nile. Upon learning of his death Isis fled to the Delta, accompanied by scorpions. We have already seen Isis in a placental role, for it was she with whom Osiris copulated while *in utero*. Therefore her flight to the Delta is symbolically comprehensible, since the Delta makes an excellent representative of the placenta. The Delta is the place where the long Nile makes its discharge, and the waters are spread out – a ready-made symbol of the placenta, into which the umbilical cord makes its discharge as the blood is spread out. While Isis waited at the Delta for Osiris, one of her attendant scorpions crept under a door and stung a child to death. Isis, hearing the lamentations of the child's mother, restored it to life. Here we have, as it were, a myth within a myth: the child destroyed at the Delta and later restored to life is a doubling of Osiris and his loss and restoration, much in the same way that the snatching away of Joseph's garment by Potiphar's wife doubles as the earlier loss of the 'Coat of Many Colors'. Isis discovered the body of Osiris and conceived a child by him while fluttering like a bird over his corpse. This part of the myth offers a likely representation of the fact that the self-as-father seems to die in the placenta and yet by his dying gives rise to the self-as-son [188]. The child born of this grisly mating was named Horus, who also has fetal characteristics, his symbol being the eye [248]. There is a part of the Osirian legend which establishes a case for regarding Horus as the resurrected Osiris: he, Horus, like the child at the Delta, was stung and killed by scorpions but restored to life by the command of Ra, the Sun God.

The coffer containing the body of Osiris floated ashore at Byblos. This place has directly uterine associations, being named after a girl who felt an incestuous love for her brother, even as Isis had felt for Osiris while in the womb of Nut. At the spot where the coffer of Osiris rested, at Byblos, a lovely Erica tree suddenly sprung up and enclosed within itself the coffer containing the body of Osiris. This tree was then cut down by the local king to make a pillar for his house. The king may be regarded as another version of the fetus, and the Erica tree as another version of the umbilical cord. This is strongly supported by what follows: Isis went to Byblos and sat weeping by a well, and to her came the king's handmaidens, whose hair she braided. As already noted above, in the story of Noah, braided hair has marked umbilical associations. When the queen saw her handmaidens' braided hair and certain other indications, she sent for Isis and made her the nurse to her son. Isis gave the child her finger to suck, and at night set him in the fire in order to burn away his mortal nature, a strange event which will inevitably remind the reader of a similar tale, of Demeter and Demophoön. Demeter is a prime symbol of the placenta and hence, of course, a suitable nurse for the 'flaming one' – in this case the infant Demophoön. Isis discovered the existence of the pillar containing the body of Osiris, and she fluttered round it in the guise of a swallow, eventually regaining possession of the coffer. But Typhon found the coffer while hunting by the light of the Full Moon, and he rent the body of Osiris into pieces and threw them in the Nile. Here again we see the reiteration of the umbilical narrative: the Full Moon is strongly placental and features in many a mythical context, and in turn this fits neatly with the tearing into pieces of the god's body. The whole story of Osiris is thus a constant reiteration of the motif of the loss and recovery of the Shining One in relation to his placental 'doubles'.

As Frazer points out, the actual resurrection of Osiris is inferred rather than described, and yet he was regarded as the sign and assurance of personal resurrection. It has been asserted that Osiris was no more than a god of the grain, an agricultural hero pure and simple, but such simple views of the mythical figures are usually the outcome of a highly rationalistic view which cannot tolerate the undertones inseparable from mythical and dream material. From the mythical standpoint, it is perfectly possible for Osiris to be both a god of personal resurrection and also an agricultural god, as previously discussed [121-122]. Insofar as he represented the purely umbilical feelings, then Osiris would truly represent the deepest intimations of loss and restoration experienced in the course of the umbilical cycle [28]. But after birth, these feelings become displaced upon the sense of a flow of energy from the body down into the earth and back. And since this displacement makes the earth into the placenta (for our feelings), then the earth itself appears to us as that dread monster into whom we are sucked and from whom we are restored. And because the processes of agriculture call for

Mythology of the Prenatal Life 49

the plunging of seed into the earth and the reaping of the uprising grain, Osiris could become naturally and spontaneously the god of this process without in any way losing his original status as god of personal (umbilical) resurrection. Indeed, far from such a superimposition being a product of primitive confusions of thought, it is the justified outcome of a wisdom far deeper than the intellectual mind can conceive solely by its own efforts.

Another prime representative of the fetal skin feeling is Abram who became Abraham, the father of the Hebrew people. His name and his adventures seem to establish him as another instance of the Shining One. Abram was born in Ur of the Chaldees, the name Ur being in Hebrew *uwr*, meaning 'flame'. He goes from Ur to Haran, a name which has associations with height, but the outline of which might easily be confused with Charan, a name having close associations with the ideas of glowing or burning. Thus we have good reason to see Abram as another symbol of the fetal nuclear feeling, an interpretation congruent with the discovery that his wife is first named Sarai and then Sarah, for both names have close umbilical associations. The name Sarai derives from the root *sar*, which has precisely the same outline in Hebrew as the word *shor* meaning 'a string' (as twisted) also the umbilical cord, the navel.[33] The name Sarah is from the same root.

[handwritten annotation: altar — implantation site ↓ ↓ Egypt endometrium]

Abram journeyed to the plain of Moreh and there he built an altar. The altar, as we have seen, is a place of blood and also of destruction, and its location upon a plain may have a subtle link with the placenta, for it will be noted that associated with the life of Abram are the 'cities of the plain' which are destroyed. This association between a plain and destruction seems more than accidental, because it is met with several times in mythology in a very suggestive way, notably in the rape of Persephone on the plain. The story of Abram tells how he built his altar between Bethel and Hai, and it is worth noting that the name Hai derives from the Hebrew word *iy*, which means 'a ruin'. The building of this altar is immediately followed by a journey down into Egypt to seek for food, a circumstance which once again presents Egypt in a placental character, as in the story of Joseph. In Egypt there takes place a remarkable little drama in which the incestuous elements are apparent, though offered in an oblique fashion.

In dream analysis, the placenta may be felt as the sister, and we know that Sara's name has umbilical associations. Therefore when we find Abram passing her off as his sister, we can see through the rationalization, which is that he had to do so to prevent the Egyptians killing him in order to possess her. What this part of the myth achieves is the linking of wife and sister, and thus it imports the sense of incest, which is strongly uterine, for reasons we have already seen. That the story of Abram's deception over Sara is a mythological device not a legend, is argued from the fact that he later employs the same ruse with Abimelech. Later still, his son Isaac played precisely the same trick upon precisely the same king. The outcome of this trickery, in the case of both Abram and Isaac, is a great accession of wealth and power immediately following. The intent of the myth is plain: with both Abram and his son, the journey down into Egypt and/or Gerar is the representation of the journey of the Shining One down the umbilical cord to the placenta, the suggestion of incest allied to the threat of death, and the return again full of power and riches. This same motif dominates the myths of Isaac, Jacob and Joseph. These supposedly chronological sequences, whatever historical basis they may have had, can be seen by their internal evidence to be symbolic repetitions of the basic story of the human ego, namely the story of the uterine life in terms of the umbilical blood and the fetal skin.

The story of Samson and Delilah is widely known, and is a good instance of a relatively incomplete myth of the Shining One, but is also one in which the uterine elements are nevertheless demonstrable. In Hebrew, the name Samson is Shimshown, and means 'sunlight', being derived from the root *shemesh*, 'to be brilliant'. The name Delilah is Delliylah in Hebrew, and is conventionally supposed to derive from *layelah*, which is a Hebrew word for 'night'. We might suppose that the myth of Samson and Delilah is merely a representation of the supposed war between the Sun and the night, or between light and dark. But even if originally it were so, we shall see that uterine elements have been imposed upon it in such a way that the Sun signifies the fetal skin feeling, while the night represents the umbilical arteries and the placenta. Indeed, in Hebrew the very word for night *(layelah)* derives from the word *luwl,* meaning 'a spiral step'; its relationship to night as a twisting or turning away from the light. It appears to me that this very particular etymology may be another instance of where the subjective elements have dominated the observations of the external senses. The simple opposition between day and night are overshadowed by the elements of opposition once felt in that 'spiral step' of the umbilical arteries [23-25] which led away from the 'sunlight' of the fetal skin feeling (Samson) to extinguishment in the 'dark night' of the placenta (Delilah).

Quite apart from the above speculations, there are umbilical and placental indications in the etymology of the name of Delilah, for Strong asserts that it derives from *dalal,* which means 'to slacken', 'to bring low' and 'to dry up'. There is also a word not too remote from Delilah, namely *daliyah,* meaning 'something dangling – as a bough', and which derives from the root *dalah,* meaning 'to dangle' or 'to let down a bucket for the drawing of water'. All these words and meanings have a varying degree of umbilical and placental association. Thus, for instance, it is the placenta, which is believed to bring on birth, so 'slackening up', or 'drying up', as a result of which it 'brings low' the majestic fetus in birth. The umbilical cord may be thought of as 'dangles' from the fetal body like a bough, and the letting down of a bucket into a well in order to draw up water makes a fair symbol of the action of the umbilical cord, which may be thought of as lowered into the placental well for the refreshment of the fetus. This tentative interpretation is greatly firmed by the realization that Sorek, where Samson discovers Delilah, means 'a vine', the name being derived from the word *soreg,* meaning not only 'redness' but also 'a vine yielding rich grapes'. In this close association with redness and the vine, Delilah's placental and umbilical nature is emphasized. If we accept this interpretation, even tentatively, the rest of the struggle between Samson (the Shining One) and Delilah becomes comprehensible.

We can then understand why Delilah encompasses Samson's ruin by cutting off his hair. This act could permissibly but superficially be interpreted as the cutting off of the Sun's rays by the night, but it also has a very definite uterine significance. As the fetal skin feeling may be partly evoked by the action of the lanugo hair [248], it may

52 *Mythology of the Prenatal Life*

also be linked with hair or hairy skins in certain myths, such as in the hairy skin of Esau and the *aegis,* an attribute of Zeus. This cutting off of Samson's hair by Delilah is further associated with placental function through the subsequent putting out of his eyes. The Bible says:

> The Philistines took him, and put out his eyes, and brought him down to Gaza ...[34]

Now, the place-name 'Gaza' is usually rendered as Azzah in Hebrew. However, in Hebrew there is a word *gazzah* which means 'a fleece', and which comes from the root *gazaz,* meaning 'to shear' (as a sheep) or 'to shave the hair'. The state of being 'eyeless in Gaza' ought to be, according to this suggestion, 'eyeless in Gazzah', meaning simply that in the loss of the fetal nuclear skin feeling (hair) there is a loss of that 'all-over-seeing' of the fetal body. This interpretation is supported by the fact that Hebrew etymology preserves a direct link between the skin and the eyes, since the Hebrew word for skin has precisely the same outline as the word which means 'to awaken' or 'to open the eyes'.

When discussing the universal myth of the Sun and the sea monster, it was pointed out that the Philistines gave credit to Dagon the fish god for delivering Samson into their hands.[35] It was in the belly of the sea monster that the solar hero lost his hair, and this serves to create not only a link between the Bible myth and the universal solar tale, but also to confirm still further the fetal nature of Samson and the placental nature of Delilah. Delilah shares with the sea monster the experience of taking the hair from the Shining One, a symbolic representation of the fact that the placenta drains the fetus of his nuclear skin feeling [28]. The placenta, however, is not merely a destroyer, it is also a restorer, as represented in the myths by the fact that the dying hero is resurrected, often by the very instrument that secured his death.

These elements of resurrection are not very clear in the myth of Samson and Delilah, but I think that there are certain oblique attempts to provide them, as I will now indicate. Before he met Delilah, Samson married a woman of Timnath, a name which in itself may have an etymological link with the Hebrew word for 'a twin'. When Samson went to Timnath to get his wife, he met a lion in the vineyards of the place and tore it to pieces. Here we have some very suggestive elements: the Sun-hero (symbol of the fetus) meets a lion (symbol of the fetal skin feeling) in a vineyard (source of wine and vines = placenta) and there tears it in pieces. It seems fairly certain that this portion of the Samson story is simply a variant of the myth of the tearing to pieces of the Shining One by the Beast – a myth which may be stated in reverse (as in the present case) without diminishing the value of the emotional associations.

The story of Samson later presents him as returning to Timnath, where he found the carcass of the lion he had slain and, behold! – there were bees and honey in it. Samson took some honey and ate it. This clearly links with the fetus feeling that he eats from the place of death, namely the placenta [31]. Shortly afterwards Samson gave a feast to which came 'thirty companions'. These may be regarded in terms of the umbilical *three* [23], akin in symbolical character to the thirty pieces of silver in the Gospel story. The bees which deposited their honey in the lion's carcass are worthy of some comment, for dreams often represent the fetal skin feeling as insects crawling over the body.[36] Freud stated that insects were often symbols for the father, a fact which may be understood if we recall that the fetal skin feeling is in some mysterious way identified with the father [186], from which would stem the equation skin-feeling = insects = father. One is reminded here that after the death of Argus, the man with the eye-covered skin, the skin of Io was perpetually stung by a gadfly. Here the insect plainly takes the place of the eyes on the skin. Moreover, the insects do not represent the fetal skin feeling in its actual prenatal state, but in the vestigial relics of it felt in the postnatal state. This fact fits both the myth of Io and the myth of Samson and the bees.

Now comes the symbolism of resurrection. Samson posed a riddle to his wife's people:

Out of the eater came forth meat, and out of the strong came forth sweetness.[37]

This riddle permits of a clearly placental interpretation, for the placenta is the 'eater' or devourer and destroyer of the fetal skin feeling, and yet it is the source of the fetal supply, so that truly it may be said that the 'eater gives meat' [32]. The placenta also is felt by the fetus to be 'strong' and yet to be the source of joy. Samson gave the people *seven* days in which to solve the riddle, and offered a prize of *thirty* sheets and *thirty* changes of raiment. Here we find new coverings offered in association with a seven-day period, and thirty items twice repeated. Further, because the people could not solve the riddle, they coerced Samson's wife into eliciting the answer, which he gave her on the *seventh day*. It is the *seven* beats of blood in the *three* umbilical tubes that restores the energy of the fetal skin, and it is this restoration which the myth seems to tell in these oblique terms. The 'changes of raiment' are in that context, of course, simply symbols of the perpetual restoration of the fetal skin energy. The Samson story concludes with the odd and seemingly irrelevant statement that Samson went out straightway and slew *thirty* men, and then gave a change of garments to them which expounded the riddle – though we have just been told that none had done so. In spite of this inconsistency, the story retains discernible uterine symbolisms.

There is an extraordinary story told by Frazer which might serve to link the Samson story with the umbilical theme, deep within the inner feelings of humanity. The story is about a man named Liongo who lived in Shanga, and Frazer calls him an 'African Samson' for reasons which become apparent in the story. Liongo oppressed his people so much that they sought his life. They bribed Liongo's nephew to ask the tyrant the secret of his vital spot, and received the reply that Liongo would die if a copper needle were thrust into his navel. The people thereupon gave the treacherous nephew such a needle, which he straightway plunged into his uncle's navel so that he died. The motif of destruction by betrayal of the weak spot is common to the story of Samson and also of Liongo. Samson's weak spot was his hair, and Liongo's was his navel. Knowing the relationship between the fetal skin feeling and the navel (umbilical cord) we can see how the two stories are symbolically of much the same order. The fundamental distinction between them lies in the fact that in the case of Samson it was a woman who twice betrayed him by revealing his riddle. The woman and the deadly riddle are well known mythic themes, and will always be found in a context which confirms her placental nature. The best-known instance is probably the sphinx-woman who sat at the gates of Thebes and rent in pieces all the young men who essayed to answer her riddle and failed.

Elements of both the Samson and the Liongo stories appear in the Norse tale of Balder, the god of light and of the Sun, whose twin brother named Hodur was somber, taciturn and blind. On the surface these two represent day and night, as do Samson and Delilah. But underneath this lie the subjective elements of the feelings of the fetus for the placenta. One day Balder was cast down by oppressive dreams of his impending doom. His father and mother, Odin and Frigga, sent far and wide to ask all things to swear not to hurt Balder, and thus they sought to comfort the young god and to protect him. All creation took the oath save the little mistletoe, which grew upon the oak at the gate of Valhalla. The servants of the great gods Odin and Frigga did not bother to ask so puny a creature, for they assumed that nothing so negligible could harm the great Sun god. Reassured by the promise of all creation not to harm him, Balder resumed his life of gaiety. Once again as was his wont he played with the other gods upon the green plain of Ida. In this connection it may be worth recalling that the plain is frequently used as a symbol of the placenta, where the destruction of the nuclear energy takes place. Here on the green plain of Ida the young gods amused themselves by hurling weapons, and Balder encouraged his companions to hurl them at him, for he had been assured that none could harm him. There was great merriment as the gods hurled their weapons at Balder. Frigga, who was spinning in Fensalir, heard the laughter and the shouting and asked a passing old woman the reason. The old woman explained that the gods were hilarious because they were hurling their weapons at Balder without bad effect, whereupon Frigga explained that all things had sworn an oath not to harm Balder – all, that is, save the puny mistletoe which grew upon the great oak at the gates of Valhalla. This was enough: the old woman was none other than Loki in disguise. Loki was the god of fire, and he hated Balder, his rival, the Sun. So he hastened to the gates of Valhalla, tore the mistletoe from the oak and, by means of his magic arts, transformed it into a hardened weapon. Thus armed, he hurried back to the plain of Ida, where he found blind Hodur leaning disconsolate upon a tree. Hodur explained that he was sorrowful because he could not see to take part in the sport of throwing things at Balder. Loki gave Hodur the fatal mistletoe shaft and guided his hand to the throwing. Hodur hurled the shaft at Balder, who gave an awful cry and fell dead. Here, as in the myth of Samson, we find the death of the Shining One encompassed through the betrayal of a secret. Also, since Loki was disguised as a woman, Balder was betrayed by a woman because Frigga, who uttered the fatal secret, also played a part.

Liongo, the African Samson, was slain by having his navel pierced. Did Hodur's mistletoe shaft pierce Balder in the navel? The myth does not say so, but when I come to consider the contents of Frazer's *The Golden Bough*, it will be demonstrated that the mistletoe is a universal symbol of the umbilical cord, wherefrom it must follow that the umbilicus is the likeliest place where the fatal blow could be struck by a mistletoe shaft.

Another well-known story of the Shining One and his placental betrayer is to be found in the myth of Jacob and Esau, represented as struggling in the womb of Rebekah. The word used for 'struggling' (namely *ratsats*) may originally have had a meaning akin to 'the jerky back and forth flow of a liquid' – which is strongly suggestive of the umbilical beat. Although in this story both twins are males, there are strong indications that Esau represents the fetus and Jacob the placenta. Esau is his father's favorite, and this acts as a means of identification. Conversely, Jacob is his mother's favorite to such an extent that she is willing to deceive both her husband and her elder son on his behalf. Everything points to Esau as representing the fetus. He is born first, with Jacob clinging to his heel, also suggestive of Jacob's placental nature and so, by implication, of the fetal nature of Esau. Esau is born covered all over with hair, a condition which is not only directly suggestive of the lanugo hair, also a symbol of the fetal skin feeling. The Hebrew word for hair is *sear*, and it is closely related to the idea of tossing and bristling hair, and to some extent with shivering. This association of ideas strongly suggests a condition of peripheral irritation, and the name Esau may be related to it, since Strong asserts that the name may mean 'sensibly felt', which would be an all-too-perfect representation of the fetal skin feeling [9]. The Hebrew *sear*, meaning 'hair', is also very closely related to the name Seir, which is mysteriously related to Esau. Moreover, it is by his hair that his father knows him, and by the mocking of which Jacob deceives the old man. Esau, we might say, was a very hairy man, and this in a very complete sense, for he was born 'all over like an hairy garment'.[38] There is another name for Esau which reinforces his fetal nature, namely Edom. Edom is exactly the same as Adam, so that Esau's identification is not merely with his own father, Jacob, but with Adam, the first father. Moreover, the name Adam in Hebrew is derived from the word *adam*, which means 'a flush of blood in the skin', an idea closely linked with the fact that the blood in the fetal skin may, in conjunction with the fetal (lanugo) hair, play a major part in the evocation of the fetal skin feeling [25, 247-248].

As perhaps to be expected, the fetal Esau has a placental twin. Jacob is primarily a placental symbol and his name comes from the Hebrew root *aqeb*, meaning simply 'the heel', referring us to the odd circumstance that Jacob was born holding onto Esau's heel. Of great importance to human feeling is the sense that the flow of blood into the legs of the fetus is only a spill-over from the flow of blood into the umbilical artery [108]. As a result of this anatomical fact a confusion is set up in the feelings as to where the placenta really is – at the end of the umbilical cord or at the end of the legs. In a word, there is confusion between the fetal legs and the umbilical arteries, and between the feet and the placenta. This confusion is the reality behind the universal myth of the hero with the lame or wounded and bleeding feet. Poetically stated, the Shining One always senses that he has the placenta at his feet, and this is the reason why Jacob is called 'the heel-catcher', which clearly reflects his placental nature. Further, Jacob's strong emotional identification with his mother Rebekah tells the same story, for the name 'Rebekah' is Ribqah in Hebrew, a name which probably derives from a word meaning 'to tie by the fetlock'. In other words, Jacob and his mother both have names which give indication of something linked or tied to the feet or ankles. Both are, in my view, placental symbols.

Jacob, moreover, is described as 'a plain man, dwelling in tents', a description which might first appear baffling, but which takes on new significance, however, when we see that the Hebrew word translated as 'plain' in our Bible is *tam*, a word which derives from *tamam*, meaning 'to complete', and is related to the Hebrew word *ta'om*, meaning 'twins'. The word for 'tents' in Hebrew is *ohel*, from the root *ahal*, to 'shine'. Behind the familiar words 'Jacob was a plain man, dwelling in tents', may thus be seen something like the following: the one at the feet was a twin, living with the Shining One. The reader will bear in mind in assessing this interpretation, that the Hebrew language lends itself spectacularly well to this type of dignified punning, so that through the very double meaning (or near double meaning) of words both the conscious and the unconscious context can be conveyed in a most extraordinary way – a way that makes no sense at all to the modern mind.

Jacob and Esau follow the conventional formula for all fetal and placental characters – the placental one betrays the fetal one. As Delilah betrayed Samson, as Loki betrayed Balder, as Eve betrayed Adam, so Jacob betrays Esau. What is more, Jacob betrays him through the act of feeding. As I showed in relation to the betrayal of Jesus by Judas, there is a strong link between the act of feeding and the act of betrayal. It derives from the fact that the placenta feeds the fetus, but at the same time 'makes him feel hollow' [21], and also by the fact that the fetus 'feeds' the placenta with blood and, in that act, is engulfed and destroyed in feeling [28, 29].

> *And Esau said to Jacob, Feed me, I pray thee, with that same red pottage; for I am faint: therefore was his name called Edom.*[39]

```
            Blastula
               |
      dismemberment = differentiation
            /   \     trophoblast
           \     /

        Jacob – Esau
        Jesus – Judas
        Samson – Delilah
```

Esau, the fetal image, depends upon the placental image for food. The English Bible asserts that he demands 'red pottage', but the Hebrew Bible simply duplicates the word 'red', and thus Esau may be conceived as saying, 'Feed me with that red redness'. That this 'red redness' means blood is clear enough, supported by the statement immediately following that 'therefore' his name was called Edom. The name 'Edom', we have seen, means 'to flush with blood'. The myth speaks about as plainly as a myth can without becoming a medical treatise, and it tells us that the result of this feeding with 'red redness' is that Esau loses his birthright to Jacob.

> *the psychic representation of the genetic pattern of the life-cycle   a sphere – buried –*

This is perhaps a symbolic representation of the fact that by taking in blood from the placenta the feeling roles are reversed and the fetus loses its nuclear sense somewhat, becoming in degree hollow in feeling, while the placenta assumes the nuclear and penetrative aspect to the same degree. All this is represented in the Jacob-Esau myth as a single event, but in fact the fetus 'sells his nuclear birthright' over and over again to the placenta with every act of being 'fed with that red redness'. Note that the Jacob-Esau myth is almost wholly concerned with the postnatal development of their mutual affect, as outlined in Part Two of *The Nature of the Self*. This myth, when analyzed *in toto*, is most evidential.

We move into a more historical atmosphere when we approach the story of Moses, and yet even there, symbolic uterine elements have been powerfully superimposed upon legend and history.[40] The name Moses is generally supposed to be derived from the Hebrew root *mashah*, meaning 'to draw out', and to be a reference to the legend that Pharaoh's daughter drew him out of the water. This in itself has dim uterine possibilities, since the daughter of the Son of the Sun is a suitable candidate for the role of placental symbol. Certainly it is the placenta, which not only 'draws out' the fetal one, but also restores him to new life. But the name 'Moses' is also alleged to be related to the Egyptian word for a son or a child, and the 'child in the water' is certainly a very apt symbol of the fetus. The flight of Moses because of a killing has a strong umbilical possibility, since the nuclear feeling seems to be related to a death in the placenta and an escape. This assertion must be understood in the sense that the nuclear element of the fetal skin feeling is felt to enter the placenta as father, to be destroyed there, whereafter it is 'reborn' and returns to the fetal body, or may be regarded as 'escaping' [84, 188]. This escape from the mother after the slaying of the father will be seen again in the interpretation of the flight of Orestes.

That Moses's flight from Egypt is a symbolic representation of the return from the placenta to the fetal body is supported in the first place by the placental nature of Egypt, as seen in the myth of Joseph, but also by the fact that Moses goes and tends the flocks of Jethro. The name has indirect associations with *yothereth*, 'a caul', and so with uterine elements. This is further symbolized by the fact that Moses comes upon the burning bush while tending the flock of Jethro. The burning bush that is not consumed makes an excellent symbol of the fetal skin feeling, not impaired in any way by the fact that the Hebrew word for bush used in this context is *ceneh*, which means 'to prick', therefore indirectly related with the fetal skin feeling as an irritation of the skin. Further, it was while he stood before this burning bush that God drew attention to the rod in Moses's hand and caused it to become a serpent. Here we have thus conjoined the sense of the fetus (Moses), the sense of the skin feeling (the burning and pricking bush), and also the sense of the umbilical cord (rod and serpent). It will be recalled that it was through the power of this magical rod that Moses had the ability to smite Egypt and to deliver the Children. In a word, the umbilical rod has the power of death and of life: it is the supreme instrument of the perpetual 'Passover'.

Turning once more to Greek mythology, we may see in the great Apollo a powerful and convincing representative of the universal Shining One, though his relationship to the Sun is said to be a late addition to his myth. However, as I have said before, through the discovery of the subjective source of the myths, we can see at once that if the original figure of Apollo showed the least fetal attributes, then his acquisition of solar associations is likely to follow as a matter of course. The same considerations apply to his epithet Lukegenes, which in addition to referencing his Lycian birthplace, may also be interpreted as meaning 'the one born of the light', thus revealing the uterine association.

Having understood the fetal nature of Apollo it seems extraordinarily appropriate that his chief temple should have been situated at Delphi, a name derived from the Greek word *delphos*, which means 'womb'. Before this temple there once stood a great stone called the *omphalos*, which means 'navel' and which marked the grave of the snake that Apollo slew shortly after his birth. The conjunction of the Shining One with 'womb-town' (Delphoi) shows the intent of the symbolism, and this is reinforced by the existence there of the 'navel' which marks the spot where the 'snake' was last known. The late Arthur Bernard Cook[41] asserted that the *omphalos* at Delphoi had a forerunner at Knossos, where it was actually reputed to mark the spot where the navel-string of Zeus fell to the ground. He also points out that when the French archaeologists found the actual *omphalos* at Delphoi, they discovered an iron shaft running through it, and this is reputed to have been the handle of a large iron knife, symbolic of the instrument which cuts the cord at birth. It is hard to see what the pedants hope to gain by adamantly insisting, in the face of so much evidence, that the word *omphalos* when used in connection with these monuments means only 'a center'. Indeed, I shall show presently that the reverse is true, namely that to the ancients every center tended to be thought of as a navel – because the sense of spatial orientation begins in the umbilical cord [34-41].

The surname of Apollo was Phoebus, which has the significance of 'shining' or 'brilliant', and it is a fact that the town of Delphoi was and still is a veritable sun-trap, and has been described thus by a modern writer:

> One's chief impressions are height, dizzy height, and light, dazzling, unbearable. The Sun god shows his power; the whole place is ablaze, and we can understand Otfried Müller dying here of sunstroke, smitten by a shaft of far-shooting Phoebus for outraging his sanctuary.[42]

Nothing could more powerfully represent the fetal feelings than the sense of height combined with the sense of overpowering light. We can well understand why Delphoi should have been termed 'the common hearth of Hellas', and why it was from there that was borne the fire from which the sacred fires of ancient Greece were relit. For the fetal fire, the nuclear skin feeling which is felt by us as a great shining, is indeed the focal point not merely of Greece in ancient times, but of all lands and people in all times, and indeed of the eternal cosmos. But not only fire came from Delphoi: there also came guidance from the 'snake woman' or 'the Pythia', who sat upon her three-legged stool and dispensed the whispers that swayed the life of Hellas. This represents in external form the fact that it is from the placenta through the navel that the deepest wisdom reaches us – a wisdom rooted in the organic life of the body and the life of nature [47-50].

There is surely a connection between the Pythia on her tripod and the pot which hung upon the tripod on the 'blasted heath' wherein bubbled the 'toil and trouble' that should fall upon Macbeth. This pot is, I believe, the image of the placenta in which a great deal of what determines our future is transmitted to us [47]. The tripod and the attendant three witches symbolize the umbilical cord, and these witches tell the future even as the Pythia did. Incidentally, the situation of the Macbeth scene 'upon a blasted heath' accords well with the placental motif for, as I have already said, and shall have occasion later to amplify, the flat place or plain is often used in a context which makes its placental symbolism perfectly appropriate.

In the light of Apollo's manifest fetal nature it is important to note his special relationship with the number seven. The number seven was regarded by the Greeks as sacred to Apollo; he was alleged to have been born on the seventh day of the month, or in the seventh month; his festivals were held on the seventh day of the month, when sacrifices were offered to him. It may appear natural that the Sun god should be associated with sevens because of the seven days of the week, but this superficial assumption would entirely miss the point as to why man should impose a sevenfold rhythm upon the fleeting sequence of the days. I have shown that this rhythm is basic to our primary sense of time, a sense which we gain through a resonance, which develops between the beat of blood in the umbilical cord and the structure of space-time [34-35]. For this reason the number seven has a very special significance for the fetal state and, hence, insofar as Apollo is a fetal symbol it is most appropriately his 'special number'.

Like the fetus, thrusting from his twin umbilical arteries, and thus appearing to pierce the placenta, Apollo was regarded as capable of shooting forth arrows with unerring aim. One is reminded of the assertion that Esau was a 'cunning hunter'. Apollo was indeed regarded as a great killer, but he is also related to the supreme healing and restorative function through his fathering of Asklepios. Now, Asklepios was regarded as a supreme healer, and in *Prolegomena to the Study of Greek Religion*, Jane Harrison recounts that he was beyond doubt originally regarded as a snake, only later receiving his more urbane human form. Jane Harrison further confirms the umbilical nature of Asklepios by pointing out that his name is believed by some to derive from a word which meant 'to coil' or 'to turn round and round', a common attribute of umbilical symbology [23-24]. The anthropomorphic Asklepios carried a snake-twined staff, a highly pictorial representation of the umbilical anatomy, a subject dealt with at length in my earlier book *The Universal Design of the Oedipus Complex*. This staff is now the insignia of the medical profession and, as I have pointed out elsewhere, what could be more essentially a 'doctor' than the umbilical cord, which serves both to detoxify the fetal blood and to recharge it with 'good medicine'!

Thus we see Apollo, the Shining One, the Lord of Seven and the founder of 'womb-town' (Delphoi), as not only a killer but, through his son Asklepios, a healer. We see him as both a destroyer and a creator of snakes, for he slew the Python right after birth, and fathered the snake Asklepios. In this combination of qualities and deeds we can gain a clear symbolic picture of the fetal skin feeling and its relationship with the umbilical cord. This picture is further confirmed when we examine the nature of Apollo's sister, Artemis. The name of the goddess seems to derive from a word which means 'uninjured, healthy and vigorous'– concepts which have the closest relationship with the placenta. The placenta, though constantly 'pierced' by the 'arrows of Apollo' (the umbilical arterial thrust), remains uninjured and provides a source of health and vigor. Constantly impregnated, she remains a virgin still, a thoroughly placental attribute [187]. Like her brother Apollo, Artemis carries a bow and arrows, and these darts bring sudden death. In spite of this she is also a healer, so that in these respects she stands revealed as the female counterpart of Apollo, a circumstance which likewise argues her placental nature, since both the fetus and the placenta are felt as 'archers' in the sense that each pierces and makes hollow the other. Yet the flow of the umbilical blood is a 'healing' flow, and thus the combination of arrow shooting and healing has a distinctly umbilical meaning. Moreover, some traditions regarded

64 Mythology of the Prenatal Life

Artemis not as the sister but as the wife of Apollo, and this imports the suggestion that she was in truth the sister-wife of the Shining One, a relationship which we already have observed in the myths of Osiris-Isis, Abraham-Sarah and Isaac-Rebekah. Artemis was called 'the stag-killer', but she also was known as the protectress of young sucking animals. Here, the umbilical reflection may be seen in the fact that the placenta is not only the 'piercer' of the fetus, but also the protectress of that 'young sucking animal', which sucks its blood supply from her through the very vein which seems to pierce him.

Thoughts of Apollo as fetal symbol evoke memories of his tragic priest at Troy, the ill-fated Laocoön. This man dared to go forth and strike his spear into the side of the Trojan Horse, whereupon there came from the sea two mighty serpents which, after entwining his two sons, seized Laocoön also in their frightful coils. The priest of Apollo, as representative of the god, inevitably assumes some of his qualities, at any rate for mythical purposes, so that we may see this struggle with the snakes as a version of the struggle of the Shining One with the umbilical cord. The representation of the father locked in the reptilian coils with his two smaller sons makes a powerful symbolic picture of the umbilical three, with the distinction between the two and the one carefully preserved [25]. To this must be added the fact that the horse appears to be a prime

[handwritten annotation: primitive stalk — Python / ↓ ↓ / umbilical cord   Asculapius (serpent)]

symbol of the placenta. The exact reason for this I cannot ascertain, but there can be hardly any doubt that the horse, and above all the centaur, is a universal symbol of the placenta, especially in Greek mythology. To this question, of the placental symbolism of the horse and the centaur, I shall return later.

In the myth of Adam and Eve we have a representation of the uterine organism as generator of both gender and consciousness. This wonderful myth, literally interpreted by the extraverted mind, has been presented to successive generations as if it were the story of the origins of mankind in an anthropological sense, whereas it is patently the story of the origins of each individual man, his

handwritten note: centaur — the intrauterine-organism / embryo ↔ trophoblast

mind and sense of gender, in the feelings of the womb and of the umbilical flow. The myth, interpreted in this way, actually asserts that the human mind and the human sense of gender are conferred upon the uterine organism by the nature of the Creator [173]. The Adamic myth symbolizes the essentials of the process by which the uterine organism becomes linked with the universal pattern of the cosmos [42]. It even hints at the fact that this uterine evocation of pattern eventually after birth polarizes the upright body, a subject which is outlined in Part Two of *The Nature of the Self*. In some cases the myth presents us with the most obvious symbolisms, but some are obscure and, save in such a plain context, would not be at all evidential.

It has already been shown that the name Adam refers to the 'flush of blood on the skin', and that in this way it serves to symbolize the fetal skin feeling both in terms of blood and 'shine'. That Adam is linked with the sense of the hairy skin is implied by the evident link between Adam and Esau, as also between Esau and Seir, which last signifies 'rough' and is derived from the Hebrew root which may be transliterated as *sa'ar*, meaning 'to shiver'. This idea of shivering may in itself be seen to contain an idea akin to the titillation of the skin, hence to be an adequate symbol of the irritation of the fetal skin by the lanugo hair. The interpretation is supported by the fact that the outline of the Hebrew word for 'hair' is identical with that of *safar*, to shiver. Moreover, it is a fact, which ought not to be overlooked that the Hebrew word for skin contains an internal link with the idea of light, since the word for skin, which may be transliterated as *owr*, has the same outline as two words concerning the eyes. One of these may be transliterated as *uwr*, and means 'to open the eyes', while the other may be rendered into English as *favar*, having the meaning of 'a film or skin over the eyes'. From many different angles the signs point to Adam as the symbol of the fetal skin feeling generated through the lanugo hair and through the blood. Adam is another instance of the 'Shining One', although not explicitly represented as such.

The name Eve is a fitting one for the placenta, since it signifies 'the life-giver'. The name is related to the Hebrew word which may be transliterated as *chayah*, meaning among other things 'to revive, nourish, quicken, repair.' That Adam and Eve together are essentially one organism [42] is symbolized in the quaint story of Eve being made from one of Adam's ribs. This myth may contain a reference to the fact that in the very earliest embryological period the blood is made very largely in the placenta, while this blood-making activity later is transferred to the bone-marrow, thus linking the placenta and skeleton by making the symbol of the former (Eve) come from an adaptation of the latter (Adam's rib). That the myth states the sequence in reverse is not important. If this suggestion seems difficult to accept, I can but assure the reader that a great deal of what I have learned about the uterine anatomy was learned first from dreams and confirmed later in external research. The record of the body's structure and function is almost certainly 'known' and recorded in the deep feelings.

a record of bodies structure and function of the transformations developmental

Be that as it may, the making of Eve out of the rib of Adam suggests a primal state of unity, which is not at all uncommon in the myths dealing with human origins. According to the primitive Aranda tribe of Australia, human beings originally existed in a highly undeveloped state: their eyes and ears were closed, and they had a small round hole in place of a mouth. Moreover, they were joined in couples, wherefore they are called by the Aranda *'rella interinia'*, which is to say 'grown-together people'. The myth states that a lizard cuts apart with his stone knife these two 'grown-together ones'. This reminds one of Plato's assertion that the original human being had a double set of organs, and was cut apart by Zeus to make two people. It is in such terms that the ancient peoples represented for themselves the dual unity situation of the fetus and placenta.

If Adam and Eve are truly the representatives of the fetus and placenta, then we would expect to find umbilical associations adhering to them. This expectation is completely fulfilled by the presence of a serpent and a tree of life in the abode of the primal pair. This tree of life that has a serpent wound upon it is an age-old symbol of the umbilical cord. The 'snake-wound tree' is simply a variant of that rod or staff associated with or entwined by snakes: the rod of Moses, the staff of Teiresias, which slew the snakes, the *kerykeion* or *caduceus* of Hermes. The fact that the Bible speaks of a single Edenic serpent does not diminish the adequacy of the umbilical symbolism, for in both dreams and myths the single serpent appears frequently in a context which is overwhelmingly umbilical. A prime mythological example of the single serpent is that which Apollo slew at Delos and buried at Delphoi (womb-town), marking its grave there with a stone called 'the navel'.

The Edenic tree with which the serpent is concerned is the tree of the knowledge of good and evil. To eat of the fruit of that tree was to become as a god, knowing good and evil. The serpent told Eve that if she and her husband ate of the tree their eyes would be opened, and they would know good and evil. But as soon as they ate they found their eyes opened to something else – the fact that they were man and woman. Here we see the plain indications that the first sense of consciousness is related absolutely and immediately with the first sense of gender. This Bible myth supports at every point the assertion made by me in *The Nature of the Self* to the effect that consciousness and sexual configuration are intimately related in their common uterine origins. The basic uterine configuration is that of nuclear penetrative power versus peripheral hollowness, a simple pattern which has in it all the primary qualities of consciousness and of sexual character. In the Adamic myth this fact is symbolized in the names of the sons. Thus the name Cain comes from *gayin*, meaning 'a lance', while the name Abel is from *habel*, meaning 'emptiness' or 'vanity'. Thus do the children, through the etymology of their names, act in an adjectival sense towards their parents, and in the birth of Cain and Abel to Adam and Eve we see symbolic representation of the fact that the outcome of Adam's thrust into his placental wife evokes the sense of a striking spear (Cain) into a receptive state of hollowness or emptiness (Abel).

The sequence of the eating of the forbidden fruit is of interest. The serpent beguiled Eve and she took and ate the fruit, whereupon she gave the fruit to Adam, so that he also ate. The serpentine umbilical arteries do 'feed' the placenta with blood, and the placenta in turn may be said to 'feed' the fetus. This poetical representation of the umbilical 'feeding' takes on a more concrete sense when we recall that in the myth of Jacob and Esau the umbilical venous flow was represented as a *feeding* of 'that red redness' to the fetal image, Esau.

serpent — endometrial arteries
apple — blood
Eve — trophoblast
Adam — embryo
good and evil — oxygen and carbon dioxide

This eating of the fruit provided by the co-operation of tree and serpent also brings death into Eden. It is a perfectly satisfactory representation of the fact that our primary sense of death is generated in the umbilical flow from the fetal body (the thrust of Cain) into the hollowness of Eve, as the woman who destroys and also gives life. With this primal knowledge of life and death, right and wrong, solid and hollow, there comes also the sense of male and female. As soon as they had eaten of the fruit Adam and Eve knew that they were naked – they became aware of the distinction of gender.

The deep and fearful sense of the cosmic origins of this knowledge is represented in the myths in terms of God's jealousy and apprehension. God is represented as saying of the Edenic pairs:

> *Behold, the man is become as one of us, to know good and evil: and now, lest he put forth his hand, and take also of the tree of life, and eat, and live forever: therefore the Lord God sent him forth from the garden of Eden.*[43]

God is also represented as wrathful towards Adam and Eve for knowing that they were male and female. Yet the earlier myth of creation in Genesis plainly asserts that this was the badge of their cosmic origins, for it was through being made male and female that they bore the image of God.

So God created man in his own image, in the image of God created he him; male and female created he them.[44]

It would be difficult for the myth to say more explicitly that God is essentially both male *and* female. It clearly says also that this is the source of the male and female nature in man and, by implication in all bisexual forms. This means to us that just as the man and the woman are respectively the agents of the sperm-point and the egg-sphere, so God bears that same nature.

$$\frac{sperm}{egg\ nucleus} \Big| \frac{arrow}{bulls\ eye}$$

This is the essence of my discoveries in dream analysis, and the point from which I commenced my inquiries into dreams: that the Creator works by the one unvarying pattern of Point and Sphere, which is to say through male and female. This discussion may be followed further by reading Chapters Four and Thirteen of *The Nature of the Self*.

In spite of the fact that man derives from God his sexual nature, God is represented as being wrathful with Adam and Eve because they became aware of that very fact. Why should it be wrong of man to uncover in himself the very impress of the divine nature? The answer seems to be that it is not the original uterine impress that is wrong, but the subsequent sexualization of it [177-180]. This leads to the creation of the most terrible incest fears, against which the mind seeks to protect itself.

Greek mythology offers a very valuable instance of divine punishment imposed upon a man who knew too much about the divine nature in sexual terms. The myth is that of Teiresias, who was blinded by Hera for knowing too much about the sexual nature. The myth states that as a boy of seven, Teiresias went wandering on the Mother Mountain of Kithairon. There, at a place where three roads meet, he came upon two snakes in copulation. Here already, we have a number of distinctly umbilical elements, as the famous umbilical seven and three are connected with copulating snakes. Teiresias struck at the snakes and killed the female, whereupon he was himself turned into a female. Seven years later, having been a girl for that period, he again came upon a similar situation and again struck at the snakes. This time he slew the male, whereupon he became a boy again. Meantime, Zeus and Hera had been arguing about sex. Zeus claimed that women had more enjoyment in the marriage bed, while Hera asserted to the contrary. In order to settle the argument, they called Teiresias up to Olympus and said to him, in effect: 'You, Teiresias, have been both man and woman; you tell us who most enjoys the sexual encounter.' Teiresias answered that the woman receives most joy, whereupon Hera in anger blinded him, but Zeus gave him inward sight as compensation.

The blind Teiresias and his second sight make an excellent symbol of the fetus. Moreover, although there is no evidence that he carried a snake-twined staff, his staff was so intimately associated with the two snakes he slew and which exerted so powerful an effect upon him, that we may think of it as the umbilical *caduceus*. The fetus is in a sense blind, inasmuch as its eyes and, indeed, all of its special senses are relatively inoperative. All his awareness is associated with the umbilical cord that is so well represented by the staff of Teiresias and the snakes it slew. That the fetus, while blind to the external world, is yet a sort of seer, is perfectly comprehensible, since the overall skin feeling and the beat of the umbilical blood do indeed confer upon him an inward vision that is entirely different from the divisive and extraverted perceptions of the special senses. The snake-killing staff is surely no other than a variant of the Edenic tree of the knowledge of good and evil. Moreover, it is plainly derived from a basic experience of gender, namely the copulating snakes and their male and female nature, which became transferred magically to their slayer, Teiresias.

The special interest of the Teiresian story is, moreover, the portrayal of the alternating feelings associated with the umbilical circulation. Teiresias is made female when he slays the female snake, and male when he kills the male snake. By this poetic imagery is represented the fact that the thrust of the umbilical arterial blood makes the fetus feel more nuclear (more male), while the thrust of the umbilical venous blood makes him feel more peripheral (more female). Teiresias is represented as experiencing this alternation just once in his life, but this mythological experience represents, I believe, that which happens constantly in the beat of the blood in the umbilical cord [27]. It is this same alternation of reversal, which is symbolized in the Jacob-Esau myth by the change of birthright between the twins. In the Adamic myth it is indicated by the slaying of Abel by Cain.

It seems to me that the anger of God against Adam is a mythological device of the same order as the anger of Hera against Teiresias. What is involved is nothing less than the relationship of the human soul to God, by which I mean the development of the impress which the cosmos makes upon the uterine organism. This impress is felt in terms of pattern – the pattern of all creation, namely the 'Nuclear Point within the Peripheral Sphere'. This pattern is the very substance of the uterine consciousness [16, 17, 18, 19], and yet it becomes also the pattern of postnatal cerebral consciousness [149], as a result of which the echoes of the one are felt in the other [151], added to which amalgam is the sexual pattern [177, 197]. Thus man is faced with the extraordinary situation that God, consciousness and sex are all intimately related in us through the constant interweaving within us of the same universal pattern.

Yet why should either the Greeks or the Hebrews feel concerned at this? They were not afflicted either by the puritanism of the Victorians or by the self-conscious libidinousness of the Freudian era. It is not a question, as I see it, of any denigration of sex in the minds of those natural people. The roots of the fear lie deeper, and are more terrible. They lie in the fear of incest. So far as we can judge, the origins of human culture lie in the control of incest. To lie with the mother or the sister is the supreme human sin because this short-circuiting of energy is a blow at the very roots of our human mental status, which appears to depend upon a prevention, as it were, of the short-circuiting of the uterine energies. Freud long ago drew attention to the great importance attached by primitive peoples to the avoidance of incest, and indicated the relevance of their social institutions to this prime purpose. Freud ingeniously asserted that this primary social organization, and with it the 'totem feast', began in some primal forest when the expelled sons of a certain primitive father banded together, slew the old man and ate him, thereafter possessing their mothers and sisters. He adds:

> *The totem feast, which is perhaps mankind's first celebration, would be the repetition and commemoration of this memorable, criminal act with which so many things began, social organization, moral restrictions and religion.*[45]

That an isolated brutish act of patricide, cannibalism and incest should be the foundation of human status, remembered forever in the breasts of all scattered humanity, is a fantastic suggestion.

Totem Feast

the inner cell mass	the totem
the trophoblast 'eating'	the feast
the inner cell mass	
at implantation	
the brothers	the trophoblast

pre implanted blastocyst	father
implanted blastocyst	son
entry of blastocyst into endometrium	entry of son into mother
	the first incest
end of pre implantation blastocystic rule	death of the father
post-implantation gastrulation etc.	

the pre implantated but attached blastocyst	the first meal
	the first wine
	the marriage at Canae
rolling over endometrium after loss of zona pellucida (+)	walking on water
" " " " " " (−)	drowning

Freud, the great rationalist, here invokes a psychological miracle greater than any of the religious mystifications against which he rightly inveighed. The whole problem is illumined by my discovery that the fetus feels itself to be not only nuclear and hence male to the uterus and the placenta, but that it feels to be that specific male, namely its own father.

More, we each feel to be not only father, but in his shape to enter mother (placenta) again and again, there suffering the loss of that 'father self' and becoming the son. And we gain this new self with each intake of blood through the umbilical vein, by which presumably is meant 'every beat of blood associated with the intake of the fetus'. This umbilical intake of refreshed blood may be regarded as the first meal and, indeed, is so felt by us inasmuch as every postnatal feeding is emotionally colored by it [29-30]. By this combination of feelings, which goes on in us without the least intervention of our postnatal consciousness, we all play out a drama which takes on the following postnatal sense: we enter the placenta as father enters mother, and there the father element is destroyed in giving place to the son aspect.

This new son aspect returns to the fetal body through the navel in an act which is essentially one of eating [189-190]. Thus the thing which Freud believed to have taken place long ago in some primal forest, leaving its impress upon the whole race of men, we each have done afresh for ourselves in that 'primal forest of the womb'. There we took part not only in the mystery of Creation, because our experience was born of the imprint of the creative pattern upon our fetal state, but also we foreknew the procreative mystery of the parental bed. Thus our fetal experiences become overlaid with our intuition of the events of the bed in which we were begotten. For this reason our fetal life is felt retroactively as an incestuous escapade [186]. I have already referred to the relationship of this fact to the so-called Blessing of Jacob in its reference to Reuben. I would add here only that it is worth noting that this incest took place with Jacob's concubine Bilhah, a name which (unconventionally) seems to be not unrelated to the word *bala*, which means 'to destroy by swallowing' – a markedly placental characteristic.

The myth of Adam and Eve may, in the light of the above, be seen as a miracle of symbolic compression. It tells us, in effect, that God is male and female, by which we understand Nuclear

74 *Mythology of the Prenatal Life*

and Peripheral. It tells us that this nature is first revealed to us through the 'primal eating', which takes place between the fetus and the placenta. It tells us that this 'eating' sowed in us the basic awareness of consciousness, sex, death and resurrection. It shows

[handwritten: the pre implantational blastocyst feeding on embryotrophe]

us that all these things were felt in terms of the distinction between the nuclear thrust (Cain) and the hollow periphery (Abel).

In less familiar terms, the myth of Prometheus gives us much the same information. It shows us clearly that the origins of consciousness are to be found in the ability of the fetus to 'steal the heavenly fire' from the cosmos in the 'hollow reed' of the umbilical cord. It likewise shows how this evocation of consciousness is bound up with the beginnings of sexual awareness. The evidence is rather scattered in the several myths of Prometheus, but the general drift of them can hardly be accidental when seen in the light of my discoveries. That Prometheus is a representative of the Shining One (the fetal skin feeling) is not to be doubted. Professor Herbert Jennings Rose has written:

> *As to who Prometheus originally was, it would appear that he is an ancient fire-god, native Greek to judge by his name, whose cult was early thrust into the background by the Oriental, but early and soon naturalized, worship of Hephaistos.*[46]

This association between Prometheus and fire may act as our first clue, because we know that there is an established relationship between fire gods and Sun gods. We have already noted the manner in which both these mythological figures, whether in their pure state or in varying degrees of coalescence, are always found in a context recognizably uterine in symbolism. Certainly it is true that there once existed fire gods who simply helped tie the primitive mind to the need for preserving fire, or who preserved a tribal memory of the invention of fire-making. But this does not in any way weaken the demonstration that such gods would in time also take on the fetal symbolism of the Shining One or the Flaming One. There are many indications that fire making was directly related to the sense of gender, since the boring stick was often regarded

Mythology of the Prenatal Life 75

shining
flaming / wet
gleaming

BI sun – god – sky   before entry

BII fire – gods – earth   after entry

attaching blastocyst — the boring stick
endometrium — the softwood
the mother cell mass
post-implantational metabolic — the flame
energy — the son

as male, the soft wood as female, and the flame as the 'son' of their 'rubbing' (copulation). This sexual symbolism is, according to Jung, strongly apparent in Hindu religion, and it is astonishing to find that the Hindu fire-bringer is called Mātariśvan, meaning the 'one swelling in the mother'. Surely there could hardly be a more emphatic description of the fetus as the 'fire bringer', which, of course, links direct with the myth of Prometheus, who was the 'fire bringer' to mankind.

That the cult of Prometheus was superseded by that of Hephaestus strengthens this interpretation, as he can be seen as the symbol not only of fire but also of fetal skin feeling. Hephaestus was reputed to have been such a weakling at birth that his divine mother dropped him from Olympus. But the gods of the sea, Thetis and Eurynome, took care of him in a cave surrounded by Okeanos, and there he lived for nine years. Nine years in the cave of the sea already has suggestive symbolic indications of the nine months which the child spends in the uterine 'cave of waters'. Later, after restoration to his parents, he was punished by Zeus for intervening in a quarrel between his mother and father. Zeus seized him by the leg and once again hurled him from Olympus. This punishment of Hephaestus for intervening in a quarrel between his parents inevitably awakens echoes in the mind of the fate of Teiresias who, in another sense, did the same thing. Hephaestus landed on the isle of Lemnos, and it was alleged that earth taken from this spot was potent to heal the bites of snakes and also to stop a hemorrhage. The priests of Hephaestus, moreover, knew the secret of how to cure snakebites. When we consider that the 'falling of the fetus' (that is, his birth) is the occasion of the first experience of hemorrhage, namely the loss of blood from the cut cord, and that the navel is a wound that may poetically be regarded as a 'snakebite',[47] we may see in this aspect of the myth a further indication of the fetal nature of Hephaestus.

the attaching trophoblast (and endometrium fused) — bleeding feet
wounding of the feet
swollen feet

early trophoblast — a Charis (charity

villus syncytiotrophoblast — Aphrodite-

B I Uranos
attaching trophoblast the genitals of Uranos

Conversation of attaching trophoblast with syncytiotrophoblast Aphrodite
bone and endometrium

This interpretation of the myth is further supported by the fact that Hephaestus is generally depicted as lame, and that this lameness is frequently ascribed to his fall from Olympus. It is a fact that the 'bleeding feet' in mythology are constantly found in a context which suggests that they symbolize the confusion between the umbilical arteries and the femoral arteries [108-110]. It is obvious that if the fetus senses its legs to be umbilical arteries and its feet to be the placenta, then the cutting of the cord at birth may be sensed by the organism as a cutting of the feet. This could not, indeed, be due to any direct neural sensations, but dreams tell very plainly that such confusion between the cutting of the cord and a wounding of the feet is indeed present in us all. The wife of Hephaestus is sometimes described simply as a *'Charis'* or as the youngest of the *Charites*. This already has strong umbilical-placental undertones, and we have had cause to consider the three *Charites* as symbols of the triple vessels of the cord. Perhaps the strongest confirmation in this symbolic matter is to be found in the assertion that the wife of Hephaestus was Aphrodite, whose character and behavior are strongly placental.

To begin with, Aphrodite was born of the foam which gathered about the genitalia of Uranus after these had been cut off by his son Kronos, and hurled into the sea. Since we know that the umbilical arterial flow is felt retrospectively as a male type of out-thrust [177], but also as a virtual draining away of the nuclear (hence male) skin feeling of the fetus, and since furthermore we know that this male-type thrust seems to end in destruction in the placenta, it is perfectly permissible symbolism to represent the placenta by a female who arises at that point, where the male genitals are destroyed. It is simply a fairy-tale way of saying that where in feeling-memory we meet with the placenta as female, we are the point where we seem to lose our sexual energy. It will be clearly understood, I hope, that I am not attributing sexual feelings or marital foreknowledge to the fetus, as has been asserted by some who have misread me and then have stated their own misrepresentations as mine. What I assert on that matter should be clear to anyone who has carefully read Chapter Thirteen of *The Nature of the Self*.

There is an old tale about Aphrodite, which says that she turned herself into a fish. This tale is scorned by scholars, it appears, but in *Smith's Greek and Roman Biography and Mythology* there are two references to it. Certainly the fish is frequently used as a symbol for the destroying placenta, as we have seen in the myths of Jonah and Samson. The placental interpretation of Aphrodite is further supported by the statement that she excited sexual passion both in men and in gods. Certainly the placenta is the pre-sexual 'wife' with whom every human being who has ever lived has experienced the origins of passion. This interpretation of Aphrodite's stimulant powers is entirely supported by the magic girdle which she possessed, and which had the power to excite sexual desire in all who wore it. What girdle it is that the placenta wears we hardly need ask, and certainly that umbilical girdle excites the first passion in us all. Both Pindar and Theocritus state that Aphrodite had the arrow as one of her attributes, a possession which would link her with the placental Artemis. Finally, the companions of Aphrodite were variously given as the *Horai* and the *Charites*, both of whom were three in number, and whose umbilical symbolical associations have already been demonstrated.

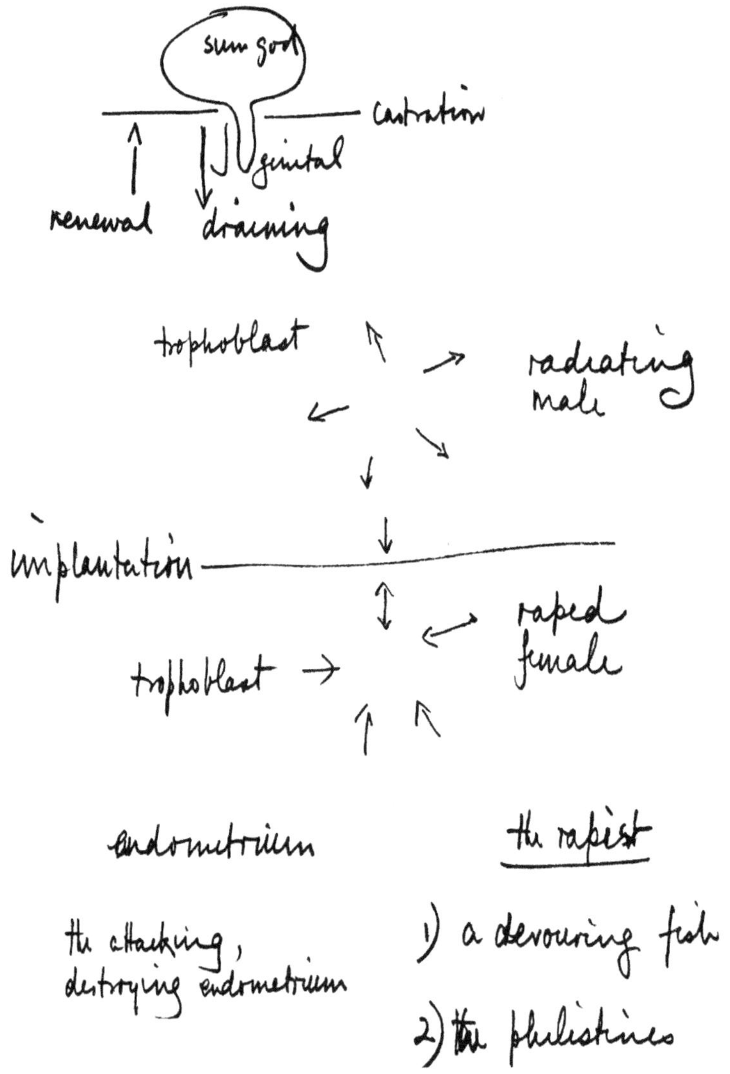

[handwritten diagram: "sun god" with arrows labeled "castration", "genital", "renewal", "draining"; "trophoblast" → "radiating male"; "implantation"; "trophoblast" → "raped female"; "endometrium" / "the attacking, destroying endometrium"; "the rapist: 1) a devouring fish 2) the philistines"]

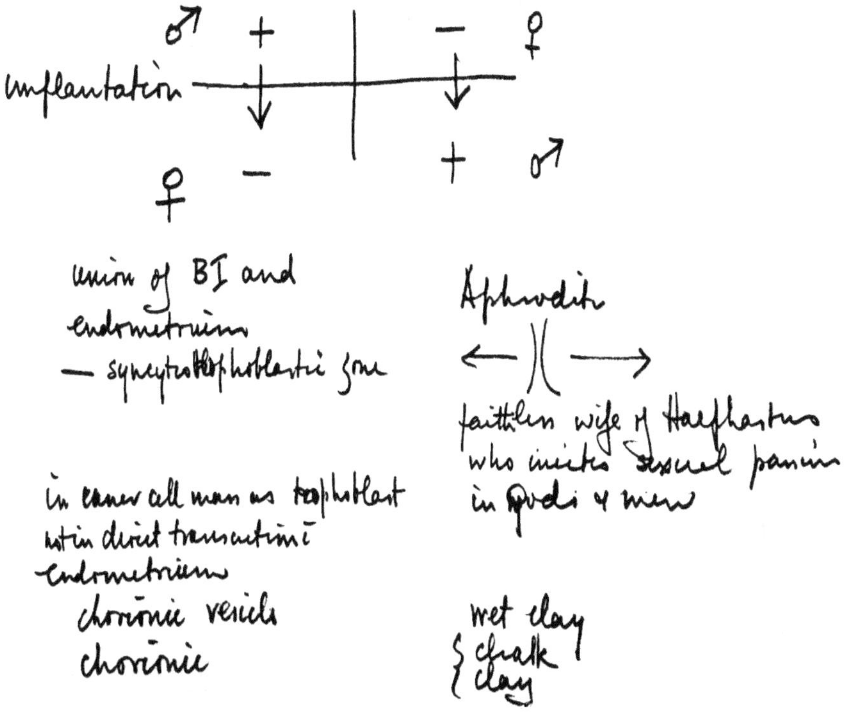

Mythology of the Prenatal Life 79

[Handwritten diagram:]

implantation: ♂ + / ↓ ; − ♀ / ↓ ; ♀ − ; + ♂

union of BI and endometrium
— syncytiotrophoblastic zone

Aphrodite ←)(→
faithless wife of Hephaestus who incites sexual passion in gods & men

in cancer cell man as trophoblast not in direct transaction i endometrium
chorionic vesicle
chorionic

wet clay
{ chalk
{ clay

Aphrodite thus can be shown to possess striking symbolic placental attributes, which makes her the natural wife of a Shining or Fiery One. In this way the fetal nature of Hephaestus is given extra support. This demonstration, in its turn, helps to establish the fetal nature of Prometheus, since if he who replaced him in the feelings of ancient men is demonstrably fetal, then the displaced figure may be assumed to represent much the same subjective elements.

Prometheus, as Shining One and thus a fetal symbol, receives his main placental counterpart in the figure of Pandora whom, at the command of Zeus, Hephaestus and Athena made and brought to life. The *Charites*, the *Horai*, Aphrodite and Hermes all contributed to the making of this highly dangerous but delectable lady, so that she was altogether shown as the product of fetal, umbilical and placental influences. For Hephaestus who made her out of wet clay is plainly fetal; Athena and Aphrodite are already shown in a symbolic placental context, while the *Charites*, the *Horai* and Hermes have been shown in a strong umbilical light. Pandora was created at Zeus's command for the specific purpose of bringing ruin on Prometheus, a fact which throws her into the same placental light that shines upon Eve, Delilah and all the other alluring-destructive female associates or enemies of the Shining One.

Pandora's name is supposed to mean 'the giver of all', which is symbolically appropriate to the primary functions of the placenta. Also, like the obviously placental Eve, she was thought of as the first woman on earth, which in a certain sense the placenta is for every human being in the deepest feelings. Pandora's most impressive attribute is her famous 'box', which was not a box at all, but a *pithos*, a large earthenware jar which was used both for the storage of foodstuffs and also for the reception of the dead.

chorionic development of trophoblast	} Pandora
the first post-implantational trophoblast	} the first woman of the earth
the endometrium	the earth
trophoblast of BII	the first <u>woman</u> of the earth, the all-giver
inner cellmass or connecting stalk	Prometheus chained to the rock
a villus	a hollow reed
uterine cavity	heaven
energy	fire
intermediate BI ↔ BII	Prometheus
BII trophoblast	the woman who would produce Zeús (B¹) supplanter

Now, my observations have shown that in dreams the placenta is felt to be at one and the same time both a place of death and a place of food [32]. The attribution of such an ambivalent receptacle to the 'first woman' and to the 'all-giver' offers the most emphatic placental symbolism.

The fetal nature of Prometheus is strongly supported by the myth of his punishment by Zeus, who chained him to a rock and set an eagle to peck at his liver by day, allowing it to grow again at night ready for another day of torture. We know that the eagle was the 'familiar' of Zeus and, therefore, knowing already of his fetal symbolism, we may suspect the eagle to be a representation of the placenta. Also, in Appendix II of this present work I shall show that the ancient zodiac used the symbol of the eagle in a position which shows strong placental associations. But all these things apart, the eagle that is set to peck at the liver of Prometheus shows this symbolism in its own right, since in a certain sense the placenta does actually 'peck' into the fetal liver with little 'pecks' of blood [27]. It should be stated here, however, that the full analysis of the myth of Prometheus cannot be demonstrated in this work, since the condition of being chained to the rock represents the transfer of the uterine feelings to the brain in the skull [155].

The supposed sins, which brought down this punishment upon Prometheus, are susceptible of the uterine interpretation. The most commonly known of these sins is his theft of fire from heaven in a hollow reed. It is sometimes said that the fire was stolen from the Sun, or from the forge of Hephaestus, but these variants would not impair the uterine interpretation, since the fetus actually feels himself to be the Sun (a fact hidden in many a dream and exposed in many a myth), while Hephaestus has already been shown to have fetal attributes. No matter where the fire was stolen from by Prometheus, his theft of it in a hollow reed immediately makes a plausible symbol of the way in which the fetus evokes the cosmic nuclear fire in his umbilical 'reed'.

Another reason given for Prometheus's punishment is that he knew the identity of the woman who should bear to Zeus a son who would supplant him. This theme of the father-son battle is common to all the major Greek gods: Ouranus was castrated by his son Kronos who, in turn, was overthrown by his son Zeus. Zeus, therefore, fearing a similar fate, was entirely in line with his whole

82   *Mythology of the Prenatal Life*

mythological lineage which, as we may now see, springs from the fact that the fetal Shining One is constantly entering a woman (placenta) and being displaced by the resultant offspring [39, 187]. The story that Prometheus knew the woman who should produce Zeus's supplanter, serves as a mythological device for identifying the two. Indeed, we already know that both Zeus and Prometheus are representations of the fetus in his state of cosmic excitation, so that this added symbolic information is useful and interesting but not indispensable.

The story that Prometheus knew the identity of the woman who should bear Zeus a father-slayer leads us straight to the mythology of Thetis and its tremendously powerful uterine symbolism. It was Thetis, daughter of Okeanos, who was the woman in question, a fact unknown to Zeus, but known to Prometheus, so the legend goes. Eventually the secret came out, and then Thetis was married to a mortal named Peleus who, naturally, could not give his bride an immortal child. Peleus, determined to get an immortal child, tried to do so by turning her own mortal offspring into immortals by laying them in the fire to burn away their mortal dross. This child-in-the-fire is patently the fetal representative whom we have already met in the tale of Isis and the King's son, and whom we shall meet again in the tale of Demeter and Demophoön. Seven children she had, and upon them she tried this fiery experiment. One day her husband, Peleus surprised her while she was trying it on her son Achilles. He cried out in terror, whereupon Thetis dropped the child and fled. Peleus then put the infant Achilles into the care of Cheiron, the centaur.

Pre implanted Blastula ĉ inner cell mass and trophoblast	the king and Queen of Heaven Zeus & Hera
trophoblast	Io heifer
transactional system between inner cell mass & trophoblast	Hermes, the messenger between gods and men
the umbilical cord, two arteries coiled around a vein	the kerykeion snakes coiled around a staff

The seven children represent the seven beats felt in the umbilical flow of blood as a result of its resonance with the cosmic beat [35-39]. The centaur is the symbol of the placenta, as we shall see again when we come to examine the Twelve Labors of Hercules. Achilles is the fetus itself, a statement that is supported by his famous heel, which, like the feet of Oedipus and the foot of Esau with Jacob clinging to it, symbolizes the sense that the foot is the placenta or a part of the cord [105]. The way in which Achilles got his weak heel is full of uterine meaning. Thetis held the child head down in the river Styx in order to give him immortality, but she neglected to submerge the heel by which she held him, so that this part remained mortal. The child held head down in the water by the heel makes a good symbolic representation of the fetus: head down in the womb and in the water, related to the placenta by the umbilical cord, that is related to the legs. Death by an arrow through the foot was also told of Cheiron the centaur. We shall later meet the river Styx as an umbilical symbol.

Now we return specifically to the myth of Prometheus. It will be seen that the one who 'steals the fire from heaven in a hollow reed', who knows the identity of the mother who bears the child that slays its own father, is none other than the fetus. It is at his liver that the placental eagle pecks. He knows too intimately the nature of the relationship between Father and Mother (Zeus and Hera, the principles of all earthly fathers and mothers), and so he like Teiresias is blind (as all fetuses may be said to be), and eventually he, like Adam, is hurled from Eden – as all fetuses are at birth! If we need still further confirmation of the fetal nature of Prometheus, we can see it in the fact that he was visited in his agony by Hermes, the Messenger of the Gods, and by Io, the heifer of Zeus. Hermes comes to ask him to reveal his fatal secret, namely the identity of the woman who should bear to Zeus a son who should slay him. Hermes, the traveler, reveals his umbilical nature by the *kerykeion* he carries, which is a snake-entwined staff that plainly signifies the umbilical cord; the wretched Prometheus, eagle-pecked and catechized by the messenger with the snake-wound staff, makes an excellent symbol of the fetus 'beset' by the placenta and the cord. To this symbolic picture the heifer Io adds her portion. Io was a woman loved by Zeus, and whom Hera therefore naturally hated. Zeus changed Io into a heifer to protect her, but Hera begged the heifer from Zeus and set a guard upon her. This guard is of the greatest possible uterine significance, for his skin was covered with eyes, the better to watch Io [11, 248]. Hermes slew the many-eyed guard, and Hermes is the symbol of that 'umbilical messenger' who carries messages back and forth between fetus and placenta. This symbolically implies that the umbilical cord is among other things destroyer of the nuclear energy of the fetal skin [23]. Hera replaced the many-eyed guard by a gadfly, which she caused to chase poor Io and to sting her perpetually on her skin, a mythological device which identifies the eye covered skin and the irritated one, and so serving to show Io as the fetal skin. This part of the myth is therefore a representation of the umbilical cycle in the course of which the fetal skin feeling is destroyed and restored. It helps to confirm that this Shining One, Prometheus, is a symbol of the fetal state.

So far we have seen Prometheus in terms of the fetus as 'fire bringer and the 'knower of the cosmic mystery' between the Father and the Mother, namely the Nuclear and the Peripheral elements of creation. We have seen him as another Adam, punished for knowing too much about the universal nature. But now we come

[handwritten notes: embryo ⇌ trophoblast / the 'messenger' between / trophoblast as destroyer / of nuclear energy of / inner all man ; gods ⇌ men / Hermes ; the many eyed guard / a godfly]

upon what is for us the most important attribute of all: Prometheus is the 'first thinker' and the giver of all those arts and sciences, which raised man above the level of the brutes. His name is supposed to mean 'the fore-thinker' in the sense of being one who foresees or fore-thinks in a prophetic sense, but if we accept the idea of him as the fetus, and the further idea that the uterine organism is the primal instrument of mind in man [150], then the name assumes an entirely different aspect. The 'fore-thinker' then is seen as a most appropriate name for the fetal Shining One in whom the first level of consciousness awakens in man. He is indeed the fore-thinker because he thinks before the brain consciousness develops.

True, this primal instrument thinks thoughts of the most limited nature. Unlike the brain, which becomes caught up into the divisive influences of the senses and all the complications of society, which employ the senses as the instruments of external understanding, the uterine organism thinks only a single thought. It knows only 'the secret of the gods', which is the relationship between the great universal Father Nucleus and the Mother Periphery [77]. It knows only the fact that from their 'marriage' it 'steals the fire' of the human soul. But this simple concept is as infinitely intensive and eternal as the complex concepts of the brain are extensive and ephemeral.

Thus it is that Adam and Prometheus are closely related. They both serve to present to us in symbolic terms the fact that it is in the womb that the first 'knowing' is done. And that this 'knowing' is born in the 'fire' of the knowledge of God, and in the discovery

chorionic disorganisation — Dionysiac madness

the first making of blood
the first pulsing, beat, throb — Dionysus
of chorionic blood vessels

blood cells beginning to move   the women of Dionysus
over the chorionic vesicle   running wild over the countryside
and metabolise cells   and tearing apart and
                                 devouring wild creatures

the destruction of cells by   tearing apart
cells and ingesting the   flaying (stripping cell
released metabolites   membrane)
                                 devouring wild animals
                                 & sacrificial beasts

                    cells   beasts
trophoblastic
the chorionic vesicle   the (chorionic) countryside

the endometrial plain (above ground)
the endometrial forest (below ground)
the chorionic countryside

  blood vessels   legs
the pounding beat of chorionic   a horse
blood vessels & the heart

  the pre circulary chorion   Pentheus of Thebes
the phasing out of the chorionic
regime by blood vessels   tearing the chorionic
  synergy between trophoblast   trophoblastic Pentheus to pieces
cardio
and circulary system   Pentheus' mother and
                                 Dionysus

Mythology of the Prenatal Life   87

of the secret that God is both Nuclear and Peripheral, Mother and Father, Male and Female. In a word, both myths confirm the truth of what is seen in the dreams of men, women and children of this day and age, namely that the uterine organism is the 'first thinker', the evoker of the 'I' which makes man higher than the beasts of the field, and at the same time is the evoker of the mental sense of sex, as distinct from the purely physiological. The myth of Prometheus beautifully symbolizes the relationship of the fetus to the cosmos as the instrument of the making of the self.

In this gallery of uterine symbolism a place must certainly be found for Dionysus, who appears to be a symbol not only of the fetal skin feeling but of the placenta also. This I say because he was certainly a Shining One, or a Flaming One, being born of the flame in which Zeus consumed his mother Semele, and yet he was an effeminate god, a fact which strongly argues the placental imagery [267]. Moreover, the fact that he was god of wine and his symbol was the vine, supports the idea that he was god of the umbilical blood. In short, he represented neither fetus nor placenta alone, but both joined together by the beating blood in the umbilical vine. Legends say that Hera maddened him and caused him to wander about almost aimlessly in the known world. This could stand very aptly for the fact that the fetal skin feeling is felt as a wanderer, which goes endlessly on and on [40]. Wherever he went he taught many things, but above all the culture of the vine and the making of wine, both of which are redolent with umbilical significance. But along with this benign and creative side there was a violent and murderous one, for the women who followed his cult were prone to bursts of madness in the course of which they ran over the countryside and slew wild creatures which they tore into pieces and devoured.

This horrible cult is surely a projection into spatial enactment of the umbilical experience in which the placenta (the woman) is felt to tear the fetal skin feeling into shreds and to 'devour' it. Moreover, the god himself was related to acts of destruction in which the procedure of 'tearing in pieces' and destroying the skin were both prominent. Thus the king of Damascus was flayed alive for opposing the culture of the vine – a suggestive link between the umbilical 'vine' and the destruction of the skin feeling. Lycurgus, who offended him, went mad and slew his own son, whom he mistook for a vine. This already lends itself to the umbilical interpretation, but an alternative legend lends itself even more, for it says that Lycurgus mistook his own legs for a vine and cut them off. The confusion of the legs with a vine and the cutting of them well symbolizes the fact that we all in degree confuse our legs with our lost umbilical arteries, and thus in that degree seem to have cut legs that are bleeding. Some of the legends say that in the end Dionysus had the wretched Lycurgus torn into pieces by horses – a further supporting item in the eyes of anyone who understands the undoubted placental imagery of the horse, which I trust the reader will come to do most thoroughly after he has read my later comments on the placental symbolisms.

To continue with the mythology of Dionysus, it is said that Pentheus of Thebes also opposed the god and for his pains was set on by his own mother, whom Dionysus made mad, and who mistook her son for a lion. She cut off his head and tore him in pieces. The tearing of a lion by its own mother is very plain uterine symbolism: the lion is the immemorial symbol of the fetal skin feeling, and the 'mother' of this 'lion' is certainly the placenta, which indeed does 'tear it into pieces' through the 'madness' of the Dionysian wine of the blood in the umbilical 'vine'.

This experience of being 'torn into pieces' was indeed the god's own legendary fate when a child. For the story told of Zeus was told also of his son, born in the fire at Thebes: the Mysteries of Dionysus held that he was stolen away as a child and torn into pieces. One version describes his dismembered parts being thrown into a cauldron, to be retrieved and restored to unity and life by the great gods. Indeed, he was called 'Dithyrambos', which Jane Harrison insists means 'twice-born'.[48] This death and resurrection motif is essentially umbilical in origin, as we have already seen.

If anything were needed to support the uterine imagery of Dionysus it is at hand in the story that Ariadne was his consort, for no being could be more emphatically placental in her imagery than this maiden whose famous thread enabled Theseus to find his way out of the labyrinth. Indeed, I shall later show that the very word 'labyrinth' has a connection with the umbilical arteries, and that indeed the labyrinth at Minos was a formalized representation of the umbilical arteries. Ariadne, as consort, and also the three Charites who attended upon the god all offer umbilical-placental

chorion — labyrinth
villi — tufts of hair
         snakes

chorionic endothelium — moon

chorionic cardio-vascular circulation — Dionysus

imagery. For there seems little doubt that the *Charites* are the same figures essentially as the *Horai* and the *Moirai*, all tending to be three in number, and all related to the Moon. Certainly in ancient symbolism the Moon is identified with the placenta as truly as the Sun is identified with the fetal skin feeling. The inchoate feelings of the lost uterine life, struggling in the depths of the mind, will project themselves upon whatever in the external world seems to offer a ready-made analogy of their configurational nature. Those who have read *The Nature of the Self*, and have understood the significance of Chapter Four and of Appendices B and O, will see that what the myth is really urging is the universal truth that what is at work inside our feelings is the impress and image of the same divine pattern which also has left its image and impress upon external creation. This radiant simplicity, allowed to shine upon the myth from a sympathetic mind, unifies man and universe, past and present in a miracle of synthesis.

CHAPTER TWO
The Mother and the Maiden

In Chapter One we showed that the figure of the Shining One is ubiquitous in the great myths, and that he invariably appears there in a context which confirms his fetal nature. Since we were concerned to show this Shining One in a uterine (symbolic) context, we were compelled to reveal in degree both the placental and umbilical symbolisms, which appear therein. Now, however, let us turn to a more specific exploration of placental symbology as such.

I trust the reader will understand that when I refer to placental goddesses the reader will not think that I am suggesting that these goddesses are mere subjective formulations of the sanguinary mass of tissue which forms the afterbirth. This would be no truer than to suppose that the Shining One is merely a projection of our memory of being a little flesh and blood organism in our mother's body. The fetal body, conjoined with the placenta and the umbilical cord, make a configurational organism [41-42] which is quite distinct in effect from their sheer organic character. Indeed, I have suggested that the fetus, placenta and cord form a sort of electrical generator and converter which acts as the resonator that tunes the cosmic pattern into the human organism [22-24]. The symbology which represents these matters in dreams and myths, is of an order that suggests a linkage between organic fact and cosmic superaddition. The Shining One is by no means merely the fetus: he is the fetal body seen as instrument of the cosmic Nucleus. Similarly, the Mother and the Maiden, which we shall now consider in terms of placental symbolism, are not to be thought of as merely uterine in the narrow sense, but as the symbols of the placenta as the link between the nuclear human being and the peripheral forces of the cosmos.

The Mother and the Maiden, Demeter and Kore (or Persephone) were respectively the wife and daughter of Zeus. Rose points out that this Maiden, Kore-Persephone, has a twofold character, being on one hand goddess of the dead and on the other hand, one of

Mythology of the Prenatal Life

the principal goddesses of the earth's fertility. In this latter role she is, as H. J. Rose points out, the younger double of her mother, Demeter. This already must strike a note with anyone who knows that the placenta is both the organ of death and of rebirth [28]. Kerényi[49] adds to this by asserting that in his view the Mother and the Maiden, Demeter and Persephone, are in reality always a double figure in a far deeper sense than that indicated by Rose. Each is the complementary half of the other, says Kerényi. However, from his context it would seem that he does not suspect that Persephone and Demeter are also the ambivalent aspects of the placenta as felt by the fetus, clamoring in our feelings for catharsis. The story of the rape of Persephone is full of placental imagery. She was gathering flowers with Athena and Artemis on the plain by Mount Nyssa when Pluton, Lord of the Dead and also called 'The Rich One', caused a marvelous flower to grow up before her. As she plucked the flower, the earth opened and Pluton, otherwise called Hades, came upon her, raped her and carried her into the depths of the earth. It will be noted that the rape took place on a flat piece of ground, or plain. As already shown, in myths and dreams we often come upon a flat piece of land or plain in a placental context: the fetus feels the placenta to have the essential character of flatness [37-40].

92   *Mythology of the Prenatal Life*

Let us look first at the companions who were with Persephone at the time of her disaster. First of all we note that the presence of two companions, namely Athena and Artemis, makes up a *trio*, an interesting detail reminding us of the importance of the number three in relationship to umbilical symbology. To this first umbilical hint the myths of Athena and Artemis have plenty to add. I have already shown in the course of dealing with the symbology of Apollo, that Artemis possessed marked placental characteristics. Let us now look at the myth of Athena, the second companion of Persephone at the time of her rape.

Athena is generally regarded as the daughter of Zeus, born from his head. But this is not the only legend of her birth. Another is that she was born of a lake nymph named Tritonis. Still another, which shows very patent placental symbology, is that she was the daughter of Pallas, who slew her father when he was on the point of raping her. This is not the last time we shall see death and rape linked together in the story of the Maiden, and we know that this makes a natural representation of the fact that the fetus feels to be the father and to thrust into the placenta, only to be 'slain' by the placenta in the very act of entering. This is powerfully supported by what follows: after having killed her father, Athena flays him and uses his skin as her *aegis*, also taking his wings and fastening them to her feet. This entirely fits the placental context, since it is the skin feeling of the 'father-fetus' which the placenta is felt to destroy. The act of attaching the wings to the feet hints at the feeling-link already noted between the placenta and the feet of the unborn child. Some versions of the myths do not represent Pallas as the father of Athena, but simply as a giant whom she slew and whose skin she took.

There is something strikingly masculine about the virginal figure of Athena, and indeed this coincidence of male and female attributes makes a striking piece of placental symbolism. The fetus feels that the placenta is not only a 'hollow female' who receives his thrust, but is also in turn the 'solid male' who returns that thrust, making him less solid [28, 29, 181]. Dream analysis shows the placenta frequently represented as a sexually indeterminate creature [267-268].

Athena bore upon her shield the image of the Gorgon's head, which Perseus severed. This also links her with umbilical elements, for the Gorgons were three in number – Sthenno, Euralye and Medusa. They had three sentries, the *Graeae*, to watch out for them – Pemphredo, Enyo and Deino. These *Graeae* had between them only a single eye and a single tooth, a symbolism which suggests an effort to represent the navel as the unitary mouth and eye of the fetal state. That is to say, before birth, the feelings which are to become associated with the eyes and the mouth [99] are centred at the navel.

Gorgons: Sthenno, Euralye, Medusa

Graiai: Pemphredo, Enyo, Deino

In Libya, Athena was thought to be the inventor of the flute, a markedly umbilical symbol. This she did in the following circumstances:

when Perseus cut off Medusa's head, her two surviving sisters made lamentation out of the mouths of the snakes that grew from their heads. Athena imitated these sounds upon a reed, and in this way created the flute. In the light of this myth, the flute appears in a highly umbilical shape, being the imitation of a snake's hiss. This is strongly supported by a further mythical element in which Athena is represented as disgusted with her invention, the flute, because its playing distorted her face. She therefore threw away the instrument, but it was retrieved by Marsyas, the satyr who challenged Apollo to a flute-playing contest on the understanding that the winner could do as he pleased with the loser. Marsyas lost, and Apollo flayed him alive. His skin was reputed to have been hung in a cave at Celanae, where it thrilled even in death to a Phrygian tune.

early chorionic trophoblast chemicals (? enzymes, hormones) which dissolve and destroy endometrial blood vessels and cells arterioles	Perseus cuts off Medusa's head snakes
reactions of arterioles around the destroyed ones	lamentation by snakes by the sisters of Medusa
sound of blood in whirling arterioles sound of first chorionic blood	the hissing of snakes imitation of the lamentation of Medusa's sisters by Athene
chorionic trophoblast spreading of blood vessels on inner surface of trophoblast	the Gorgon's head appears on Athene's aegis playing the flute distorts her face

Mythology of the Prenatal Life 95

Since the name of Phrygia is derived from the Great Mother, the skin of Marsyas in thrilling to a Phrygian tune well symbolizes the relationship between the fetal skin and the womb [9]. The fact that Marsyas was alleged to have composed the Hymn to the Great Mother adds support to this present view of Athena in a uterine setting. The conjunction of the umbilical flute of Athena, the figure of Apollo, and the skin that thrills to the Great Mother's influence – all these serve to show that Athena is highly uterine in symbolism, and therefore a natural companion of the placental figure of Persephone.

The rape of the Maiden by Pluton lends itself to interpretation in umbilical arterial terms, since the umbilical arterial thrust is felt not only as a sexual assault [183], but also as an excretion [182]. Pluton, as God of Wealth (wealth = gold = feces) who rapes the Maiden, thus embodies several aspects of the umbilical arterial thrust into the placenta, and when his role as Lord of the Dead is added, we can understand it as the thrust into the placenta seeming to encompass the destruction of the fetal nuclear elements [185].

Demeter, the mother of Persephone, mourns her daughter's loss with a terrible intensity, and begins a search for her. She finds two witnesses to the rape: one is the Sun, who saw it and the other is Hecate, who heard the Maiden's cries. Naturally the Sun 'sees the rape', for the Sun is the symbol of the Shining One, thus representing the nuclear skin feeling which, since it is the 'rapist', inevitably 'sees it'. That Hecate is the second witness we understand at once when we see a little of her umbilical characteristics. Hecate is the goddess of the crossroads, and it was a custom of the Greeks to set up small statues of her at such intersections. For the ancient peoples, a crossroad would have evoked the feelings associated with the 'cross-over' or twist of the umbilical arteries. For this reason it was that Teiresias met his palpably umbilical snakes at a crossroad, while Oedipus slew Laius at a similar place.

A further umbilical circumstance related to Hecate is the fact that she was frequently portrayed as a goddess with either three bodies or three heads. The myth of the witness of the Sun and Hecate to the rape of Persephone is a highly plausible way of saying that the nuclear fetal feeling, through its umbilical dynamism, carries out the 'rape of the placental Maiden'. In that context the Sun symbolizes the nuclear fetal feelings, while Hecate represents the umbilical dynamism.

music — of the spheres — blastulic
— of hissing snakes — endometrial
— chorionic
umbilical

chorion | Marsyas
contrasting sounds \ embryo | Apollo
embryonic and chorionic — flute competition between
blood circulation Apollo & Marsyas

In his work on the Kore, Carl Kerényi states the symbolic function of Hecate in the following words:

> *The classical figure of Hecate stands stiff and strange in the Greek world, built up on a triangle, and with faces turned in three directions. They tried to get rid of the stiffness of these Hecate statues by breaking up the triune goddess into three dancing maidens. Later times were to stick more rigidly to the characteristic number '3' than did the classical age of Hesiod. The fact that Hecateia were set up at the crossing of three roads and that these places were held especially sacred to Hecate does not militate against the Hesiodic or cosmic conception of the number 'three': all crossings of three roads point clearly and obviously enough to the possibility of dividing the world into three parts.*[50]

Kerényi's words may be used as a means of 'illumination through criticism'. The number three may be regarded as 'cosmic' in the sense that it is through the three tubes of the umbilical cord that the fetus gains from the cosmos

the entrance to the uterus from the uterine canal

the crossroads

Mythology of the Prenatal Life 97

the primal sense of the pattern of creation [23, 289-290]. The setting up of *Hecateia* at places where three roads meet confirms her cosmic aspect in the sense of this book. Kerényi's comments would not explain why it was that Hecate dwelt not only at crossroads, but also by tombs and near the blood of murdered people. Seen in umbilical terms, all this fits together into a single pattern, for the umbilical 'crossroads' are the point of 'death' for the fetal nuclear energy, and are the point also at which the sense of self is felt to be 'murdered'. Jane Harrison, faced with the mysterious Greek sense of triplicity, makes here an honest confession:

> In the ritual of the lower stratum, of the dead and of chthonic powers, three was, for some reason that escapes us, a sacred number. The dead were thrice invoked; sacrifice was offered to them on the third day; the mourning in some parts of Greece lasted three days; the court of the Areopagus, watched over by deities of the underworld, sat ... on three days; at the three ways the threefold Hecate of the underworld was worshipped.[51]

Why this constant recurrence of the number three? Jane Harrison, having admitted that she did not understand it, made the suggestion that perhaps it had something to do with the fact that the Greeks changed over from having only two seasons and recognized three. She adds that three figures make a better-balanced statue. But we have a more telling source of these widespread triplicities, namely the umbilical impress in the depths of the human self. That this should be projected upon the earth itself is not surprising when the facts are known [122-125], for we know that the earth itself takes on the lost placental feelings for the postnatal organism. *The earth itself becomes all that the placenta once was – the great maternal monster, which swallows the hero and yet restores him.* Behind all the gods and demons of the underworld are the primal feelings of the fetus for the placenta, for they are the outcome of the projection of those same feelings upon the earth.

Perhaps the most astonishing piece of evidence for my contentions is the fact that in her search for her daughter, Demeter was commonly depicted as using a chariot drawn by two snakes. Arthur B. Cook writes:

> *The scene of her quest was common on sarcophagi of Roman date; and here she is seen holding a torch and drawn by two monstrous snakes usually winged near the chariot-wheels, or in more agitated guise holding two torches and drawn by snakes winged at the neck. Sarcophagi of the former type show the snake's tail twined about the hub of the wheel, which takes the form of a lion's head. This detail perhaps, points to the solar character of the vehicle in question. For Greeks and Romans alike, therein agreeing with the Egyptians and the nations of the nearer east, looked upon the lion as an animal full of inward fire and essentially akin to the sun. The lion on Roman military standards was interpreted as a solar emblem. The Mithraic sun-god was figured with a lion's face. The sign Leo was called 'the house of the sun', and – be it noted – the sun was in Leo when Persephone was carried off. What is perhaps more to the point, it was Helios that took pity on Demeter and told her where her daughter was to be sought. Did he not also lend her his chariot for the search?*[52]

I would interpret this as follows: it was by the forward thrust of the two umbilical arteries that Hades raped Persephone, so that Demeter, in following her daughter, is impelled by the same two 'snakes'. Hence the twin-snaked chariot, simply a direct symbol of the umbilical arteries. That it was lent by the Shining One, whether figured as Sun or lion, is perfectly to the point, since it is the drive of the fetal nuclear energy down the umbilical arteries that both 'rapes Persephone' and 'carries Demeter'.

When at length Demeter finds Persephone, the Kore, the ravished daughter, she invokes the aid of Zeus to recover the girl. Pluton at last agrees to let her go, but by a trick dooms her to spend one third of the year with him in the underworld, but only the other two thirds above with the gods. Here we see umbilical symbolism: the back and forth passage of the Kore between upper and lower worlds being divided into three parts, with the added aspect of two versus one. In assessing the symbolism of this part of the myth we might do well to remember that Zeus and Pluton (Hades) may be simply two aspects of the Shining One. Zeus and Hades were brothers, Zeus having the sky as his kingdom, and Hades the underworld while a third brother, Poseidon, ruled the seas. Sometimes Hades was called 'Zeus of the Underworld'. The presumption is that when Hades rapes Persephone, it is really Zeus who does it, whereupon at once he becomes the Zeus of death. In other words, Zeus symbolizes in this context the fetal nuclear feeling as it is in its full power in the fetal body, while Hades represents the same nuclear feeling in association with the thrust into the placenta (rape), with the sense of loss there (death), and with the sense of excretion (gold). Hades-Pluton as a brother of Zeus, concerned at the same time with rape, wealth and death, is too apt a symbolic coincidence to be so merely by accident.

Zeus BI had the scepter his kingdom
→ god of the sky/uterine cavity
Hades — God of the inside of the endometrium

The recovery of Persephone by her mother, and the bargain for the threefold division of her presence, is clearly a representation of the cycle of loss and recovery felt in the triple tubes of the umbilical cord, but imposed upon the earth and the life of plants [120-125]. The cyclic rise and fall of the vegetation makes a very powerful symbol for the representation of the umbilical cycle. The deeper we probe, the more apt the symbolism appears. The vegetation which grows upon this planet is a direct response of the earth (as part of the planetary periphery of the Sun) to the energy flowing out from the Sun as nucleus. The plant rises up to seek the rays of the Sun, and when at length it falls to earth again it becomes manure for the new plant. If we keep in mind the fact that the Sun is the prime symbol of the Shining One, then the cycle of plant life takes on a very strong umbilical character. For as the umbilical vein thrusts the blood up towards the fetal body, so the stem of the plant lifts up the sap to meet the solar radiation, becoming in the process the source of all man's food. Just as the umbilical arteries are the vehicles of excretion and of death, so the falling of the vegetation becomes akin to excretion through dying and becoming waste. The agricultural process contains a great deal of ready-made symbolism upon which the primitive and ancient mind may hang the umbilical feelings.

No wonder that a prime symbol of the umbilical cord is the serpent on the tree, for the serpent as readily symbolizes the umbilical arteries as does the tree (or any of the higher plants) symbolize the umbilical vein. Indeed, this symbolism of the tree is plainly evident in a myth concerning Erysichthon, son of Triopas. Erysichthon cut down trees in a grove sacred to Demeter, for which crime the goddess inflicted him with insatiable hunger. Obviously, the fetus would be insatiably hungry if he cut 'the tree of the mother', namely the umbilical cord – and especially the umbilical vein! This myth clearly represents the tree as the umbilical vein, and by linking the tree in this way to Demeter and her power to curse by starvation, it helps to support the assertion that Demeter is the placental counterpart of Persephone. The endless interweaving of myths can be seen in the fact that some attribute the cutting of Demeter's trees to Triopas himself. The name Triopas itself is suggestive of the umbilical 'three', and his birth also reflects the uterine atmosphere, since he is shown as the son of Poseidon upon Canace, who was killed by her father for unnatural love for her own brother, and who thus herself is another version of the incestuous placental sister-wife.

The feeding relation of Demeter as placenta to the fetus as Shining One is told in a myth that is closely related to that of Isis. When Demeter arrived at Eleusis, she offered her services as nurse to the son of the local king. The child, Demophoön, grew up under her care entirely without ordinary food, being nourished by Demeter from her own breast and a diet of ambrosia. Every night she laid the child in the fire in order to burn away his mortal nature. This myth shows very plainly the relationship of the placenta as 'nurse' to the 'burning' child or the Shining One, the fetus. In these terms we may see Demeter as the maternal aspect of the placenta, wherefrom the Shining One, the divine child, is born again and again through the act of feeding. For, as I have shown, the Shining One feels itself not only to feed from the umbilical vein, but also to be born through it, so that as he 'feeds' so he is also 'reborn', and as he is 'reborn' so he 'eats himself', even as Kronos devoured his own children [32]. But this 'feeding from the dead children of his own body' cannot take place unless the placenta is 'raped' by the Shining One, in the very act of performing which he dies. That the Shining One is reflected in both Zeus and Hades is confirmed by Jane Harrison, who tells us that when Demeter appealed to Helios to tell her who ravished Persephone, she discovered that the ravisher was none other than Helios himself in the form of Hades.

This strange combination of marriage and death must inevitably remain an enduring puzzle to those who do not know of the uterine facts underlying the myths. Thus Kerényi writes:

What are difficult to understand, because they appear to have no precedent, are the strange associations. There is, for instance, the strange equation of marriage and death, the bridal chamber and the grave. Marriage in this connection has the character of murder: the brutal ravisher is the god of death himself.[53]

In the light of my discoveries, this mythological equation of marriage with death presents a seamless and undeniable association. Because the umbilical arterial thrust, which 'marries' the fetus to the placenta, it carries the fetal nuclear feeling to destruction. At the very moment that the umbilical arterial flow arouses in the fetus the sense of 'raping' the placenta, it also awakens in precisely the same degree the sense of being sucked down into a monster and destroyed. Thus, the placenta is both the bridal chamber and the grave. The equation of marriage with murder we can also readily understand. For the same arterial thrust that 'rapes' the placenta also is felt as an act of destruction in a dual sense. Not only does the fetus feel to pierce, to 'hollow out' and destroy the placenta, but also the placenta seems to destroy the piercer. Thus the ravisher, in a certain rather heavily poetic sense, may be said to be death itself.

Clearly, both the Maiden and the Mother may here be seen to represent the placental functions. Kerényi, however, carries his treatise on myth beyond the sphere of Greece to the Indonesian archipelago. There he finds material so confirmatory of my thesis that I cannot omit some mention of it. The myth concerns a divine maiden called Hainuwele, who sometimes is called Rabie.[54] Rabie was wooed by Tuwale, the 'Sun-man', but her parents rejected him. Shortly afterwards the earth opened and swallowed the girl, who cried out as she sank:

> *Tuwale is fetching me! ... When it is evening three days from now, look up at the sky, all of you, and you will see me appearing as a light.*[55]

The villagers went home and for three days kept the feast of the dead. On the evening of the third day they looked up at the sky, and for the first time the full Moon rose in the east. Here we have distinct placental elements. The Sun-man, representative of the Shining One, abducts the girl. That she is the placenta is made clear by the fact that she becomes transmogrified into the Moon. Sun and Moon stand together as ancient symbols of the fetus and placenta, as may be seen in the way in which Apollo and Artemis were related to the heavenly bodies: when Apollo was regarded as identical with the Sun or Helios, nothing was more natural than that his sister should be regarded as Selene or the Moon, and accordingly the Greek Artemis is, at least in later times, the goddess of the Moon.[56]

Tuwale, the Sun-man, and the Maiden, who is the Moon, make entirely satisfactory symbols of the fetus and the placenta. The real evidence of the uterine nature of this Indonesian myth is to be found in the ritual with which it is associated. The descent of Rabie or Hainuwele into the earth is represented in a dance which reveals the most telling umbilical associations. Kerényi describes it thus:

> *The dance itself is the means of her descent. The men and women alternately form a huge ninefold spiral. It is a labyrinth, the original model and later the copy of the labyrinth through which men have to pass when they die in order to reach the Queen of Hades and be ordained to human existence again. Hainuwele stands in the middle of the labyrinth, where a deep hole has been dug in the earth. In the slow convolutions of the spiral dance, the dancers press closer and closer towards her and finally push her into the pit.*[57]

The huge dancing spiral represents the beat of the spiral umbilical arteries, which carry the blood down into the placenta. Here we see again the relationship of the dance-rhythm to the umbilical beat; the 'noise of beating feet', which bore the infant Zeus away is echoed in the Indonesian rite when the feet of the dancers stamp the earth down over the luckless girl playing the role of Hainuwele. Kerényi links this Indonesian myth with the rites of Persephone and Demeter in the following words:

There are accounts of the introduction of a chorus of maidens in Persephone's honour in Rome which lead us to conclude that similar dances were performed in the Greek or Graeco-Italian Kore cults. The accounts refer to the number of dancers: they were thrice nine, and there is also a mention of a rope, which they held in their hands in order to form a continuous row. It is difficult to think of this as a dead straight line with no windings at all. Scholars have pointed out that dances were performed in Delos with the help of such a rope. The most important of these dances is the one that Theseus is supposed to have danced with his companions on the Apollonian isle after he had extricated them from the labyrinth. It was done in honor of Aphrodite, by which was meant Ariadne, whose nature coincides both with Aphrodite's and Persephone's. The dance was called the Crane Dance, and its convolutions were so involved that our chief source calls them an imitation of the windings of the labyrinth. In this ritual dance the rope probably played the same part as the thread in the fable of Ariadne. For the Greeks the spiral was the key-figure of the labyrinth, though it is usually stylized in angular form.[58]

The number of dancers, with three as its common denominator, is the least significant element in this quotation. The winding spiralling convolutions of the rope, the location of the dance at the Sun-god's birthplace, the link with the rescue of Theseus from the spiral labyrinth – all these lend weight to the umbilical interpretation of the material.

The most important of all these associations is perhaps the myth of the rescue of Theseus by Ariadne from the cave of the Minotaur. Theseus entered the labyrinth to slay the bull-man who resided there, and depended for his safe return upon the thread paid out to him by Ariadne who, we can see, is also the placental Aphrodite. A. B. Cook, in his *magnum opus* tells us that the Minotaur was sometimes represented with a skin spangled with stars, a circumstance which serves to link him with the fetal skin.

Before leaving the present discussion of the Mother and the Maiden, mention of Persephone will be made, in a story which offers some extremely clear placental symbolism. This old tale asserts that although she was his daughter, Zeus desired to possess her, which he finally did in the shape of a serpent. As a result of this incestuous union Persephone bore a son who was called Zagreus, but Hera had him lured away by Titans who tore him to pieces and ate him. Athena, however, managed to save the child's heart and this she took to Zeus, who swallowed it and then begat the child again upon Semele.[59] Since it was by Semele that Zeus also begat Dionysus, and since Dionysus also was lured away, torn to pieces, eaten and restored, we see already in this old Orphic tale the lineaments of Persephone's placental nature. Persephone is the representative of the placenta, which seems to be entered by the Shining One (Zeus) through the agency of the umbilical serpent. As a result of this entry the Shining One is felt to be torn into pieces, and yet a part of him is saved and eaten by the Shining One, which is to say that the resurrection through the umbilical vein takes place in relation to the sense of restoration of the fetal blood. And from this restoration through eating (of the heart) the process is repeated all over again. These old tales are forever interwoven, and yet forever they remain one and the same. There is but one myth, though its representations and variations are many.

With regard to the incestuous elements in the above story, note that the reason for them was probably not clear even to the ancients themselves, and is certainly not clear to modern scholars, as can be seen in the words of H. J. Rose:

> *A certain number of the unions of gods are marriages with relatives in the first degree, full sisters or daughters. This was never allowed in Greek society, and we must explain such cases, as it seems to me, by supposing that the connexion between a god and a goddess was explained by some as that of brother and sister, or father and daughter, by others as that of husband and wife. The ancients themselves noticed this anomaly, and were puzzled by it, in later times.*[60]

H. J. Rose states that 'in later times' the ancients were puzzled by this incestuous tendency on the part of the gods. But in 'earlier times', perhaps the ancients were still close enough to the deep prenatal feelings to enable them to create external representations of those primal feelings – representations upon which later generations could create in semi-dreamlike fashion an ever-growing variety of gods and goddesses, heroes and heroines. Precisely the same thing occurs every night in dreams all over the world. And anyone who seeks to understand the origins of these tales on a purely archaeological basis is simply repeating on the highest level of mental activity a rarefied version of the kitten's mistake when he pats behind the mirror to find the 'other kitten' he sees therein.

To those who have glimpsed the source of the myths, the meaning of the persistence of incestuous relations between the gods is plain: they are all variants of the fetal Shining One and the placental Mother-Maiden, between whom there is felt in each one of us before birth the very essence of the incestuous feeling, for reasons explained in *The Nature of the Self* [188].

CHAPTER THREE

The Golden Bough

In Chapter One, I showed how mythology is full of representations of the fetal skin feeling as a cosmic instrument. In the second chapter I demonstrated a similar ubiquity for representations of the placental functions. Now I will endeavor to point out a similar ubiquity for representations of the umbilical cord. Here I have somewhat forestalled myself, because in seeking previously to show the fetal and placental nature of certain symbolisms I have also been obliged to deal with certain umbilical ones. Nothing could serve my purpose better than the great work of Sir J. G. Frazer who collected a vast amount of mythological and anthropological information under the general influence of the myth of Aeneas. In demonstrating that 'the golden bough' is simply a representation of the umbilical cord, a clear instance of the umbilical symbolism will be shown, which also underlines the complete unity of the myths. For if Frazer can bring vast collections of material under one head, and if I can follow by showing its basically uterine character, I shall have carried the spirit of his vast unification yet a step farther into a concentrated synthesis.

In the year 1890, Sir J. G. Frazer published his famous work on primitive religion, called *The Golden Bough*. This title refers to that golden bough which Aeneas plucked from the tree in order to gain the right to visit his father in the underworld:

Yet none the shades can visit, till he tear that golden growth, the gift of Pluto's queen, and show the passport she decreed to bear.[61]

I have already shown that although the underworld, the abode of the dead, is naturally represented as below the earth's surface, yet preceding the earth's role in this respect is the role of the placenta, which is also the place of death. Clearly, the 'golden bough' may be seen as a symbol of the umbilical cord. I have shown several instances where the symbolic reference to the umbilical cord takes the form of a tree or branch, so that we need have no fear that we are putting any *prima facie* strain upon the symbolism of the golden bough of Aeneas, especially when we treat it only as a preliminary hypothesis. Our hypothesis strengthens when we know that this golden bough is really the mistletoe:

> As in the woods, in winter's cold, is seen, sown on an alien tree, the mistletoe to bloom afresh with foliage newly green, and round the tapering boles its arms to throw, laden with yellow fruitage, even so the oak's dark boughs the golden leaves display, so the foil rustles in the breezes low. Quickly Aeneas plucks the lingering spray, and to the Sibyl bears the welcome gift away.[62]

We have met the mistletoe before as a symbol of the umbilical cord, for we saw that it was a shaft of mistletoe which alone could kill Balder, to whose myth I now revert. The use of the mistletoe as the fatal instrument in the struggle between Light and Dark imports a strongly umbilical element. One might suppose, indeed, that the myth of Balder began as a simple personification of the 'struggle' between Light and Dark, Day and Night, and in the human relationship to Fire which played a mediating part, as he became able to control in degree their power over him. One might then suppose that upon this basic myth the uterine elements would be later imposed by the human feelings, since these are literally created out of a similar struggle, namely between the nuclear Shining One (the fetus) and the dark and destroying periphery of the womb. Yet on the other hand it is just as likely that the uterine myth came first, and that the external elements of Night and Day from the very beginning were subsidiary to the uterine feelings at the core of the self. It is a question of the primacy at any given stage of man's development of the inward feelings or the outward perceptions. We have already seen in the Hebrew myth of Samson, that Delilah, whose origins and behavior are most emphatically umbilical and placental, has a name which is commonly derived from the word for Night, and which yet has distinctly umbilical and placental associations. This would suggest that perhaps in the minds of earlier men the two categories, the outward and the inward, were literally inseparable.

    The investigation of the Balder myth is pursued here to develop the notion that the mistletoe shaft is the symbol of the umbilical cord, and that the 'golden bough' is of precisely the same symbolical order. The very first steps of this pursuit of the meaning of the myth would seem to be firstly to discover the grounds on which the mistletoe should have been singled out for this symbolical role, and secondly to determine what significance there may be in the legend that the mistletoe grew upon an oak at the gates of Valhalla.

Firstly, the mistletoe is a parasite. So also are the placenta and the umbilical cord. Indeed, the whole uterine organism is like a parasite upon the maternal body. Yet seen or felt, from the standpoint of the fetus itself, it is the placenta which is a parasite, especially in respect to the umbilical arterial flow. But note that not just any mistletoe is important: both in the myth of Balder and also the story of Aeneas the mistletoe grows upon an oak. It was an oak tree that was important. This is no casual association, as may be seen from the fact that the whole Druidic religion appears to have been centered around the ritual cutting of a mistletoe bough from an *oak tree* and no other. The question therefore inevitably arises as to why an oak tree, of all the trees of the forest, should have been selected. The oak was thought to be specially related to Zeus, and in ancient Italy every oak tree was held sacred to Jove, the Roman Zeus. Because the oak tree exceeds all other trees in its conductive powers, it is more frequently struck by lightning than any other tree. Both the Romans and the Greeks regarded with holy awe any spot where lightning had struck. Such places were enclosed and regarded as sacred:

> *In Greece a place that was struck by lightning became a spot not to be trodden on, unapproachable.*[63]

It is easy to understand that if the oak tree appeared frequently to be associated with the creation of such holy places, then the link between the heavenly fire and the oak would develop over time. The oak itself would be the fire-tree, and thus the symbol of the Shining One. The parasite growing upon the Shining One plainly makes a remarkably apt symbol of both the umbilical cord and also the placenta. It is in this fashion, I believe, that the mistletoe can be seen in its role as symbol of the umbilical cord.

Now we have to consider why the Balder myth places the mistletoe at the gate of Valhalla. If we could find anything in the nature of Valhalla to suggest that it symbolizes the womb, it would be most appropriate. For then the gate of Valhalla would be symbolic of the 'gate of the womb', the mother's vaginal opening – it is certainly true in a rough poetic way that we last knew the umbilical cord at that very gate. That is to say, if we think of how our feelings must run back in ever-diminishing complexity to the moment of birth and beyond, we can see that to trace back in our feelings to the last experience of the umbilical cord, is to retrace our mental steps back to the immediate postnatal moments when we were still at 'mother's gate' and still linked by the 'parasite growing from the navel'. With such an idea in mind, if we survey the myth of Valhalla, we shall see that it does yield no small enlightenment.

We are told that the walls of Valhalla were fashioned of glittering spears, which illumined the whole hall, recalling here that the fetal skin feeling is sensed not only as a 'gleam' or 'glitter', but also as the essence of nuclear, hence a spear-like piercing energy. Those favored warriors who attained Valhalla spent their days alternating between feeding and fighting. They fed upon the flesh of the divine boar Saehrimnir, who was daily slain and as regularly restored to life. This eternally slain and resurrected boar makes an excellent symbol of the placenta, which is felt by the fetus to be constantly slain by the arterial umbilical in-thrust, and as constantly revived in its maternal and nutritive aspect. As soon as dinner was over, the inhabitants of Valhalla rushed off to battle, there to deal and to receive terrible wounds. But when once again the dinner horn sounded, their wounds were miraculously healed, and back they went once more to eat of the dying and reviving boar. This constant cycle of eating and wounding clearly represents a process which may be linked to the sense of the relationship between the fetus and the placenta. For the fetus constantly deals out his 'piercing thrusts' through the umbilical arteries and is also constantly wounded, yet in the same cycle of events is restored by feeding. Indeed, the fact that the source of food was a divine boar, itself no mean thruster and wounder, may appear poetically significant.[64]

Valhalla may thus be seen to symbolize the uterine life, especially in the sense of the nuclear fetal polarity and its umbilical reversals. And the oak tree may likewise be seen as the representation of the fetal nuclear feelings. Thus the mistletoe on the oak at the gate of Valhalla appears as a highly plausible symbol of the umbilical cord on the fetal body at the entrance to the maternal body.

This heavy Nordic mythology appears to have a reflection in lighter vein in English folk customs at Christmas time. Christmas is pre-eminently the 'Day of Birth' and has been from ancient times, since it is on the twenty-fifth day of December that the Sun, having rested at the winter solstice, begins its annual climb out of the depths of winter. Not only the Christian Feast, but also a number of folk-customs of varying antiquity, have been apportioned to this day. What can we suppose of the little man in the red coat who comes down the chimney on Christmas Eve? Is he not the representative of the baby in the act of being born? And when he comes down the chimney, does he not fill stockings and deck a tree? While Father Christmas does not deck the tree with its candles and spangles, by implication it is he who provides the wherewithal of Christmas. We can perhaps see the symbolic identity between the Christmas tree covered with lights and shining spangles, and the oak tree that is lit up by the lightning bolts of Zeus, as both trees represent the fetal skin feeling. As to the filled stocking, here again is a reference to the fact that at birth the umbilical feelings are assumed largely by the legs. The presents in the stocking are in essence of the same order as those on the tree, and this may clearly be equated with the idea that the fetal nuclear feeling does indeed involve not only the skin but also the umbilical arteries and the legs.

A folk custom which supports this view of the chimney in relationship to the womb and the legs is this: a homesick boy was cured of his malaise by placing salt in the hem of his trousers and making him look up the chimney. Salt is the symbol of the blood, and when placed in the trousers it symbolizes (in this particular context) the umbilical arterial blood in the legs. The chimney is the mother's birth canal, and so by this rough device of sympathetic magic, the boy is made to feel restored in some degree to his old place 'up the chimney' (in the womb) where indeed he did have 'salt in his legs' (the symbol of the umbilical cord).

In such a context, as in the descent of Santa Claus, the family hearth is manifestly the entrance to the mother's body – and its natal exit! Thus the gate of Valhalla and the Christmas hearth are not so far apart. Here, perhaps, is the mistletoe's special relationship to Christmas, to be found not far from the Christmas hearth on that day, even as the fatal Norse mistletoe was found not far from Valhalla's gate. Moreover, the use of mistletoe at Christmas is in keeping with this view of its nature, for it promotes the kiss between males and females, and so fleetingly and superficially plays a pseudo-umbilical role, since the first 'long kiss' between the 'first male and female' was through the umbilical cord, and may be said to have 'ended on Christmas Day' – the day of the birth.

According to Frazer, in Mabuiag, an island in the Torres Straits, it was believed that a pregnant woman could be made to bear twins if she touched or broke a branch of a mistletoe-like parasite. Considering the widespread superstitions about twins, which we have good reason to understand as symbols of the uterine organism [255], we can see in this primitive belief a plausible link with the umbilical nature of the mistletoe. This belief is saying, in effect, that the twins are fetus and placenta, linked by the 'navel-string' or umbilical cord. By touching the parasitical symbol, the sense of the navel-string is imported, so, *ergo*, twins may result. Obviously this is not the mental process by which the primitive man arrives at such conclusions, but is simply a representation of the pattern of feeling-associations involved in the belief. Similarly, the mistletoe is felt to be a panacea for all manner of disease. The umbilical cord is before the ridder of poisons and the giver of life, and the mistletoe is the umbilical cord – therefore the mistletoe is a great healer and a remedy against all poisons. Pliny said that the Druids made a potion from the mistletoe and believed it to cure barrenness and to antidote poisons. Naturally! The mistletoe is the umbilical cord, and the umbilical cord evokes the first sense of sex and reproduction, and is the instrument for excreting the poisons of the fetal body. Hence the mistletoe fosters reproduction, cures all ills and clears away all poison. We know that the Greeks regarded the umbilical cord as the Great Healer, as witness the healing powers of the snake Asklepios and the clear (if formalized) umbilical nature of the *caduceus*. We are not therefore surprised when Frazer tells us that in Breton, Welch, Erse and Gaelic the name of the mistletoe may still be translated as 'the All-Healer'.

Having indicated some reasons why the mistletoe, and hence the golden bough of Aeneas, may be considered as symbols of the umbilical cord, I would like to turn the reader's attention again to J. G. Frazer's masterpiece. It is surely a commentary upon the absolute divorce of the modern mind from the real content of the feelings that Frazer could write his enormous work, replete as it is with symbolic references to the uterine feelings, without ever once making even a poetic linkage between the symbolism and its obvious internal referent. It is the more astonishing that this should be so, since Frazer did not have to invent the links: they lay dormant in the mythopoeic operation of the ancient mind. The whole of ancient mythology can be seen to be full of such associative links. So completely is the modern mind cut off from its own origins, and diverted into spatial and intellectual channels, that the most blatant symbolism did not awaken in J. G. Frazer even a flicker of this suspicion. Through the whole book, he assumes that the ancient and primitive man was a fool, and that therefore his marvelous myths and rites could have no other explanation than being a childish effort to compel or induce nature to carry out her immemorial cycles. Yet in spite of this blindness which is, of course, not peculiar to him, Frazer weaves unwittingly an umbilical thread through the whole of his vast work, sometimes tenuous to the point of disappearing, but manifest nonetheless. One can only suppose that in addition to the rather forced conscious linkage which he sought to maintain through his eleven volumes, the natural and unconscious one was nonetheless operative in a ways that would most likely have affronted his intellect.

As he himself shows, when Frazer began his masterpiece, he had no intention of carrying it into its eventual length. It was to be at first, as its title reveals, an effort to explain the *'strange rule of the priesthood or sacred kingship of Nemi and with it the legend of the Golden Bough, immortalized by Virgil, which the voice of antiquity associated with the priesthood'*.[65] The kingship or priesthood of Nemi was the core of the whole vast and scholarly undertaking, and it is this core which I propose to analyze next, showing it to be replete with the most exact mythical and ritual symbolic representations of the uterine life.

First, let me give a condensed version of Frazer's description of the 'priesthood or sacred kingship of Nemi'. Lake Nemi is an upland lake, situated in the Alban hills, not far from Rome, and formed in the crater of an extinct volcano. A temple of Diana stood on a flat wooded stretch to the north of the lake. It was here, in this wood and in association with this temple, that a tragic drama was perpetually enacted down into historical times. In the sacred grove there grew a certain tree, and around this tree in ancient times a furtive figure prowled, carrying a drawn sword and peering anxiously about. This figure was the priest of the wood of Nemi.

Why was he armed and furtive? Because it was said that some day a runaway slave would come to Nemi and free himself by breaking off a branch from that sacred tree. He would then engage the priest in single combat and, if he could, slay him. If he succeeded, he in turn would become the priest of the wood of Nemi, and would likewise prowl about the tree to guard his life and his precarious tenure of priestly office.

Frazer tells us that, according to the ancients, the fateful branch which the runaway slave sought to break from the sacred tree in Nemi was identical with the golden bough which Aeneas plucked from the tree in order to gain the right to descend into the underworld. The fact that the branch could be plucked only by a runaway slave could be linked with the flight of Orestes. Indeed, the worship of Diana at Nemi was reputed to have been instituted by Orestes. Diana was an original Italian divinity whom the Romans completely identified with the Greek Artemis. From votive offerings found on the site of her temple at Nemi, she appears to have been conceived of not only as a huntress but as a goddess of human fertility, having the power to aid conception in women and also to give them easy delivery of the child. On the site have been found many models of the genital organs of both sexes, including wombs, and other generative representations.[66] At Nemi she bore the title of Vesta, which, as Frazer asserts points clearly to the maintenance of a perpetual fire in her sanctuary there. Here in Nemi, it would appear, this sacred fire was tended by vestal virgins, as had been a common practice in Latium from earliest times. Diana was also the goddess of vines. Diana did not, however, reign alone in Nemi. She shared the holy spot with two lesser divinities. Egeria the water nymph and wife of Numa was worshipped here, and she was associated with a stream which bubbled up from the rocks and flowed away over the pebbles. Here, pregnant women offered sacrifices to Egeria because she was believed to have the power to grant easy childbirth. The second lesser divinity of Nemi was named Virbius, by legend identical with the Greek hero Hippolytus. Hippolytus learned the arts of the chase from the centaur Cheiron, and spent his days hunting with Artemis.

Proud of his companionship with Artemis, Hippolytus spurned the love of women, for which Aphrodite caused Phaedra, his stepmother, to fall in love with him. He then spurned her wicked (incestuous!) advances, and in a jealous rage she accused him falsely to his father Theseus. Theseus prayed to his father Poseidon to avenge him, and the god sent a fierce bull to attack the youth as he drove his chariot by the seashore. The horses bolted and Hippolytus was killed. But Diana, because of the love she bore the youth, begged Asklepios to bring him back to life, and bore him off to Nemi where he was entrusted to the care of the nymph Egeria. Here he was worshipped as a god, and because of his death at the hooves of his horses, all horses were excluded from the wood of Nemi. Frazer notes: 'It was unlawful to touch his image. *Some thought he was the sun.*'[67]

Here we may note an important element reported by Frazer. Hippolytus appears to have originated in Troezen, where his untimely end in the chariot accident was mourned. Every year a sacrificial festival was held in his memory, and his fate was mourned by single girls who also dedicated locks of their hair to him before marriage. Both youths and maids of Troezen were said to have been forbidden to wed until they had shorn their hair in honor of the sad Hippolytus, for whom there was no resurrection at Troezen. Frazer links this sacrifice of the hair with the custom of boys going to Delphoi to offer their hair to Apollo, and he also mentions the custom of Argive maidens shearing their tresses and offering them to Athena. Megarian girls similarly laid clippings of their hair on the tomb of Iphinoe. He gives several other instances of the 'sacrifice of hair' on the eve of marriage. At the annual mourning for Adonis at Byblos, women were required either to shave their heads or to prostitute themselves to strangers. Frazer remarks upon this choice in the following terms:

> *It is clear that the goddess accepted the sacrifice of chastity as a substitute for the sacrifice of hair. Why? By many people, as we shall afterwards see, the hair is regarded as in a special sense the seat of strength; and at puberty it might well be thought to contain a double portion of vital energy, since at that season it is the outward sign and manifestation of the newly-acquired power of reproducing the species.*[68]

We shall see later on that there is a simpler and much more concrete explanation, which derives from the deepest human feelings and needs no such cerebration as is implied in Frazer's explanation. One final element in Frazer's description of Nemi must be noted before I proceed to demonstrate the uterine elements involved. A double-headed bust was discovered in the temple of Diana at Nemi. Both faces are of similar type, but one is the face of a young and beardless man while the other is that of an older man with a tossed and matted beard. Leaves, believed to be oak leaves, are plastered on the necks of both figures, and apparently also under the eyes of the younger man. When viewed in profile, Frazer says, the moustache of the older man presents the aspect of an oak leaf.

It will now be my task to show that all this material related to the golden bough and the temple at Nemi, its divinities, rites and legends, is infused with strongly uterine symbolism. I shall show that there is a consistent umbilical motif underlying the mysterious drama of the priest of the wood of Nemi, and that all the related mythology points to the same interpretation. As in all mythological material, and indeed in all dream material, there is no 'proof' to be found in any isolated element. But when the whole material is surveyed with an informed eye, a flickering uniformity is to be seen covering the whole. This uniformity is, I assert, the inward memory of the uterine life seeking to find and indeed to create representations of that life which is forever lost, but which forever cries deep in the emotions for expression and restoration.

First of all let us consider the Lake of Nemi itself. It is set high up in the hills, and is formed in the crater of an extinct volcano. Here we have a geographical symbolism ready made for a uterine drama. The womb is a lake, as represented so frequently in dreams where the likely context is uterine. The womb, moreover, is an 'extinct crater' where once we were identical with the nuclear skin feeling which has so close a connection with shining, gleaming, sunlight and fire. The womb is frequently represented in dreams as a high place, which I have suggested is due to the fact that it is the place which we leave at the dawning of the sense of gravity and falling. A volcanic crater filled with water, moreover, links together two aspects of water and fire which, though physically incompatible, are not so in the uterine sense, for the mysterious nuclear 'gleam' or 'sunlight' upon the skin of the Shining One is linked with the sense of being in the uterine waters. This uterine link between water and fire is strongly supported by an ancient Christian baptismal rite in which a burning brand was first doused in the water of the font before being used to baptize the child. The burning brand signifies the fetal skin feeling, while the water is the amniotic fluid.[69]

Once we recognize the nature of Diana's cult we shall not be surprised to find her temple in a uterine setting, for her whole worship was concerned primarily with the womb and its fruits. She was firmly believed by the ancient Romans to aid conception and to give easy release from the womb, while all about her temple have been discovered models of the human genitalia, including wombs and also the images of pregnant women. Insofar as she represents the womb, her relationship to the vestal fire is evident, for *the womb is the organic instrument for the evocation of that undying fire which is the nuclear energy of creation*. This aspect of the vestal fire is emphasized by the fact that, as Frazer shows, it was fed with oak wood. That is to say, that very oak which, when it grew, attracted so often the nuclear fires of Zeus, the heavenly Shining One, also provided when cut down the perpetual fire on Diana's hearth.

Here we consider the sacrifice of the hair which Frazer linked, though tenuously, with the sacred fire. The fetal skin feeling is frequently associated with hair, in dreams and myths, as seen in the myth of Samson, the Shining One, in whose hair the virtue resided. We have also seen it in the myth of Esau and in his appellation Seir – in both cases the idea of hair is connected to the fetal state. The fact that the maidens in Troezen sacrificed their hair to the chaste young Hippolytus is of special interest because it was this very same Hippolytus who, in the form of Virbius at Nemi, was regarded as being identical with the Sun. Thus, as in the case of Samson, we have a link between hair and the Sun – that is, between the hair all over the fetal skin and the sense of being the nuclear 'shining' focus. The various instances given by Frazer of the sacrifice of hair at puberty strengthens this interpretation, as noted in Frazer's suggestion that the hair was in ancient times regarded as the seat of strength, and that at puberty it might be thought to contain a double portion of vital energy. All such rough approximations are transformed once we know that the fetal skin feeling is the origin of all male feeling and that this is transferred at puberty in large measure to the genitals [175-181]. For then we see that the appearance of hair at the genitalia is not merely a physical fact of puberty, but also is a ready-made symbol of the transfer of the fetal nuclear 'male' feelings at the genitals. In such terms, the sacrifice of hair to a representative of the Shining One (be he called Hippolytus, Virbius, Apollo or Adonis) may be seen as a symbolic recognition of the public accession of the umbilical polarities to the genital regions.

Thus we can see both geographical and ritualistic reasons for regarding the temple of Diana at Nemi as the representation of the womb, where the primary drama of every man is laid and which thus clamors in our depths for some kind of recognition or projection.[70] The Lake of Nemi itself offers a beautiful and poetic representation of that high 'lake' in which we lived our lives before birth, and which is frequently represented in modern dreams in just such terms even by one who has never actually seen a body of water situated in the heights [315]. Diana's temple makes an impressive symbol of the womb, especially when we consider that it was the location of the vestal fires, a telling representation of the nuclear 'fire' as felt upon the fetal skin. And the presence at this same sacred spot of Virbius-Hippolytus, patently a Shining One, tends to complete the uterine symbolism. On such a stage we naturally look for some play-out of the umbilical drama [26], and we are by no means disappointed when we analyze the drama of the Priest of the Woods of Nemi, which I propose now to attempt.

The first thing that strikes us is that the claimant to the priesthood of Diana at Nemi was required to be a runaway slave. It is true that Diana was, in Italy, the protectress of escaping slaves, but under this fact there lies a deeper meaning. I have observed again and again in modern dreams a tendency to represent the fetus as a slave or prisoner, and the act of birth as an escape from bondage. Such observations were made well before I knew about the story of the Nemean wood, and indeed before I knew anything about the functions of ancient goddesses as protectors of slaves. Wherever I have found in dreams the figure of a fugitive from bondage of any kind, the context tends to suggest that it is a residual memory of the struggle to escape from the womb. Although felt as a heavenly abode before birth begins, it is in retrospect sensed as a prison insofar as the feelings concern birth and its struggles. The runaway slave of Nemi may thus be seen as the symbol of the fetus.

In this light the plucking of the mistletoe or the golden bough from the tree represents the cutting of the umbilical cord and, likewise, the fetal self from the maternal 'tree'. The slaying of the old priest by the new then represents the undoubted fact the child, in the act of being born into the world as a human being, brings on the death of the earlier fetal self. There is no doubt that this feeling is a very real one yet in spite of that, the interpretation offered above would prove a very shallow one because it would miss the fact that the experience of birth summates in the feelings all that has already been known of escape, death and restoration in the course of the umbilical flow [31-32]. For in the umbilical cord every pulse of blood evokes among other things the sense of restless escape, the 'slaying' of the old father sense [187] and the 'birth' or emergence of his successor. This is an important matter because, were we to insist on regarding the drama of Nemi only as a birth drama, it could have no possible relationship with such myths as those of Orestes, as ancient opinion insisted it to have.

Also, as a simple representation of birth, the drama at Nemi would have little or no association with the mysterious double-headed bust found in the ruins of the temple. But if the cycle of slaying and being slain is basically a representation of the umbilical drama, then we can discern a simple meaning in the double-headed bust. The old man represents the nuclear energy that is destroyed, or about to be destroyed, in the placenta. The young man represents the new emergent nuclear energy to which the placenta gives rise. And this, I believe, is what the drama at Nemi fundamentally represents: *the cycle of death and resurrection, which perpetually takes place in the umbilical circulation.* As I have said earlier, the fetal state has its static aspect, namely that of the fetal body as nucleus within the uterine surround. This static state is wakened into dynamic activity by the umbilical circulation, which constantly brings the two extremes into synthesis. So also the temple of Diana, dreaming in the woods by Lake Nemi, represents the static picture of the womb. It is the cyclic drama of murderous succession which awakens the picture and adds to it the dynamism of the umbilical cord. This suggests, of course, that Diana is more than the womb – that she is also the symbol of the placenta. And this can be demonstrated without transgressing the mythological picture if we remember that the womb and the placenta are largely identified in the fetal feelings [42].

In seeking to understand Diana's nature we have only to recall what we have already seen of the character of Artemis, for they are one and the same. Artemis is the life-giving maiden who in spite of penetration remains uninjured. She is the sister of the Shining

One, Apollo, whose temple was at the Place of Wombs (Delphi) and who slew the umbilical snake and buried it under the Navel Stone *(omphalos)*. Artemis sends plagues and death with her arrows, and yet the very evils she could inflict were also the ones she could cure. Her powers of healing were marked: it was she who healed Aeneas when he was wounded and carried into the temple of Apollo. Everything about her fits into place in a plausible symbolism of the placenta. Diana as the nurturer of the vestal fire is a beautiful symbol of the uterus. But Diana, huntress and counterpart of Artemis, is no less a symbol of the placenta.

The link between Aeneas and the golden bough of the sacred tree in Nemi is verified with Aeneas symbolizing the fetal nuclear feeling, which can only get into the place of the 'dead father' via the umbilical cord. It alone enables the nuclear fetal feeling to penetrate into the placenta, where this feeling is destroyed and, indeed, becomes the 'dead father'. In other words, as the nuclear fetal feeling is identified with the father, then that same feeling when destroyed in the placenta is the 'dead father'. Thus the journey of Aeneas – down into the underworld and back – is a journey which can only be taken through the mediacy of the golden bough. This journey symbolizes the perpetual movement of the fetal skin feeling down into the placenta and back – a journey which can only be made through the medium of the umbilical cord.

If I seem to be reading too much into the story of Aeneas, it is only because its author, Virgil was a cultivated Roman who was mentally far removed from the primitive Achean and Mycenean people from whom he drew the elements of his tale. For this reason the cultured tale of *The Aeneid* appears in terms which belong far more to the conscious mind than to the deep feelings. In short, *The Aeneid* is the product of a mind for which the myths were already more poetry than subjective fact. A very different mental atmosphere can be felt at once in the myth of Orestes, which ancient opinion linked also to the drama in the Woods of Nemi. Here the umbilical drama stands out in stark and bold terms.

The story of Orestes is briefly thus: he was the only son of Agamemnon and Clytemnestra, and when Agamemnon returned from Troy, he did not meet his son Orestes, but was murdered by his wife and her lover Aigisthos. This part of the story alone has strong uterine undertones. Aigisthos, for instance, was represented as begotten of an incestuous affair, as having been exposed by his mother and brought up by a goat, whence his name. Here already we have markedly uterine elements. The fetal drama is essentially an incestuous one, since the placenta is both sister-wife and mother, and the nuclear sense seems to enter the placenta and to create itself there as child. The wicked mother who exposes her child is not only the symbol of the womb, which exposes (gives birth to) the child, but also of that earlier perpetual drama of placental destruction. That the goat is the fetal symbol we have already suspected from the fact that Zeus wears the goatskin unshorn as his *aegis*. So the incestuous child who is exposed by his mother and rescued by a goat makes a very plausible symbol of the umbilical cycle.

If Aigisthos is a fetal symbol, then Clytemnestra may naturally be suspected of being placental. That she kills her husband is congruent with this symbolic context, since the fetus is sensed as the male counterpart (husband) of the female placenta, and is perpetually 'killed' by her with every beat of the umbilical blood. That Aigisthos was incestuously born, and was also the lover of Clytemnestra, delineates the same general theme. In a myth, as in a dream, it is necessary only to bring the requisite elements together, as the actual logical framework matters little. In the myth of Orestes, there are three representatives of the fetal nuclear feelings, namely Agamemnon, Aigisthos and Orestes, each of whom appears to symbolize a different aspect of the primal complex. Thus Agamemnon represents the fetus as 'husband' of the placenta, by whom he is destroyed. Aigisthos represents the fetal (hairy) skin feeling and the elements of incest and betrayal involved in its relationship with the placenta. Orestes imports into the picture the sense of the piercing and destruction of the mother (as placenta) and the 'flight' from the placenta back along the umbilical vein to the fetal body. The placental symbolism of Clytemnestra, already strongly implied by the nature and behavior of the males to whom she is related, is heightened by the legend that she trapped her husband in his bath, threw a net over him and then stabbed him with a trident. The husband in the bath and the net well symbolize the nuclear-feeling fetus 'trapped' in the 'watery net' of the amnion. The act of stabbing him with a trident is a splendid symbol of the destructive placental activity carried out through the instrumentality of the three-tubed umbilical cord.

Mythology of the Prenatal Life 121

Against such a background, the myth of Orestes is plainly umbilical in tone. Learning that his father Agamemnon has been slain by his faithless mother, Orestes went and slew her and her lover Aigisthos, then fled from the scene and went to Delphoi, whither he was pursued by the *Erinyes*. Here he was rescued by Apollo who advised him to take refuge with Athena. When he was eventually accused before the court of the Areopagus by the *Erinyes*, Orestes pleaded that he was encouraged by the oracle at Delphoi to slay his mother. In this light we see Orestes as the symbol of the nuclear fetal energy which thrusts down the umbilical arteries and penetrates the placenta (mother) and thus 'makes it hollow' – that is, destroys it, whereafter it returns again to the fetal body and

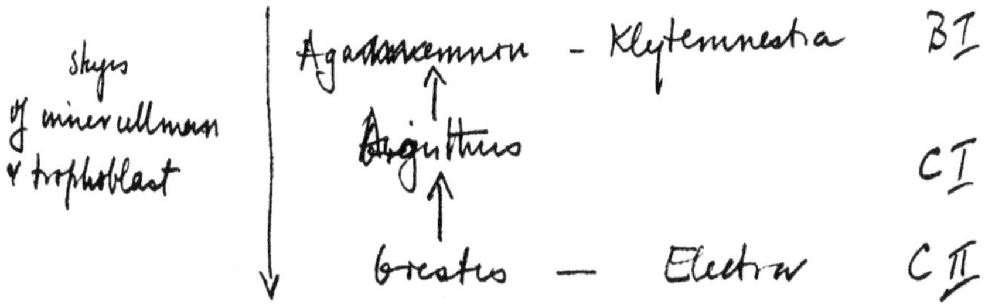

[handwritten margin note: skyus of miner ullman & trophoblast]

[handwritten diagram:
Agamemnon — Klytemnestra   BI
↑
Aigisthus   CI
↑
Orestes — Electra   CII]

its nuclear skin feeling. Orestes, in slaying his mother, symbolizes the fetal thrust into the placenta. In slaying Aigisthos, he enacts the thrust into the placenta by the nuclear energy which thus also feels itself to be destroyed. The rescue by Apollo at Delphi symbolizes the manner in which the journeying nuclear energy returns to the fetal skin through the umbilical vein. Of course it is the Delphic oracle which incites Orestes's dreadful deeds, for that very oracle is the servant and mouthpiece of the umbilical Python.

We can understand also why Orestes was represented as clinging for sanctuary to the *omphalos* at Delphoi, while about him the *Erinyes* of his dead mother clamor for vengeance. Jane Harrison calls the *omphalos* the 'the life-stone', a title appropriate for our uterine considerations: to the umbilical vein the navel is indeed the 'life-stone', just as the umbilical arterial flow is symbolized by the phallus and the spear. Hence, the navel is the pathway to doom and

[handwritten: the embryo slays the chorion]

122   Mythology of the Prenatal Life

also the pathway to life, as well as having other ambivalent roles. The umbilical nature of the flight of Orestes is also reflected in the ancient portrayal of the *Erinyes* as snakes.[71]

Miss Harrison further reminds us that Aeschylus in *The Choephori* tells of Clytemnestra dreaming that she gave birth to a snake and suckled it. In this context Jane Harrison writes:

> The snake is more than the symbol of the dead; it is, I believe, the actual vehicle of the Erinys.[72]

The umbilical cord is indeed the actual vehicle whereby the memories of death and incest in the placenta 'pursue' the nuclear feelings (Orestes) to the 'life-stone' of the navel. We need hardly be

[handwritten annotation: the embryo and placenta supercedes the chorion / Orestes and Electra slay Klytemnestra]

surprised to find that there existed a legend to the effect that Orestes died of a snake-bite, for every fetus does so 'die', and his successor (the postnatal organism) bears the mark of that bite throughout life! These umbilical undertones beneath the story of Orestes explain the ancient belief that the drama of Nemi was instituted by Orestes. For if the drama in the wood at Nemi is a play-out of the umbilical cycle by human actors, and if Orestes symbolizes that cycle, then the runaway slave of Nemi was carrying on what Orestes had initiated.

That Diana symbolizes not only the womb but also the placenta is supported by the presence of Virbius as her consort at Nemi. This god has two aspects, namely a static and a dynamic aspect, which subtly modulate the nature of Diana herself into two aspects, namely uterine and placental. As Virbius at Nemi, the god represents the fetal skin feeling. He was 'thought to be the Sun' and, in this aspect was akin to the vestal fire which burned in the temple. He was in this sense the Shining One, placid and nuclear, and in relation to him, Diana was the womb. But we find that Virbius was originally Hippolytus the consort of Artemis, closely related to Diana. It was as a result of his attachment to Artemis that Hippolytus brought upon himself the wrath of Aphrodite and eventually death at the hooves of his horses, a fate which also helps to confirm his fetal nature, since the horse and the centaur are frequently found in mythology in a placental context. The reason for this symbolism is by no means clear, and the judgment is based solely upon its persistent appearance in a context which amply justifies that conclusion.

The wrath of Aphrodite was aroused by a false accusation of incest against Hippolytus, a further piece of support for the interpretation here given. When Diana learned of the death of Hippolytus she begged Asklepios (the healing snake!) to bring him

the start of blood circulation in the chorionic vesicle

embryo experiencing input from chorionic circulation as persecution

the life stone

the embryo

Klytemnestria gives birth to a snake

Orestes persecuted by the Erinys

the connecting stalk

Orestes

back to life, which he did, thus symbolizing once again the power of the umbilical 'serpent' to restore the power of the slain Shining One. These facts enable us to see Hippolytus as the symbol of the dynamic umbilical aspect of the fetal nuclear feeling. Destroyed by the placenta (symbolized by Artemis + Aphrodite + Horses), he is brought to life again through the cord (Asklepios) even as he was also in part destroyed through its action. It is in this way that I see Virbius and Diana as the symbols of the fetal skin feeling in relationship to the womb, while as Hippolytus and Artemis they represent the same elements in dynamic (umbilical) interaction.

We have seen that the Temple at Nemi and its priestly-drama, as well as the ancillary legends, all have a general uterine and umbilical cast. Therefore the function of the golden bough, which alone permits the fulfillment of the cyclic drama of death and succession, adequately responds to the umbilical interpretation as the umbilical cord is that essential 'branch' or 'bough' without which the cyclic drama cannot be carried on. When this bough is linked with the mistletoe, as in the myth of Balder, its umbilical symbolism is clearly demonstrated.

The fundamental base of Frazer's *magnum opus* may thus be seen to rest upon uterine foundations and the themes of his book may be read as 'the Umbilical Bough'. It seems significant that Frazer saw indications in this drama in Nemi that primitive man believed that in order for new life to emerge, there must be a death and a destruction. It must not be a mere negative fading away through senility, but rather a positive and violent slaying with the full intent to promote new life. Though, as he himself admits, his application of this principle to his great work was at times faltering, yet we may see in the very titles of the majority of his volumes the basic theme which forms the veritable core of the human sense of self. *The Dying God; Adonis, Attis, Osiris; Spirits of the Corn and the Wild; Balder the Beautiful* – all these evoke sacrifice and resurrection, and the human reaction to the cycles of sowing and growing, of day and night, winter and summer. These cycles themselves take place in the world outside of man, but Frazer is concerned with the subjective reactions of primitive and ancient man to them. These reactions he interprets as merely the efforts of an essentially ignorant savage to account for and even to control the cycles of loss and restoration, or to propitiate the gods presumed to be responsible for them. This is the inevitable assumption of one who supposes that primitive man is an empty vessel who must be filled from outside by experience and education.

However, as soon as we see the reality of the umbilical core of the 'I', and recognize that the basic cycle of the self is one of perpetual loss and restoration, in which the inherent nature of the cosmos is echoed – then we can see that neither primitive man nor little child are empty vessels, but both are nuclear echoes of the cosmos itself, which can see the outward cosmos only in terms of what it is. Modern man outgrows this experience and becomes fascinated through the outward senses and social semantics into an almost hypnotic extraversion. But he goes through it as a child, just the same, and never really escapes from it, since all that experience and education overlay but do change that original sense of 'I', of self.

Frazer achieved a great work of syncretism, bringing together vast masses of primitive, ancient and folk material under a single head. But he could not bring them to synthesis because he never at any time recognized that the golden bough, the mistletoe, is essentially the symbol of the subjective aspects of the umbilical circulation. He himself confessed:

> *The book grew on my hands, and soon the projected essay (on Nemi and its implications) became in fact a ponderous treatise, or rather a series of separate dissertations loosely linked together by a slender thread of connexion with my original subject. With each successive edition these dissertations have grown in number and swollen in bulk by the accretion of fresh materials, till the thread on which they are strung at last threatened to snap under their weight.*[73]

Had our distinguished author known that the thread connecting all primitive rite and religion is that triple thread, the umbilical cord, which creates the very subjective powers by which external events can be known and strung together into a meaningful whole, then he would have found himself consciously in possession of a chain of enormous strength which no amount of analysis and digression could snap.

This brief glance at the essence of *The Golden Bough* seems to demonstrate that primitive religion was everywhere a collective effort to perceive in the frequently hostile cycles of external nature some sign of the humanizing presence of those cosmic cycles, which have formed the core of the self. For man needs to know that the God whose pattern he once 'saw' through the 'single eye' of the fetal navel is present also in the harsh world of space. In modern man, this need is greatly obscured by extraversion and by material success, as a result of which he lives very much in a Fool's Paradise. Primitive man, whose hold upon physical existence was infinitely more precarious than our own, had infinitely more opportunity and more need to remember the Golden Bough.

CHAPTER FOUR
The Traveler and the River

We have thus far considered the mythological pictures concerning the fetal nuclear feeling, the placenta, and also the umbilical cord. I now propose to examine the mythology of that nuclear self, who seems to travel back and forth along the umbilical cord, experiencing the most tremendous adventures as he goes [40, 41, 83, 84]. This is the 'great traveler' referred to above, in the title of this chapter, and the umbilical cord is in part the great river. I say 'in part' because the river of the umbilical cord is really the instrument by means of which the unborn organism intuits that vaster cosmic river that flows forever in the invisible cosmos, whose influence the turnings of the visible cosmos show forth. The beat of blood in the umbilical vessel acts, as I have shown, as a sort of 'tuning fork' or 'resonator' through which the beat of time is impressed indelibly into our most primal feelings. In other words, in some strange manner, the miniscule flow of blood between the fetal body and the placenta imitates the vast flow of the wider cosmos. Whether this was 'an evolutionary accident' or part of some vast teleological design is here beside the point. I propose in this chapter to try to show that mythology contains powerful evidence in support of what I have learned direct from dream analysis by my methods. Before proceeding to consider that evidence I will give an outline of its general nature.

The mythological theme of which I speak concerns a great traveler who goes about the world and beyond it, performing mighty deeds. He is frequently related not only to the Sun and its daily and yearly rounds, but also to a specific river or rivers in general, which upon investigation turn out to represent the cyclic movements of the heavenly bodies or even the Milky Way and the constellations. This traveling hero or god has usually been considered as only a representation of solar or cosmic motions dimly perceived. In the words of C. G. Jung:

> *The wandering is a representation of longing, of the ever-restless desire, which nowhere finds its object, for, unknown to itself, it*

> seeks the lost mother. *The wandering association renders the Sun comparison easily intelligible; also, under this aspect, the heroes always resemble the wandering Sun, which seems to justify the fact that the myth of the hero is a Sun myth. But the myth of the hero, however, is, as it appears to me, the myth of our own suffering unconscious, which has an unquenchable longing for all the deepest sources of our own being; for the body of the mother, and through it for communion with infinite life in the countless forms of existence.*[74]

The wandering of the mythological hero is partly a search for the mother, representing as it does the umbilical flow which once connected the fetal self to the mother (placenta). Importantly, however, the hero also signifies the response of the umbilical energies to the *cosmic rhythms*. This theme of 'wandering' also offers a sharp and specific depiction of the nuclear fetal energy connecting with the solar fire, traveling forever down the umbilical road to the mother, and back again. The solar hero is not merely the symbol of the fetal skin feeling or the umbilical affect. He is also the symbol of the cosmic pattern and beat to which they are attuned in the human feelings.

Although this dual aspect of the solar hero was deliberately ignored in earlier chapters, for simplicity of description, the truth is that the solar hero or the Shining One is not merely a representative of the fetal skin feeling and its umbilical dynamics [9, 20], but is equally a symbolic representation of that cosmic process which is imprinted upon the fetal feelings. This was hinted at when discussing the nature of Zeus in earlier chapters, but will now be brought out sharply as the dual nature of the prime myths of the hero are demonstrated. The prime mythological Hero will be seen to contain the following elements:

1. The Hero is a great traveler, who goes about doing great works, and above all teaching and creating.

2. He is represented in such symbolic circumstances as to leave no doubt that he is the symbol of the fetal nuclear feeling which constantly travels between the fetal body and the placenta.

3. At the same time Hero is shown as being related to cosmic entities or processes in such a way as to make it clear that he is also the symbol of the cyclic flow and return of the universe.

Interpreting these facts in the light of my discoveries in dream analysis, I conclude that the Hero is ultimately and properly the *symbol of the resonance between the uterine processes and the cosmos.* He is the 'end product' of the processes whose symbolisms we have studied in the foregoing chapters; the hypostatization of the human sense of selfhood which results from the resonance between the cosmic and the umbilical beats. This is not easily demonstrated to the modern mind, which knows nothing of the inner contents of its ego and unfortunately, in large measure, cares little about it. The average human being today is hardly able to believe that the great mythic themes – say, of the dramatic pilgrimages – are really encapsulated in the depths of his own mind. It might be said that men and women today are so used to their 'egos' that they take them for granted, and simply cannot be easily persuaded that these 'egos' once existed in quite different form, namely before birth and also during infancy, but especially before birth. The average person vaguely senses that his 'I' is in his head or, at any rate, more or less inside him. He can with some difficulty believe that before birth it was, on the contrary, sensed rather outside the body, namely on the skin, in the movement of the blood and especially in the umbilical cord and placenta. The adult 'I' is sensed as something relatively formed, not to say fixed, and contained more or less in the organism. The fetal 'I' is sensed as something entirely fluid, subject to periodic reversals, and as likely to appear to the fetus as its enemy as to appear as its own selfhood – especially when it seems to re-enter the fetal body through the umbilical vein as invader. Yet once these strange, fluid and peripatetic elements of the fetal selfhood are grasped, the 'adventures of the hero' become remarkably intelligible.

As far as ancient Greece is concerned, Herakles was the most famous of heroes:

> *The traditions about him are not only the richest in substance, but also the most widely spread; for we find them not only in all the countries round the Mediterranean, but his wondrous deeds were known in the most distant countries of the ancient world.*[75]

This ancient fame has come down to us in the present time, for no mythological figure is better known than Herakles or Hercules. In everyday language we speak of 'herculean strength' and, less commonly, of great tasks as the 'Labors of Hercules'. Rose calls

Mythology of the Prenatal Life 129

him 'the Greek Samson', a character whom we have already seen as representative of the fetal skin feeling, and whose journey to Timnath vineyard and the slaying of the lion there we have already discussed in uterine terms. I shall now attempt to show that this wandering hero is the representation *par excellence* of the human soul that is evoked or generated out of the cosmos as a result of the resonance between the umbilical and the cosmic beats. The story of Herakles fulfills all the symbolic requirements of the prime mythological Hero figure:

1. He is a great traveler.
2. He is closely involved with all manner of uterine symbology.
3. His journeys are closely related to a cosmic flow and beat.

Herakles was a mighty traveler and voyager, as made clear by the ascription to him of the Twelve Labors, all of which involved him in travels of one kind or another.[76] They were, in fact, acts performed in order to gain a prize – the prize in this case being immortality. The doing of these mighty works, and the ceaseless journeying which it demanded of him, makes it possible to say that Herakles offers one of the most perfect examples of the hero as traveler.

[handwritten annotation:]
Hera - M_1 pre implantation
Zeus - $F_{1,5}$ last stage of blastula

His fetal nature is no less demonstrable, as I shall now attempt to show. However, no particular order of approach to this theme can be followed, because of the vast complexity of the mythology. The myth of the Theban birth of Herakles gives us our first clue. Alcmene, wife of Amphitryon, attracted the attentions of Zeus, who disguised himself as her husband and thus possessed her, making the night three times its usual length for his amorous purposes. Later in this long night Amphitryon himself returned home and possessed his wife, who was puzzled by his double appearance. The outcome of this double mating was the birth of twins. The first-born was called Alkides, later renamed Herakles by the Pythia at Delphi – a significant fact for anyone who has appreciated the uterine nature of that holy place. The second twin was called Iphikles. The myth soon makes it clear that Herakles and Iphikles represent the fetus and the placenta, just as Jacob and Esau have been shown to be. Rose writes of Herakles and Iphikles:

> *In this story we have a very widespread belief, firstly that twins are apt to be in some way remarkable, or that one of them is, and secondly that one of the two is the child of a god or spirit of some kind, not of the mother's mortal consort.*[77]

```
              ⎛ Zeus       ⎞
Alkmene  ⚭  ⎝ Amphitryon ⎠ ─────── Hera
                │
        ┌───────┴───────┐
    Iphikles          Alkides
                      Herákles  ← Pythia at Delphi
```

The learned professor could understand the deeper meaning of this 'very widespread belief' by realizing that the source of all mythology is the uterine evocation of mind from the cosmos! Then he would know that to the ancient mind, or indeed anyone willing to see, twins meant always the 'uterine organism' of fetus and placenta, and that the one who was the child of a spirit or god was the fetal nuclear element – that is to say, not merely the flesh and blood baby, but the fetus as the nuclear element of the uterine cosmic resonator.

the zona Pellucida = the womb of Nut
                     the sky Goddess

inner cell mass and   Osiris and Isis
trophoblast

The truth of this may be glimpsed in the Peruvian belief that one of each set of twins was a son of the lightning. The Baronga, a Bantu tribe, call the mother of twins Tilo, meaning 'the sky', and the twins themselves are called 'children of the sky'. One is reminded by this of the fact that the manifestly uterine twins Osiris and Isis lived and copulated before birth in the womb of Nut, the sky goddess. Manifestly there is a very close connection between the myth of Herakles' birth and the Peruvian belief since indeed Herakles, as son of Zeus, was a son of the lightning. By such means are the 'uterine twins', the fetus and the placenta, symbolized: Herakles is the fetal Shining One, son of Zeus, son of the lightning, while the insignificant Iphikles is the placenta. This uterine imagery is emphasized by the myth that Hera sent two serpents to attack the children in their cradle, but that Herakles choked and killed them with his bare hands.

A variant of the myth is even more telling: Amphitryon put the snakes in the cradle, whereupon Iphikles 'ran away' while Herakles faced them and slew them. Amphitryon thereby knew which child was son of Zeus. It is not indifferent poetic imagery to say that 'the placenta runs away from two snakes' while 'the fetus faces them', because in fact the fetus does feel to thrust through 'twin snakes' at the placenta. The same general motif, though in a very different external form, may be recognized in the terrible jealousy, which Hera inflicted upon Herakles because he was Zeus' bastard, and the torments to which this gave rise, the most fearful (and at the same time the most evidential for the present context) being the madness she brought upon the hero, causing him to slay his wife and children in a fit of Hera-sent madness. The hero's slaughter of his wife is perfectly comprehensible in umbilical terms, because the umbilical arterial thrust evokes in the fetus feelings that the placenta is not only his (pre-sexual) wife, but also his perpetual victim. The same motif has already been seen quite differently expressed between Adam and Eve, but in their case projected into the terms of sons Cain and Abel. The slaying of the children may be similarly interpreted, since the fetus feels to be not only constantly 'reborn' (as its own child) from the placenta, but also to 'eat that self as it is so born' through the umbilical vein. This terrible ambivalent aspect of Herakles has its representations also in the conjunction in his nature of strength and bravery with gluttony and lust, which also are comprehensible in uterine terms, since the fetal skin feeling is the core of the self and its strength, while the fetus might be poetically described as concerned wholly with 'drinking' and 'sex', through the umbilical flow.

132   Mythology of the Prenatal Life

The second marriage of Herakles and its shocking culmination strongly argues his fetal nature. He woos Deianeira and, in order to get her, fights Achelous. This Achelous exhibits the most marked umbilical character: he has the power to change his form, being not only a river, but also a man, a bull and a snake. In this threefold form, Deianeira confesses, he has wooed her again and again:

> *A visible bull, sometimes, and sometimes a coiled gleaming snake, and sometimes partly man...*[78]

Achelous is thus a prime symbol of the fetus, which is frequently in mythology represented unmistakably by a bull. The umbilical significance of the coiled, gleaming snake needs no interpretation. This combination of bull and snake, indeed, calls to mind a story of the incestuous relations between Zeus and his own mother and incestuously begotten daughter. In order to possess his mother, Zeus turned himself into a bull, the result of this incest being a daughter, Kore. In turn, in order to possess this girl, Zeus turned himself into a snake, as a result of which the girl gave birth to a bull. Hence: *'Bull begat Snake, Snake begat Bull.'*[79] Here we see a crude representation of the fetal 'bull-feeling' thrusting into the placenta as mother, resulting in the re-creation of the same 'bull-feeling' in the cyclic reversals of the cord. In this way, to continue with the myth of Herakles, we see Deianeira as the placenta and Achelous as the fetus. Herakles attacks Achelous and breaks off his thrusting horn, taking away both the horn and the girl, a typical mythological stratagem for showing that Herakles is the successor to Achelous, and thus becomes himself the fetal representative.

$$\text{Zeus} \rightarrow (\text{bull} \leftrightarrow M)$$
$$\downarrow$$
$$\rightarrow \text{snake} \rightarrow \text{Kore}$$
$$\downarrow$$
$$\text{bull}$$

$$\left. \begin{array}{l} \text{bull} \\ \text{snake} \\ \text{partly man} \end{array} \right\} \rightarrow \text{Achelous} \leftrightarrow \text{Deianeira}$$

The rest of the story contains highly concentrated symbolism. A centaur, Nessus, tried to assault Deianeira, and Herakles shot him. As the centaur lay dying he told Deianeira to take some blood from his wound and, should Herakles cease to love her, to smear it on his garment, whereupon his love for her would revive. In due course Herakles turned to another woman, whereupon Deianeira did as Nessus had bidden, and smeared the centaur-blood upon Herakles' garment. This contaminated garment caused such pain that he tore feverishly at it, but the garment had so stuck to his body that he tore away great pieces of his flesh and died. The assault upon Deianeira by Nessus and the shooting of the centaur by Herakles is a myth within a myth, so to speak – a representation in miniature of the sense of assault and counter-thrust felt by the fetus in respect to the placenta. The centaur is a markedly placental symbol, as is the horse generally, so that the blood of the centaur smeared by Deianeira (herself already a candidate for the placental role) upon the garment of the hero, resulting in the tearing of his skin, is an excellent symbol of the fact that the action of the placenta, via the blood, is felt by the fetus as a 'tearing to pieces' of his skin feeling. By such symbols is Herakles confirmed as the representative of the fetal feeling.

Additionally, his Twelve Labors and the travels associated with them represent the constant journeying of the fetal nuclear energy to the placenta and back. One extra pointer to the uterine nature of Herakles may be found in the legend that, after slaying his wife and children, he went to Delphoi and asked advice from the Pythia, who sent him to serve Eurystheus for a period. It was at the behest of this Eurystheus that Herakles performed his Labors, so that it can be said that these Labors were indirectly organized by the Pythia. When we remember that the Pythia may be regarded simply as 'the snake woman', living at 'womb-town', the uterine nature of the Twelve Labors seems still more plausibly confirmed.

Let us now examine the 'Twelve Labors of Herakles' in the light of prenatal symbolism:

FIRST LABOR: The Fight with the Nemean Lion

In the mountain valley of Nemea lived a monstrous lion, the offspring of Typhon and Echidna. When Eurystheus ordered Herakles to bring him its skin, he found the lion in its cave, slew it with his hands and took its skin, whereafter it became the symbolic dress of the hero Herakles.

Greeks and Romans alike, therein agreeing with the Egyptians and the nations of the nearer east, looked upon the lion as an animal full of inward fire and essentially akin to the Sun.[80]

The lion is a symbol of the fetal skin feeling, and also an excellent symbol of the Shining One, in this fashion the shining solar orb is linked directly with the hairy skin. The Nemean lion had other symbolic links with the uterine state, having been born of the union of Typhon with Echidna, both of whom demonstrate placental attributes. Typhon is the Greek equivalent of the wicked Set who betrayed Osiris, the Shining One, and destroyed him. Echidna was a blood-sucking monster, half-maiden and half-serpent, spiritual kin to the Sphinx of Thebes who fornicated with young men and tore them to pieces, another placental representation as mentioned in the story of Nessus. Another such confirmatory tale asserts that Selene (the Moon) produced the Nemean lion out of a foam-filled basket. This association echoes something often seen in dreams, namely a baby covered with iridescent bubbles which, upon investigation, yield the sense of the tiny pieces of shining skin feeling [247, 248]. The very first Labor of Herakles may thus be seen in a very plausible uterine light.

$$\text{Selene} - \text{blastule}$$
$$\downarrow$$
$$\text{foam-filled basket}$$
$$\downarrow$$
$$\text{Nemean lion}$$

SECOND LABOR: The Fight with the Lernean Hydra

In a swamp in the country of Lernae dwelt a fearful water-snake, also one of the offspring of Typhon and Echidna, and hence sibling to the Nemean lion. Herakles was ordered by Eurystheus to destroy the monster. He shot at it with burning arrows, and slashed off its head or heads, but new ones grew as fast as they were destroyed. Hera sent a giant crab to help the Hydra in her fight against Herakles, but the hero stamped it underfoot. He then slew the monster and dipped his arrows in its blood, making their wounds incurable.

The parentage of this water-snake is immediately suggestive, since we know that both Typhon and Echidna are prime placental symbols, as the following pages will amplify again and again. The use of burning arrows against the monster by this partly solar hero reminds us of the arrows of the 'far-shooting Phoebus', the lord Apollo, of whose fetal nature we have seen so much evidence. Insofar as they represent the light-shafts of the Sun, the arrows of Apollo can without exaggeration be described as 'burning arrows'. That the heads of the monster grew as fast as they were severed presents us with a good representation of the anxiety and frustration frequently perceptible in dream symbolism, namely a primal fetal sense of hopelessness born of the fact that no matter how hard he thrusts at the placenta, it inevitably thrusts back at him – indeed, the one seems to evoke the other. The giant crab sent by Hera makes another excellent placental symbol, for the zodiac sign of the crab is related to the Moon, a prime placental representation. The fact that Herakles slew this crab by stamping upon it with his *feet* reminds us that the fetus feels its umbilical arterial thrust to be related to the legs and feet, while the dipping of the arrows in the monster's blood reminds us that it is the same blood which is taken from the placenta and thrust back into it again. The contest of Herakles with the Lernean Hydra is thus powerfully symbolic of the struggle between the nuclear energy of the fetal skin and the placental functions.

[handwritten note: Wine = blood / Dionysos - foetal circulation]

THIRD LABOR: The Struggle with the Kerneian Stag

This creature was dedicated to Artemis by the nymph Taygete. Ordered to catch it and bring it alive to Eurystheus, Herakles wounded it and carried it away on his shoulders. But on the way home he was met by Apollo and Artemis, both of whom severely upbraided the hero for daring to wound a creature sacred to Artemis.

Already we have seen Artemis in a strong placental light, so that a stag dedicated to her tends to assume the same color. However, the creature also symbolizes the fetal nuclear feeling in the state of being held by the placenta, for it was represented as having golden antlers and brazen feet, both of which could readily signify the umbilical arterial thrust. We know that the thrust of horns, whether of a bull or of a ram, are found in mythology in a markedly umbilical arterial context, and a stag's horns may similarly be considered, as amplified by the emphasis upon the feet. This is supported by the fact that Herakles was ordered to bring the creature back alive. It will be noted as we survey the Twelve Labors that in some cases Herakles is ordered merely to destroy the creatures he is sent out to find, and that in some cases he is ordered to bring them back alive. In the cases where he is asked to retrieve the creatures, the creature perhaps represents not so much the placenta itself as the fetal nuclear feeling 'in the grip of' the placenta. However, the placental nature of the Kerneian Stag (which is sometimes called a 'hind'!) is seen in the mythology of Taygete who gave it to Artemis. In one tale, Taygete was another maiden whom Zeus pursued, but who was saved from the god by being turned into a cow by Artemis. We shall return to explore further what this maiden-become-cow or heifer signifies.

In any case, the female pursued by the Shining One in this context symbolizes the placenta, and the intervention of Artemis on her behalf supports this interpretation, as does the transmogrification into a cow – we may recall that Zeus's wife Hera was called 'cow-face'. Moreover, the transformation of a girl into a cow because of Zeus's attentions reminds us of Io, whose uterine nature was indicated in the first chapter. The wounding of this stag with an arrow is in line with umbilical imagery, and the meeting with Apollo (the Shining One) and his consort Artemis links together the diverse elements of the prenatal picture represented in this story. Apollo and Artemis are both arrow-shooters and healers, they 'shoot' and 'heal' one another as do fetus and placenta, which explains their deep feelings about Herakles wounding the stag. Here is another representation of the umbilical-placental struggles of the Traveler.

FOURTH LABOR: The Erymanthian Boar

This creature also had to be brought back alive by Herakles. He chased it and eventually caught it and carried it off. In the course of this chase, the hero met the centaur Pholus to whom Dionysus had sent a cask of choice wine. Herakles opened the cask, and the scent of the wine attracted the other centaurs who besieged his haunt. Herakles chased them away to the house of Cheiron, whom he mortally wounded by mistake.

The boar itself, as a fearsome creature with piercing tusks, makes a plausible symbol of the placenta. It accompanies the conflict with the centaurs, lending to this Labor a strong placental symbolism. Pholus, the centaur with the Dionysian wine offers a strong symbol of the placenta and its blood, which indeed is 'sent to it' by the divine (fetal) child. The clustering of the centaurs to the smell of it conjures up the sense of the 'blood-drinking' monsters, the vampires and all their kind. The slaying of Cheiron with an arrow adds to the picture, for Cheiron is the supreme Centaur who 'taught the heroes of Greece' from his refuge in a cave. This last matter might seem irrelevant but for the fact that I have found consistent evidence in dreams which shows that the placenta conveys certain information to the fetus, quite distinct from its biochemical refreshment [47-50].

Selene — blastule
↓
foam-filled basket
↓
Nemean lion

The teaching centaur in the cave with the hero thus makes an excellent representation of the placenta in its role as an *organ of heredity*.

FIFTH LABOR: The Cleaning of the Stables of Augeias

Eurystheus imposed upon Herakles the task of cleaning out the foul stables of King Augeias in a single day. Augeias was a son of Helios and, like his father, had great herds of cattle. To achieve this task, Herakles diverted the great rivers Alpheus and Peneus through the stables and in this fashion washed them clean in a single day.

One of the tasks of the umbilical cord is to carry away the fetal waste through the two umbilical arteries, and it is this function which is symbolized by the Fifth Labor. We shall meet the Sun-god's cattle again in the course of our examination of the Labors, noting their manifestly uterine nature. These cattle of Augeias are linked with the Shining One, Helios, father of the king. The excrement of these cattle may thus be regarded in a quasi-poetic sense as the excrement of the Shining One. The mythological background of the river Alpheus seems to support this imagery. Alpheus was represented by Pausanias as a passionate hunter, but he was no less a passionate hunter of the female, for he chased the nymph Arethusa and also, some say, Artemis herself. Plutarch called him a son of Helios, whereas he is commonly known as a son of Okeanos and Tethys. The Fifth Labor represents the cleansing thrust of the rivers, a mythological association with the passionate thrusting of the male towards the female. In this way, it serves to represent the two main aspects of the umbilical arterial thrust through the 'twin rivers' of the Shining One.

SIXTH LABOR: The Killing of the Stymphalian Birds

On a lake near Stymphalos lived great flocks of man-eating birds, which slew men with their arrow-like feathers and also by their excretions. Eurystheus demanded their death or expulsion, and this task Herakles accomplished by killing them with arrows, some say, or by expelling them.

The Stymphalian birds shot men with feather-arrows just as Herakles shot them, which makes a plausible representation of the fetal-placental conflict in the back-and-forth thrust of the umbilical blood. Birds which both devoured men and slew them by excreting can be given a *rationale* in placental terms, for the placenta actually devours the fetal skin feeling through the excretions of the umbilical cord. The umbilical arteries are the instruments both of the fetal excretions and of the destruction of the fetal skin feeling.

SEVENTH LABOR: The Capture of the Cretan Bull

> King Minos of Crete had a mad bull loose in his land (for reasons which need not be considered here), and Eurystheus sent Herakles to capture it and bring it back. This he did, but let the bull go again, whereafter it wandered to Marathon, where Theseus eventually slew it.

The Cretan bull was a dazzling white creature which Zeus had sent his son Minos. The queen of Crete conceived an unnatural passion for this bull, and by it had a monstrous child, half-bull and half-man, which was called the Minotaur and was shut up in a labyrinth specially built to house it. Herakles caught the bull and took it away, but it eventually landed in Marathon. A dazzling white bull sent by Zeus to the king of Crete already has strong uterine indications, especially when we recall that in Cretan myth the Sun itself was regarded as a bull. For the bull is simply another variant of the Shining One, while the woman he possesses is yet another version of the placental image. The white, shining bull reminds us that Zeus himself wore the form of a white bull when he sired a bull-child with his own daughter, Kore. So do the myths weave their uterine associations endlessly on and on, yet ever revolving around a simple set of subjective elements. The appearance of Theseus in the tale of the seventh Labor imports umbilical elements, since the famous labyrinth in which the Minotaur lived is also an umbilical representation. Thus we see that the Cretan Bull, manifestly a double of the Minotaur, both being forms of Zeus himself, is the fetus, while the labyrinth is the umbilical cord.

There is a subsidiary myth concerning Minos and his wife Pasiphaë, mother of the Minotaur. This couple had a son, Glaukos, who fell into a barrel of honey and was suffocated. An oracle who was consulted as to his whereabouts (for his body had not been found) said that a marvelous creature had been born among the herds of Minos, and that he who found this creature would also find the child. The marvelous creature turned out to be a calf that changed his color *three* times a day. The boy lost in the honey-barrel is the fetus, which feels to be 'lost in the placenta' and the 'one' who 'finds' him is the triply changing polarities (color) of the umbilical flow.

To continue with the myth of Theseus and the Minotaur: it was told how Minos, having had the fearsome Minotaur imprisoned in the labyrinth, demanded of Athens a yearly sacrifice of seven youths and seven maidens to serve as its food. Theseus, hearing of this, offered to be one of the seven youths, and to use this chance to slay the Minotaur. He went to Crete, where the daughter of Minos, Ariadne, fell in love with him and gave him a sword wherewith to slay the Minotaur, and a thread which she would roll out as he went in, so that he could safely find his way back from the tortuous windings of the maze.[81] Theseus went into the labyrinth and slew the Minotaur, and indeed, the thread of Ariadne led him back out again. Ariadne, as we have seen, is a prime symbol of the placenta, and closely linked with Artemis, Aphrodite, the Kore and Persephone. Her thread is the 'straight' umbilical vein which 'leads the hero back' from the labyrinthine windings, which represent the helical windings of the umbilical arteries.

But who is the Minotaur? In this context, he symbolizes the fetal skin feeling, as described previously, but this interpretation is also supported by the fact that his skin was frequently represented as spangled with stars, whence his name Asterios or Asterion, meaning 'the starry one'. At other times his skin was represented as covered with eyes, which links him with other fetal representatives such as Argos and Osiris. But how can the fetal skin feelings be identified with a creature who plays such a placental role as the Minotaur, living at the end of the labyrinth (umbilical arteries) and devouring the seven youths and maidens? It must be remembered that in the umbilical cycle, the polarity of the fetus and the placenta become reversed: the fetus feels at one moment to be the nuclear one and at the next, the hollow one. *Thus we find this reversal of roles in the myths as between the fetal and placental functions. The reason why seven girls and seven boys* are selected annually to be sacrificed to the Minotaur seems to lie in the need to represent the umbilical *sevenfold beat* and its male-female reversals. We saw the same thing in the tale of Teiresias who, at intervals of *seven years*, through killing snakes, became first a girl and then a boy again. The same was also seen in the explanation of Pharaoh's dream, where the *seven years* and the

Mythology of the Prenatal Life 141

reversal from plenty to famine were linked with the 'great river'. In a similar vein is the tale that Dionysus was sent away to be brought up as a girl.

The nature of the labyrinth is extremely interesting in the light of this book. The name derives from the Greek word *labrys*, simply 'a double-headed axe'. At first sight there seems to be little connection between a maze and a double-headed axe, but the umbilical association is not difficult to discern. It stems from the fact that the *labrys* became strongly linked with the thunderbolt, presumably in the following manner: the ancient peoples believed that a lightning strike was literally an actual bolt hurled by the sky-god. When axe-heads of Neolithic origin were found, they were assumed to be the remains of the lightning bolts hurled by this god. This led to an ultimate belief that these were double-headed axes, and the double axe became strongly associated with the horns of a bull. To quote A. B. Cook:

> To grasp the real meaning of this combination (of the double axe set up between a bull's horns) we must bear in mind:
>
> (a) That the bull was the theanthropic animal of the Cretan Zeus, torn asunder in his service and buried in his name.
>
> (b) That ritual horns appear to have originated in the shrine of a buried bull, regarded as a centre or focus of life.
>
> (c) That the vital force of the divine beast was gathered into its horns, so that any object placed between them would be quickened to the uttermost. Was not this the right position for that dread weapon, which constituted the might of the Almighty?[82]

If the bull is Zeus, the Shining One, and if the Shining One is in turn the representation of the fetal body and its nuclear fire, then what relationship would the horns of that bull have to the fetus? Surely the horns would symbolize the thrust of fetal nuclear energy through the umbilical arteries! And if the divine Zeus in the sky, hurling his lightning-bolts is to be fit this context, then his lightning also, like the umbilical arterial thrust, should be dual in character. Hence the bolt of Zeus is a double axe that is clearly related in ancient thought to the dual thrust of the horns of the divine bull, which is plainly a fetal symbol, being among other things torn to pieces in the way that all fetal gods were. Cook states that the ancients felt the lightning strike to be helically twisted, a feeling which links with the umbilical arterial pattern. Thus the *labrys* or two-headed axe may be associated with the helix of the umbilical cord, and this becomes a *labyrinth*. The fetal hero, in order to traverse the umbilical pathway, must find his way through this dangerous labyrinth, and to return safely, must have the 'straight thread' of the umbilical vein. We are told that after his deliverance from the labyrinth, Theseus and the youths and maidens he had rescued from the Minotaur, Daedalus showed them how to weave a circling dance for the gods that resembled his own entrance into and exit from the Labyrinth. Cook writes:

> *In Cretan ritual, the Labyrinth was an orchestra of solar pattern presumably made for a mimetic dance.*[83]

What the dance really imitated is plain: it was the helical dance which we all have danced in the umbilical blood, and which cries out in our feelings for some kind of recognition in the world of external events. This is further substantiated by the Indonesian dance described in the chapter on the Mother and the Maiden.

It is in such complex terms (though essentially simple at root) that we may understand the meaning of the Seventh Labor of Herakles. Behind the myth of Theseus and the Minotaur we may see the myth of Herakles and the Cretan bull. We know that Theseus sought and desired to imitate the achievements of Herakles, and in this particular instance Theseus has acted to amplify the Labor of the Cretan bull, which we now see as one more representation of the journey of the Traveler down the umbilical arterial labyrinth and back again in triumph.

EIGHTH LABOR: The Capture of the Mares of Diomedes

> These horses were fed by their master on human flesh, and Eurystheus ordered Herakles to fetch them to him. Herakles captured the mares, killed Diomedes and flung his body to the mares to be eaten, whereafter they became tame.

A distinctly placental element is evident here, when we recall that horses often appear in such a placental context. To the Greeks, this creature was always seen as rather uncanny, and it seems clear that they felt the horse to represent in the external world whatever it is in the feelings that is derived from the uterine experience of the placenta. The horse as a placental symbol has been seen in the myth of Hippolytus, a Shining One whom the horses killed, so that horses were not allowed in the precinct of his shrine. It is in keeping with this symbolic aspect of the horse that it should be represented as eating human flesh, since the placenta is felt as blood-sucker or devourer of the fetal self. And since the placenta is felt primarily as female, it is even more to the point that these carnivorous horses of Diomedes should be mares. The fact that Diomedes was eaten by these mares suggests the idea that the fetus is 'owner' of the placenta, which devours him.

NINTH LABOR: The Capture of the Amazonian Girdle

> Hippolyta, the queen of the Amazons, had a girdle which Eurystheus (or some say his daughter) wished to possess. Herakles was sent to fetch it and, after certain adventures, killed the queen and took her girdle.

This desirable girdle was said to have been given to Hippolyta by Ares, the father of the Amazons, to show that she was superior to all other women. The Amazon perhaps represents the male aspect of the placenta – namely its thrust through the umbilical vein. This interpretation is supported by the peculiar legend that the daughters of the Amazons had their right breasts cut off, thus leaving them single-breasted. In dreams one frequently finds images of the placenta overlaid by images of the breast – a not unnatural overlay since, in marked degree the one is the successor in function to the other. And when this overlay manifests in dreams, it sometimes takes the form of a single-breasted woman, whether or not the dreamer has familiarity with Greek myths. Another element of Amazonian myth, which supports their placental character, is that if they bore a male child it was sent to its father to be slain. This may well be a symbolic manner of stating that when the self is 'reborn' from the placenta it travels up the umbilical veins to be 'devoured' by the fetal body [190]. Also, the Amazons are said to have been fathered by the god of war, Ares, which surely could stand as a symbol of the militant (therefore 'male') and thrusting aspect of the placenta. The desired girdle, therefore, may be seen as symbolically akin to the fabulous girdle of Aphrodite, which kindled sexual passion for those who wore it, and which Hera borrowed in order to recaptivate Zeus. The name Hippolyta, of course, derived as it is from the Greek word for 'horse', adds its quota of support by linking the girdle to the (placental) horse.

TENTH LABOR: The Capture of the Oxen of Geryones

This Labor, like the Ninth, carried Herakles far afield – this time to the very lands of the setting Sun. It carried him to the island called Erytheia, which name means 'the reddish place' and has reference to the fact that it lay under the rays of the setting Sun. Here lived the fearful monster, Geryones, who kept a herd of red oxen. These pastured together with the oxen of Hades, guarded by the herdsman Eurytion and the two-headed dog Orthros. After many adventures Herakles slew Geryones, Burytion and Orthros and drove the cattle home to Eurystheus, as commanded. Eurystheus promptly sacrificed them to Hera.

Geryones has been described by Smith in *A Dictionary of the Bible*, as a fabulous king of Hesperia, a being with three heads, and possessing magnificent oxen in the island of Erytheia, the 'Red Island'. This 'red island' inhabited by a three-headed monster is already significant, for the placenta might poetically be described as 'an island of blood' dominated by three vessels. This interpretation is supported by the fact that Geryones was brother to Echidna, that half-serpent woman whose foul offspring dominated the First and Second Labors of Herakles. The relationship of 'Red Island' to the rays of the setting Sun and the West generally links it with that dreadful monster which nightly swallows the Sun-hero for rebirth in the East. This monster is none other than the projection of the placenta upon the 'sunset place'. The red cattle of Geryones represent the fetal blood, and their pasturing with the herds of Hades signifies the fact that in the placenta the fetal and the maternal bloods come into close relationship [19]. As the two herds feed together in the red lands of the West, so the fetal and the maternal bloods may be said to 'feed together', since each makes a transfer to the other. The two-headed dog as guardian of the herd of Geryones symbolizes the dual excretory sense of the umbilical arteries: a dog is a strong anal symbol, and the two-headedness of this dog implies a dual function. Cook has told us that in Homeric times the Sun-god was looked upon as the owner of cattle:

> He had seven herds of oxen and seven fair flocks of sheep in the island of Thrinakie. In each herd or flock were fifty oxen or sheep, as the case might be. They were not subject to birth or death ...[84]

The Shining One is here represented in terms of animal qualities – brought down to earth, as it were, and linked to flesh and blood. Thus, these cattle of Geryones represent 'the cattle of the Sun', the Shining One, the fetal blood and nuclear feeling, in the placenta. It is this blood and this 'possession of the Shining One' that the Traveler (Herakles) must bring back again. And, behold! When he does so, they are sacrificed to Hera – which may be understood as meaning that the blood, hardly having arrived in the fetal body, is 'sacrificed' again down the umbilical arterial tubes. The seven flocks and seven herds of the Sun, though not specifically indicated in this Heraklean myth, signify that in the background of the ancient mind the cattle and sheep represented the migratory aspect of the blood, and thus the sevenfold beat associated with that perpetual (umbilical) migration [37-40].

ELEVENTH LABOR: The Recovery of the Golden Apples of the Hesperides

> These golden apples had been given to Hera as a wedding present. They were placed under the guardianship of the dragon, Ladon. Accounts as to their location vary, but some assert that the abode of the Hesperides lay in the West. This Labor was especially difficult, since Herakles had no idea where the apples were. In the course of his travels he came to the river Eridanus, whose nymphs told him how to wrest the secret (of the location of the apples) from Nereus, the Old Man of the Sea. He finds them, slaying the dragon who guarded them.

Hera, as wife of Zeus, the Shining One, may be at least suspected of having placental associations, in which case her 'wedding present' might well be a symbol of the umbilical thrust of the fetal 'male' into the placental 'female' [177]. Thus the golden apples have symbolic relevance, since we know that gold as a symbol of the feces is common currency in dreams and in myths.

Hera ? ≡ mother

Ladon ? ≡ placenta

Also, the umbilical arterial flow (that same flow which in another sense becomes the 'wedding present of Hera') is felt as excrementory. Support for the umbilical nature of the golden apples is given by the story that Prometheus was chained to the rock for '*three myriads of years*' or for 30,000 years, being released from that bondage by Herakles as he passed by in his search for golden apples of the Hesperides.[85] Here we have the *umbilical three* in two distinct appearances, which, when linked with the passage of Herakles and his release of the fetal figure Prometheus, refers to the umbilical flow of the fetal nuclear feeling being 'released from a static condition'. Note that this also has direct relevance to the postnatal sense of the skull as womb [155].

purification
sacrifice
libations

placenta → endometrium
old
death
← new
rebirth

The Apples of the Hesperides were apparently associated with the toys used by the Titans as they lured away the infant Dionysus to be slain and torn to pieces and eaten. Clement of Alexandria says of this:

> *The mysteries of Dionysos are wholly inhuman, for while he was still a child and the Kouretes were dancing round him their armed dance*

the Titans came stealthily upon him and lured him with childish toys and tore him limb from limb while he was yet a babe. Thus does the Thracian Orpheus, the poet of the Rite recount: 'The cones, the rhombos and the limb-bending toys and the fair gold apples of the Hesperides'.[86]

We know that the divine child is always led to death and destruction down the umbilical arteries, so that whatever seems to lure or conduct him down that *'via dolorosa'* is *prima facie* of umbilical arterial association. Thus it would appear that in the ancient mind the Golden Apples of the Hesperides held some association with the sense of the 'drawing away' of the fetal energies to destruction. These umbilical apples of the Hesperides lie under the guard of the dragon Ladon, also represented as the offspring of Typhon and Echidna, those manifestly placental monsters. We shall return later to the significance of the river Eridanus and its nymphs, showing that they have the closest mythological relationship with the sense of the Traveler in his cosmic aspect. Here again in this Eleventh Labor we have a symbolic representation of the endless cycle of the umbilical blood, by which the 'golden apples' are borne away to the western sunset world of the placenta and brought back again by the Traveler. H. J. Rose points out that:

> ...the original legend no doubt signified to begin with that Herakles won immortality – the fruit of the Tree of Life – by his exploit.[87]

This neatly sums up the symbolism, in two senses. Firstly, when the umbilical traveler reaches the placenta and completes the work there, he inevitably finds again the 'tree of life' which is none other than the umbilical vein. Secondly, the constant repetition of this umbilical cycle and its work is the source of the living individual soul. We have seen that the role of the placenta transcends the biochemical alone, being a place where the new elements of mind that are to be the soul-stuff of the baby engage in a struggle with the mental elements active in the mother's blood [47-50].

TWELFTH LABOR: The Capture of Kerberos

This is the only one of the Labors that is expressly mentioned in the Homeric poems, perhaps the most terrible of all the tasks, and one which Herakles could not have accomplished, had not Athena and Hermes guided and befriended him.

148 *Mythology of the Prenatal Life*

In this Labor, he performed the typical heroic task of the 'Harrowing of Hell'.[88] One tale describes how he fought with Hades himself and wounded him, which H. J. Rose thinks may suggest that Herakles' task was to conquer death and win immortality. Many embellishments have been added to the original story, such as that before undertaking this Labor, the hero Herakles had to be purified from the guilt of murdering the centaurs. According to an Orphic tradition, Herakles compelled Charon to ferry him over the river Styx in order to reach the monster Kerberos. One legend describes how Herakles slew one of the oxen of Hades in order to give the ghosts blood to drink. He then captured Kerberos, who originally was described (by Homer) simply as 'the dog', though later he became known as another child of Typhon and Echidna, described either as 'many-headed' or as 'three-headed', with the tail of a serpent. His task was to guard the gates of Hell, whereto he admitted the ghosts of the dead, never letting them out again. As Herakles returned to the earth's surface with the monster he saw a white poplar growing; he wreathed himself in its boughs and brought it to show Helios. This poplar had been planted by Hades in memory of Leuke, daughter of Okeanos, whom Hades (Pluton) had carried down as his lover. Having shown the monster to Eurystheus, Herakles took it back again to hell.

Here we have some complex mythology in a highly compressed form, shorn of any embellishment. It may be seen to describe the journey of the fetal nuclear energy into the placenta and back again, in terms of the postnatal thrust into the earth and its reciprocal upthrust [225]. Since the sense of loss and destruction in the placenta is the origin of our human sense and fear of death, the Hero-Traveler who experiences and survives this (placental) experience does 'conquer death' because he is the symbol of our own sense of perpetual loss and restoration in the umbilical cord. We can understand in this context why Herakles should need the help of Athena and Hermes, as placenta and umbilical cord respectively.

[handwritten note: Hermes the snake twined staff = umbilical cord / Athena = placenta]

The stories of Hermes are as complex as those of Herakles, and would require a chapter to themselves if their full umbilical nature were to be demonstrated. He is also a great Traveler, the messenger of the gods, and he carries the snake-twined staff, an obvious formalized representation of the umbilical cord. His magical *caduceus*[89] drives the souls of the dead and raises them – a powerful umbilical meaning in the light of this work. The legend of the aid given to Herakles by the placental Athena and the umbilical Hermes makes a wonderfully apt symbolic statement that the Traveler does his traveling precisely by the instrumentality of these uterine organs. That he had to be purified of the murder of the centaurs before embarking on this Twelfth Labor we also understand, for the centaur is itself a placental symbol, and the importation of it into this context is simply another instance of the endless dreamlike association-process of the primitive and ancient minds.

The presence of the legend of Herakles and Charon also supplies another strong umbilical element, since the back and forth rowing of Charon is reminiscent of the umbilical cycle – a myth within a myth. This rowing back and forth in the underworld is set in an avowedly umbilical context in the Grimm brother's tale of *The Devil with the Three Golden Hairs,* which I have analyzed elsewhere [263-266]. Kerberos, the three-headed dog with a serpent tail, whose task it is to let the souls of the dead in and keep them there. He symbolizes the umbilical cord and placenta in its relationship to the excretory aspects of the umbilical flow, specifically related to the sense of death [31-32] and also projected upon the earth itself [120, 121]. Kerberos is the placental monster which devours the sense of self and seeks to hold on to it, so that his capture by Herakles symbolizes the 'victory' of the fetal nuclear element over the forces of the periphery. The poplar, which Herakles saw on his journey back from hell, refers to the umbilical vein by which the blood returns from the placenta to the fetus. That he showed the tree to Helios is simply a way of showing that the umbilical venous tree is the way back to the restoration of the Shining One. That the poplar was planted by Hades in memory of a girl he bore down into hell links the tree directly with Persephone, synonymous with Demeter, and thus to her trees and to the umbilical vein, as explained in our analysis of the fate of Erysichthon (see Chapter Two).

The Twelve Labors are often seen as simply representing the annual cycle of the Sun, considering the purely astronomical view, while others see the parallel with the astrological signs of the zodiac at work in the formulation of these Labors, a theme to be explored further in Appendix II, where the superimposition of the umbilical experiences upon the solar cycle is discussed. We turn now to the third element perceived in the mythology of Herakles, namely that symbolic component which relates him to the rhythms of the cosmos. For the Traveling Hero is the symbol not only of the travels of the fetal blood, but also of the vast cosmic movement with which it resonates, and out of which resonance the core of the self is created. This cosmic movement is represented in the Heraklean myths by that great river called Okeanos, and by its tributaries and associated currents.

When Herakles went out to perform the Tenth Labor, the capture of the oxen of Geryones, he sailed to the West upon the mystical stream of Okeanos, riding the river in a golden cup which, at the point of an arrow, he had compelled Helios to give him. It was by means of this golden sun-cup that Herakles reached the 'Red Island', and in this same cup he bore the oxen back again after he had captured them. This golden cup represents in part the orb of the Sun itself, being related to the golden boat upon which, so the ancient Egyptians believed, the Sun-god traveled daily from East to West. Even in this part of the myth there is, however, at least a hint of umbilical imagery, for the umbilical thrust into the fetal body is felt as a wound, and in the discussion of the zodiac we shall see that the arrow of the Archer represents this very thing. Since the in-thrust of the umbilical venous blood is the counterpart of the arterial thrust from the fetal body, it is easily and poetically represented by the arrow which compels the Shining One to yield the vehicle of the journey to the placenta. But what is this great river, Okeanos, upon which the golden boat sails? It is certainly not an ordinary river. Rose asserts that it began in the Greek mind as a means of explaining the larger environment of the ancient world, where the earth was felt to be a flat place with the dome of the sky overhead, while all around the plain of earth there flowed a mighty river. This was Okeanos.

But Okeanos was more than a river, or became so: he was the great begetter, a god greater and more primordial than Zeus, whose summons he would not obey. He was married to Tethys, and by her he begat 3000 sons (all rivers) and 3000 daughters. These 3000 sons and daughters strike an umbilical note, amplified by the Homeric assertion that he begat only three daughters, Thetis, Eurynome and Perse. Moreover, two of these three women, Thetis and Eurynome, cared for Hephaestus when he was dropped from Olympus. Hephaestus is himself a Shining One, as we have seen in Chapter One, so that his reception by these two symbolizes the fact that the Shining One (the nuclear fetal feeling) is 'cared for' by the two umbilical arteries when it is 'expelled' from the fetal body. However, we are more concerned here with the Great River as a representation of that cosmic flow and counter-flow which the umbilical flow registers – that is to say, with which it comes into some form of resonance [38]. That Okeanos was indeed the representation of this cosmic flow is by no means only my own suggestion, as the following excerpt will show:

> ... 'back-flowing Okeanos', the very 'source of the gods', was not originally a terrestrial river forming the circumference of a discoidal earth, but, as E. H. Berger has maintained, a celestial stream of stars. I should indeed venture to suppose that in pre-Greek times, before the rise of geographical speculation, the river Okeanos simply meant the Galaxy.[90]

The journey of Herakles in the solar cup upon the river Okeanos to the 'Red Island' in the West, presents us with a combination of celestial and umbilical symbology, which supports my contention that *the self is the product of the resonance between the umbilical and the cosmic rhythms.* Herakles is thus the prime symbol of that selfhood – the product of this resonance.

Herakles' relationship to rivers is not limited to his journey upon Okeanos. Recall his association with the river Achelous, lover of his wife Deianeira before Herakles met her. The relationship between Achelous and Okeanos is established: Achelous was one of the 3000 sons of the great primal river. He made love to Deianeira in three forms: as a snake, as a bull and as a man down whose beard a glistening river flowed. Herakles breaks off the great horn of Achelous and carries it away, along with Deianeira. As Jane Harrison says, this represents the fact that Herakles is the fully humanized form of Achelous himself. Herakles and the glistening river are one. This glistening river that is son of Okeanos is surely none other than a representation of the great river of the sky. Yet it is a river closely linked to umbilical symbology, for it is both fetal bull and umbilical snake, having the power to make love to a woman (Deianeira) whose placental characteristics have already been demonstrated. This link between Okeanos and other rivers is by no means mere supposition, for A. B. Cook tells us that ancient lore specifically linked the Nile with Okeanos, and by implication all other rivers:

> *The Nile is described in the Odyssey by the remarkable adjective Diipetes, which properly denotes a river 'that falls in the Zeus', 'in the clear Sky.' This description would apply with strict accuracy only to the Milky Way, but might be extended to all rivers conceived as rillets of that great flood.*[91]

So far as purely mythological links are concerned there was a direct link between Okeanos and the Nile, for Neilos, the god of the Nile, was a son of Okeanos by Tethys. This enables us to amplify our conceptions of the myths of Osiris and of Joseph (see Chapter One), for we see that the Nile probably symbolized not only the umbilical flow but also the cosmic flow. Thus Osiris, borne away by the river to the Delta, was like Herakles riding not only the umbilical flow but also the cosmic flow – the symbol of their conjunction through resonance. Joseph taken down into Egypt thus came to the Land of the River, for Egypt never was and never has been anything else but the Nile and its alluvial borders. And this river has the atmosphere of the celestial flow and its link with the umbilical. There are signs to link Hebrew thought to such a concept:

> *And out of the ground made the Lord God to grow every tree that is pleasant to the sight, and good for food; the tree of life also in the midst of the garden, and the tree of knowledge of good and evil. And a river went out of Eden to water the garden; and from thence it was parted, and became into four heads. The name of the first is Pison: that is it, which compasseth the whole land of Havilah, where there is gold; and the gold of that land is good: there is bdellium and the onyx stone.*[92]

In these verses from Genesis one may discover strong symbology of both a cosmic and an umbilical character. The word used for the *great river* of Eden is in the Hebrew *nahar*, a name which strongly links with the Nile. But the word *nahar* derives from a primitive root *nahar*, meaning 'to sparkle'. Significantly enough, from this same root is derived a word *neharah*, meaning 'light' and even 'daylight'. This 'light river' is described upon the first mention of the Tree of Life and the Tree of Knowledge of Good and Evil, which have distinct umbilical significance in the context of the myth of Adam and Eve. This 'great river' is linked (though not etymologically) with the Seven Days of Creation as described in the first chapter of Genesis. In such a view, the seven days are not events done once-for-all-time but a continuing creative series, representing the sevenfold rhythm of the cosmos which the fetus senses in the beat of umbilical blood [38]. In this context it is significant that light is presented as having a special relationship to the first and the fourth days of creation, since in the first, daylight is created; in the fourth, the Sun and the heavenly bodies. This symbology links well with the fact that the sevenfold rhythm of the umbilical cord is represented in dreams as two linked fourfold series [62].

The great river of Genesis breaks into four parts, only the first of which, Pison, yields any possible etymological links with our themes:

> *The name of the first is Pison: that is it which compasseth the whole land of Havilah, where there is gold; and the gold of that land is good: there is bdellium and the onyx stone.*[93]

The name 'Pison' may derive from the root *puwsh*, which means 'to spread out', a concept which could be a symbolic description of the action of the blood in the umbilical arteries and the placenta. The name 'Havilah' is Chaviylah in Hebrew, apparently meaning 'circular'. Okeanos was a circular river, although even more specific is the fact that the name probably derives from the root *chiyl*, meaning 'to twist or whirl in a circular or spiral manner'.[94] Another possible etymological link is to be seen in the fact that the name Chaviylah may have some relationship to the word *Chavvah*; which is the Hebrew name of Eve, who plays the placental role to the fetal Adam. The reference to the 'gold of Havilah' is suggestive of an excretory symbolism, while the word for 'bdellium' in Hebrew derives from the word *badal*, meaning 'to divide'. A river which 'spreads out', which 'twists in a spiral manner', which is also related to gold and to a sense of division, certainly has strong claims to be regarded as an umbilical symbol. For the 'river of blood' from the fetal body may be said to 'spread out' in the placenta after twisting in a spiral manner in the umbilical arteries. Moreover, it is felt as an excretion (gold) and to the experience of division whereby the 'father' element is divided from the 'son' element [186-187].

Let us turn again to the myth of Herakles, for we have yet to consider the nature of the two rivers Alpheus and Peneus which he drove through the stables of Augeas, and which we have already seen to have symbolic affinity for the twin umbilical arteries. Have they also an affinity for the great cosmic river? They both are sons of Okeanos, though this perhaps carries little weight, since all rivers essentially were thus represented. But there are other factors which suggest a more specific relationship between Alpheus and Okeanos and Herakles. Alpheus was that passionate lover-river who fell in love with the nymph Arethusa. The nymph fled to Ortygia and changed herself into a well, but Alpheus went underground and united with her, as the well. There was an ancient belief that a cup thrown into the river Alpheus would eventually appear in the well of Arethusa. Do we see here a link between this cup flowing in the river Alpheus and that golden solar cup in which Herakles journeyed to the West? Arethusa was the name of one of the Hesperides, who in the earliest legends of the Greeks were described as living on the river Okeanos in the extreme west, and whose umbilical-placental symbolism we have already noted.

It was in his quest for the golden apples of the Hesperides that Herakles encountered another magical river, namely the Eridanus, whose nymphs gave the word that enabled him to trace (via Nereus) the location of the golden apples. This Eridanus was called 'the king of rivers' and we need not be surprised to find that he was another of the 3000 sons of Okeanos and Tethys. But what really alerts us to something still deeper is the myth of Phaethon, whose name means 'the Shining One', which recounts how this son of Helios fell from the Sun's chariot into the river Eridanus. A. B. Cook suggests that the name Eridanus appears to have meant 'River of Life', and that it was at the outset nothing less than the Milky Way. He quotes approvingly the statement of Hyginus that the constellation Eridanus was once named as both the Nile and also Okeanos.[95] In this way, we can see certain signs that Okeanos, Eridanus and even Alpheus are symbolically closely related. All three figures link with the journeys of Herakles for the reasons repeatedly stated.

There is yet one more river associated with the journeys of Herakles, and that is the Styx over which Charon ferried him when he embarked upon his Twelfth Labor, to fetch the monster Kerberos from hell. Styx was a daughter of Okeanos and Tethys, and was by others described as a branch of the great river itself. She was alleged to flow seven times around the nether regions. What renders the river Styx of special importance in this context is the fact that her waters became the seal of the oaths of the gods. When one of the gods was to take an oath, Iris fetched up a cup of water from the Styx and the god poured it out as he swore his oath. Iris is the rainbow and her name derives either from a word meaning 'messenger' or from a closely allied word meaning 'to join'. Sometimes she was identified with the rainbow itself, but at other times the rainbow was regarded only as the pathway upon which she traveled to link earth and sky – even as Herakles traveled upon the stream of Okeanos!

Here is a story which parallels that of Noah and the rainbow, whereby God swore to never again drown the world. Apparently the god of the Hebrews, like the gods of the Greeks, swore their binding oaths upon the rainbow. Why should this be so? I suggest that it is because the rainbow is the symbol of that basic unity which unites the fetus with the placenta, whose instrument is the umbilical cord. This is the primary covenant. Why should the rainbow symbolize the umbilical cord? Because it was felt to be the link between the Father Sky (the Shining One) and the Mother Earth, whose cosmic natures are felt to be in resonance with the fetal nuclear feeling and the peripheral feeling of the placenta. This view of the rainbow has already been explored in the myth of Noah and here, in the symbology and associations of the river Styx, one may see a clear representation of the umbilical flow and the cosmic flow in combination.

CHAPTER FIVE

The Significance of Salt

An hypothesis has now been offered to account for the fact that the umbilical flow seems to evoke the basis of mind from the cosmos, and that the mechanism of this evocation is the electrical circulation of energy between the fetal heart and the placenta through the umbilical cord [22-24]. It has been suggested that these uterine electrical energies are conducted by electrolytic means, and that the sodium chloride in the blood provides the basis for this conduction [22]. The common name for sodium chloride is, as most people know, the word 'salt', by which is meant the common salt used in our food. As is well known, salt is the subject of a number of traditional superstitions – are these two things related? Is it possible that the many superstitions concerning salt spring from a deep primal perception that salt plays a major role in the creation of the primary feelings? Do we somehow know, in the depths of our feelings, that it was the activity of the sodium and chlorine ions which, by their electrolytic functions, provided the means either for the generation of the nuclear fetal skin feeling or for its dynamic reversals in the umbilical cord and placenta? With these general questions in mind I have surveyed some of the traditional beliefs concerning salt, and I summarize here what I found. I offer no conclusion, but I feel that the reader will be struck by the fact that a great number of superstitions concerning salt may be interpreted in the above terms. My main source of information on this subject was an article by that famous Freudian, Dr. Ernest Jones, who writes:

> In all ages salt has been invested with a significance far exceeding that inherent in its natural properties, interesting and important as these are. Homer calls it a divine substance, Plato describes it as especially dear to the Gods, and we shall presently note the importance attached to it in religious ceremonies, covenants, and magical charms. That this should have been so in all parts of the world and in all times shows that we are dealing with a general human tendency and not with any local custom, circumstance or notion.[96]

From this article, nine separate headings have been condensed below, and these nine aspects of salt-superstition will be explored in the light of the present book. Since many of the superstitions concern blood or urine, it might be supposed that they are based simply upon an external perception of the general saltiness of bodily fluids. However, this explanation simply does not adequately cover the facts and will be amplified in the light of our subject matter.

1. Salt is traditionally associated with mind, knowledge, wisdom and learning.

The personified figure of Wisdom was frequently depicted holding a salt-cellar. The heavenly Sophia, whose name signifies wisdom, was represented in mystical tradition by the element *sodium*, her color being yellow, the color of burning salt. In ancient times, wit was often referred to in terms of salt. In Italy the combination of salt and bread is known as *Lumen Christi,* the Light of Christ. In the mythical lore of Finland, Ukko, god of the sky, struck fire in the heavens and a spark fell into the waters and became salt.

The mysterious link felt to exist between salt and consciousness may be at least illuminated by the supposition that it is through the electrolytic qualities of salt that the primary patterns of feeling are woven into the anatomy of mind. The Finnish myth of the origins of salt serves to link the salt in the water with the fire of the sky-god, which in turn directly serves to link the lightning with salt dissolved in the blood. Here we may perceive a link between Zeus, the sky-god, the Shining One, and salt. The *Lumen Christi* also suggests a link between salt and light and the Shining One. The word 'lumen' may signify an aperture through which light enters, which serves to portray salt as the instrument of light.

Additionally, note the fact that the placenta has been revealed as a sort of teacher [47-50], the elements of knowledge being transmitted from the maternal blood through the umbilical blood to the fetus. This transmission, according to the electrolytic hypotheses noted above, would involve the agency of salt. Therefore the association of salt with primary wisdom and learning may be due not only to the fact that the whole electrolytic circulation of umbilical blood evokes mind from the cosmos [39-40], but also to the fact that actual information is transmitted through the blood (or salt in the blood) from the placenta to the fetus.

2. Salt is traditionally associated with the establishment of covenants, with marriage and with the establishment of pacts of friendship, loyalty and brotherhood: in this connection salt is a substitution for blood.

In traditional ceremonies, blood may be shared by the contracting parties either by mixing a little of their blood or by the sucking of a little blood from a wound. Or a little of the blood of each of the parties may be shared by them after dilution with water or wine.

This direct association of salt with blood both strengthens and weakens my hypothesis. It strengthens it by demonstrating that salt and blood are equivalents in the primal imagination. It weakens it by suggesting that in this case salt is not directly sensed as important, but as a mere substitute or symbol for blood. The drinking of salty liquid may also have another explanation, namely that our very first drink was highly saline, since *in utero* we have all taken gulps of the salty amniotic water. On the other hand, we have already seen good reason for supposing that the blood of the Covenant is not just any blood, but is definitely related to the umbilical flow. One very definite piece of evidence as to the function of salt in the umbilical cord comes from a superstition of the Peruvian Indians, and is taken by Jones from Frazer. The indigenous Peruvian people appear to have been quite disturbed by the birth of twins, asserting that one of them is 'the son of the lightning', abstaining for six months both from sexual intercourse and the eating of salt should twins be born into their immediate family. Here is a suggestive association of feelings. We have already seen that twins were regarded by primitive and ancient people as representing the uterine organism. One of this pair is naturally the fetus, who is felt to be the Shining One, and who may therefore be felt very naturally as a son of the lightning in a semi-poetic sense. The umbilical link between this uterine pair is apparently associated with the electrolytic action of salt, and that link is felt to be involved in most dangerous experiences, among which is most prominent the element of sex and incest [186-190]. Hence, it is understandable that primitive people might feel endangered by both sex and salt when in the immediate presence of the actual epiphany of this uterine pair in the flesh. In order to escape the curse of incest, therefore, they will have nothing to do either with sex or with salt. That sex and salt are felt to be closely related will

Mythology of the Prenatal Life 159

be made clear in point Seven of this discussion, below. Certainly we are free to assume that salt is the proper cement of covenants because it is a substitution for blood. But below this perception which is relatively near to the surface of consciousness, there is perhaps an underlying and deeper intuition of the feelings of that wholeness (the wholeness of the uterine organism), in which the electrolytic functions of salt play a leading role.

3. Salt is traditionally related to money and wealth, a fact which is reflected in the word 'salary' and in the phrase that a man is 'worth his salt'.

Here is a direct link not only between salt and income in the widest sense, but also between salt and excretion, for money and wealth have powerful excrementory associations. Jones even goes so far as to assert that the word 'salt' has direct excrementory and dirty associations, of which the French word *'sale'* (unclean) is an indication. The link between money and salt also provides the link between salt and excretion, since salt = money = excretion. Wealth is frequently referred to in terms which have distinctly excretory associations: 'he stinks of money', 'he is filthy rich' and 'filthy lucre'. These associations are passed on to salt through its link with money.

Yet salt is traditionally used for the purpose of savoring food, and without 'being worth our salt' and thus getting some 'salary', we cannot eat. Salt has thus a distinctly ambivalent significance in terms of ingestion and egestion. Salt is the symbol of give and take, in terms of eating and excretion. Why is this? The explanation would derive naturally from the circumstance that salt is the electrolytic agency by means of which the primary senses of egestion and of ingestion are created. The umbilical cord is the first instrument of give and take, and in the cord we feel both to excrete and to eat, the placenta being similarly sensed as both the eating pot and the excreting pot [29-30].

4. Salt is traditionally used as the instrument or pledge of immortality, and has been called 'an emblem of the immortal spirit', partly related to its use for embalming in ancient times.

This explanation does not cover such strange customs as the Welsh rite of 'sin eating' in which the local 'sin eater' ate bread and salt off the coffin and so took upon himself the sins of the deceased. The relationship of salt to the dead and to immortality contains ambivalent elements akin to those seen in its association with ingestion and egestion. That salt is symbolically related to death is clearly brought out in the myth of Lot and the fate of Sodom and Gomorrah. A great battle takes place by the salt sea in the Vale of Siddim and in the final drama of the plain, Lot's wife became a pillar of salt. In classical times, Jones tells us, the salt-cellar was regarded as a holy vessel associated with the temple in general, but especially with the altar. This must appear significant in view of the undoubted placental meaning of the altar as the place of blood and sacrifice. We can thus understand that salt should also be an emblem of immortality, for the umbilical circulation (in which the electrolytic function of salt is involved) not only brings death to the Shining One, but also resurrection. And this seems to accommodate naturally the strange custom of the 'sin eater'. For we have seen that the restoration of the fetal nuclear feeling is directly related to the first 'eating', namely of the fetus via the umbilical vein. Thus the eating of salt at the bier of the dead seems to signify that by taking in salt (blood and salt's electrolytic function along with it) the fetus lifts the blight of death and is renewed – that is, so to speak, it eats its own past and in so doing, renews it.

5. Salt is likewise traditionally associated with movement.

It was once a widespread custom to carry salt on the person while moving from one house to another. Dr. Jones states that the poet Burns, when he moved house, was escorted by relatives bearing a bowl of salt. As we have seen, the first journey known to the deepest feelings, upon which all later sense of moving is erected, is the journey of the fetal nuclear feelings in the umbilical cord. Certainly it is in the umbilical cord that we make a perpetual move from 'house to house', which is to say from the fetal to the placental location. Dr. Jones quotes Schleiden as linking the word 'salt' with a Sanskrit word *sar*, meaning 'to flow'.[97]

6. Salt has in the past been extensively used for medicinal purposes, and Dr. Jones links the Latin word salus, meaning 'health' with the Latin sal, meaning 'salt'.

No doubt salt does indeed have medicinal uses, and yet one can hardly suppose that its therapeutic use was so widespread as to identify it as a panacea. But if the present hypothesis is correct, and the superstitions concerning salt spring primarily from its electrolytic function in the umbilical cord, then we can well understand that salt might become traditionally regarded as the medicine *par excellence*. For the umbilical cord has been thus regarded – witness the myth of the snake Asklepios. Even today, as mentioned before, the two snakes on the rod (the *caduceus* of Mercury) are the symbols of the whole art of modern healing as practiced by orthodox medicine. However, what we are concerned with here in this superstition concerning the universal healing properties of salt is not any actual biochemical virtue that is demonstrable in modern medicine. It is rather an equation of the following order: the umbilical cord is the feeder and detoxifier of the fetal body, a form of overall healing. Related with this is an electrolytic process which results in the evocation of primary consciousness. This electrolytic process is related to salt. Somehow this indirect relationship is intuited in the primary consciousness, so that the deepest feelings of the human being continue to equate the aforesaid overall healing process with that salt which permits the electrolytic process whereby mind is evoked out of the cosmos.

7. Salt has been regarded as promoting sexual desire as well as fecundity.

Salt, Dr. Jones tells us, became the symbol of procreation, and he gives several instances of the typical use of salt for curing barrenness. One of these may be mentioned: the putting of salt into the pockets of the bride and bridegroom. The ancient belief was that salt had the power to arouse sexual ardor. The word 'salt' was formerly used of animals in heat, as well as for human lust. Dr. Jones suggests that the word 'salacious' may be another derivative from the root '*sal*'.[98]

The circulation in the umbilical cord is the instrument of the primary marriage, as we have seen clearly in the myth of Adam and Eve. And insofar as the salt in that circulation is the agency of the primary feelings of gender, we can understand why salt should be regarded as an arouser of sexual passion. Moreover, since in the umbilical flow the Shining One seems to enter the mother (placenta) as father and to be reborn as son, we can understand the deep feeling that salt furthers procreation. Indeed, in this specific sense, salt would be related to the primary sense of procreation known to man. There is also an etymological link between the word 'salt' and several words signifying aggression, a fact which strongly supports the present thesis, since the umbilical cord is the instrument not only of the primary marriage, but also of the primary sense of thrust. Thus the word 'assault' derives from *adsaltare*; the word 'assail' from *adsalire*, both of which have links with the word *sal*. Allied words are 'sally', 'salient' and 'exult'. In the light of what has been written concerning the primary feelings of the umbilical arteries, this may appear extremely significant, for in these feelings are evoked the primary sense of going forth (sallying), penetrating the placenta (assault) and with it a definite sense of exultation.

8. There exists a probable etymological link between the root word for 'salt' and the Latin words for leaping and dancing.

Dr. Jones suggests that the Latin verbs *saltare* and *salire*, which mean 'to leap' or 'to dance' both are derived from the root *sal*. He further suggests that *saltus*, meaning 'leap' may have the same origins.[99] Since it is from this same root that the word 'salacious' is alleged to derive, we can see that the leaping of the male upon the female may have a close connection here. Moreover, the mating of animals is frequently preceded by a courtship dance. Human dancing also has distinct, if mainly sublimated, associations with sexual feeling. Owing to the close connection which I have shown to exist between the legs of the fetus and the umbilical arteries, the beat of the blood in the umbilical cord is identified with (or confused with) the beat of the legs in dancing. In these terms we can very well understand why dancing or leaping might be related with the feeling for the activity of the salt, and emerge in such etymological links as those noted above. The relationship of the beating of the feet to sexual intercourse is also suggested in the old phrase 'to tread', used as a description of the male upon the female. In this phrase we can see signs of the link between the primary coital rhythm of the umbilical arteries and the feet of the unborn child. It is perhaps significant that the *Kouretes* who bore away the infant Zeus with 'noise of beating feet'[100] were called by the Romans, *Salii*, meaning 'the leapers'. Thus Jane Harrison writes:

> *Denys of Halicarnassos in his full and interesting account of the Salii saw that Kouretes and Salii were substantially the same: 'In my opinion', he says, 'the Salii are what in the Greek language are called Kouretes. We (i.e. the Greeks) give them their name from their age, from the word koupol, the Romans from their strenuous movements, for jumping and leaping is called by the Romans salire.'*[101]

The evocation of the nuclear, male feeling of the fetus [175] is closely related to the sense of rhythmic movement such as we know in the form of dancing. This is because the nuclear feeling of the fetus is evoked not only through its own leaping movements in the womb, but also through the rhythmic beat of the blood in the umbilical cord, closely associated with the fetal legs [108]. That is why a close connection exists between the leaping, or leg motions of the *Kouretes* and that primary maleness which is stressed in their name. Whereas the Greek name for the *Kouretes* stressed their maleness, the Latin name stressed their rhythmic motion. Since it is in the electrolytic action of the salt in the blood that this leaping or beating produces the aforesaid nuclear sense of maleness, we see here a logical reason why, in the deep feelings, salt should be associated with the *Kouretes* in this indirect etymological fashion.

9. Salt has always had a close relationship with rank, protocol and procedure.

Dr. Jones points out that 'the laying of salt at the table was in the Middle Ages a tremendous ceremony'. He goes on to say:

> *With the Romans it was a matter of religious principle that no other dish was placed upon the table until the salt was in position. Rank and precedence among the guests were precisely indicated by their seat above or below the salt and their exact distance from it.*[102]

The primary sense of relationship is evoked in the umbilical circulation. It is the act of umbilical feeding which determines who is nuclear and who is peripheral, who is male and who is female – in a word, determines the basic scale of values. This is shown not only in the myth of Adam and Eve, but also in that of Jacob and Esau. The position of supreme importance is the nuclear (central) position, with which is linked the idea of maleness, for reasons already shown. Conversely the position of inferiority is the peripheral one, with which is linked the idea of hollowness and femaleness. This does not properly signify that woman is inferior to man, for though she is peripheral to the man in her genitalia, she is nuclear to him at the head [198-201]. Here we consider not the relative virtues of man and woman, but the *configurational values*. Inevitably that which is nuclear and focal contains the virtue of the whole and is thus felt as the superior position. This human sense of relative values is most certainly related to the first consciousness evoked in the umbilical cord. Since that evocation seems to depend upon the electrolytic action of the salt in the blood, we can quite understand the deep feeling-basis for the symbolic role of salt as a marker of precedence.

The above commentary will not of course appear congruent in every detail, just as no single piece of symbolism can by itself be convincing, whether it be taken from dreams or from myths. My own procedure has been to let the mind range freely over a number of pieces of evidence with a view to seeing if it can detect any signs of a drift of meaning which corresponds to the hypothesis at hand. The idea behind this method can be gathered by reading Appendices H and P of *The Nature of the Self*. As the mind roves over a variety of material it can soon, with a little training, learn to observe the drift of the symbolism. A mass of symbolism is seldom seen to tell a consistent and highly evidential story – this is true both in dreams and in myths. Very few myths have the consistently meaningful character of the full tale of Jacob and Esau. Even the Gospels, in their manifestly mythological portions, do not possess it to the same degree.

While no myth or set of myths can 'prove' anything, when a consistent pattern is seen at work behind a variety of ideas, that pattern asks not be ignored. And when the perception of those patterns is dependent upon the existence of hypotheses from still older discoveries, and this process of hypothesis and observation permits the construction of a pattern such as set forth in *The Nature of the Self*, to ignore the evidence seems utterly unintelligent. It is the constant growth of the plausible into the demonstrable which brings 'proof' in this subtle field, where the grosser experiments of the laboratory are inapplicable.

The Old Testament offers some striking symbolism involving salt, in which can be traced a most persuasive umbilical lineament. The link between salt and destruction is shown many times, awakening an echo in any mind aware that the fetal skin feeling is 'destroyed' by the (presumed electrolytic) action of salt. This echo is considerably amplified by the fact that this destruction is largely related to a plain, or flat place, which we know to represent the placenta [37], where the fetal nuclear sense seems to be destroyed [39]. As we have seen, this relates to the electrolytic action taking place in the salt of the blood [22-23], so that in this way the stage is set for the sense that salt is related to a flat place where destruction is experienced.

If one transfers that set of ideas into the atmosphere of the Old Testament one is reminded of the adventures of Lot, whose wife was turned into salt for daring to look back at the *destruction upon the plain*. This is perhaps not a fortuitous association, for the context shows the drama of Lot as a representation of the experience of the Shining One in the electrolytic action of salt in relationship to the placenta. The name 'Lot' seems to be derived from the Hebrew word *luwt*, which means 'to wrap up', and which may thus be taken tentatively as a symbol of the fetus, which could be called, with some poetic license, the 'wrapped up one'. Given this tentative interpretation, it is easy to see the relevance to Lot of a 'salt wife', for that is what Lot's wife may be said to have become. For this 'salt wife' makes a good symbol of the placenta, in relation to which the fetus may be said to invoke a primary sense of marriage through the action (at least partly) of the salt in the umbilical flow. This general idea seems to be reflected by an old Spanish compliment of calling one's sweetheart 'the salt-cellar of my love'. That the salt-cellar is also a symbol of destruction and blood we have seen already in the fact that the salt-cellar was in ancient times emblematic of the altar, which in turn we have seen as a symbol of the placenta. Thus the link between the 'salty' lover or wife and destruction is to be seen in contexts other than the biblical. Lot's wife and her saltiness and destruction were clinked closely to the 'flat place', a 'placental symbol.

In Genesis 19:24-26 we read:

> ... *the Lord rained upon Sodom and upon Gomorrah brimstone and fire from the Lord out of heaven; and he overthrew those cities, and all the plain, and all the inhabitants of the cities, and that which grew upon the ground. But his wife looked back from behind him, and she became a pillar of salt.*

When one recalls that this destruction was linked with the guilt of sexual sin, in which the element of homosexuality was paramount, one may see a constellation of ideas which yields significance when viewed in the light of *The Nature of the Self*. Then we see the plain and its cities as symbols of the placenta; the destruction wrought on the plain represents the destruction of the Shining One in the placenta; the homosexual 'sins' are closely related to the sense which the placenta in retrospect acquires [267-268]; the changing of Lot's wife into a pillar of salt represents the electrolytic action of the salt in the blood by means of which all these mental elements are first evoked. The 'sins of the cities' have been referred to as homosexual in character, but we also should recall that in the myth of Lot that there is a strong incestuous element which well represents the other pre-sexual experience which the fetus gains in relationship to the placenta [185-187]. The representation of incest in the tale of Lot takes the form of the copulation of Lot with his daughters. The story also has distinct uterine elements, for the father is discovered by his daughters lying in a cave, drunk with wine. The womb is frequently symbolized by a cave, and wine is a common symbol for blood. Therefore the myth may be saying that the incest is felt to take place in the uterine cave through the action of the blood. Nor must the element of triumph in this incest be missed, for it is through this incestuous copulation that rebirth takes place after the terrible destruction on the plain – a very strong fetal-placental motif.

The destruction of Sodom and Gomorrah takes place not only in connection with 'sexual sin' and with the creation of a 'salt wife', but it takes place upon a plain that is distinctly related to a salt sea. This salt sea is also a dead sea in which nothing lives, and this detracts nothing from the placental symbolism. Whether or not there is any historical kernel for this tale of burning cities is beside the point. Every man and woman has, by postnatal retrospection to uterine times [185], committed 'sexual sin' with a 'salt wife', and has likewise, through the course of that experience, been destroyed upon the placental 'plain' or plane, afterwards being restored to new life through the very same primary incestuous act.

The Old Testament contains several myths or legends concerning a mysterious slaughter in a 'valley of salt'. It can hardly be accidental that every one of these mass killings is of either Edomites or

Seirites, names which at once remind us of the symbolic forms of the fetal skin feeling to be found elsewhere in the Old Testament. The Edomites link us direct with Adam, whose name and myth we have seen to establish him as the fetus, or its nuclear skin feeling. The Seirites link us, through the etymology of the name, with the hairy aspect of the fetal skin. Both Edomites and Seirites come into a focus in the manifestly fetal personage called Esau, whose nature we have already examined.

There are four accounts of slaughter of Edomites or Seirites in 'the valley of salt', thus in 2 Samuel 8:13, we read:

And David gat him a name when he returned from smiting of the Syrians in the valley of salt.

In 2 Kings 14:7, we read of Amaziah:

He slew of Edom in the valley of salt to thousand ...

Another slaughter of Edomites in a 'salt place' is recorded in 1 Chronicles 18:12, thus:

Abishai the son of Zeruiah slew of the Edomites in the valley of salt eighteen thousand.

The Book of Chronicles also contains a report which may be a repeat of the story reproduced above from the Book of Kings, but which clearly states the identity of the Seirites and the Edomites. This is from 2 Chronicles 25:11:

Amaziah strengthened himself, and led forth his people, and went to the valley of salt, and smote of the children of Seir ten thousand.

Genesis 14:3 contains a strange and confused story about the vale of Siddim 'which is the salt sea'. I have paid special attention to the Hebrew etymology since the key to the meaning of the Hebrew myths lies largely therein. The etymology of the names of people and places in this story does indeed yield a degree of correlation with the elements of the uterine drama. Although the symbolic content of this old tale is not consistent, it is a matter of surprise, given the age and diversity of the original legends, that anything has come through at all. The Bible story and the etymology of the names are tabulated below:

ETYMOLOGY OF NAMES

Genesis 14:1 And it came to pass in the days of Amraphel king of Shinar, Arioch king of Ellasar, Chedorlaomer king of Elam, and Tidal king of nations;	The name 'Amraphel' may be from the Sanskrit *amarapala*, meaning 'guardian of the immortals, and the name 'Shinar' from *seniyr*, meaning 'pointed'. Taken in conjunction, the two names have a certain 'nuclear' flavor. The name 'Arioch' may derive from *ariy* meaning 'a lion' – a creature representing the fetal skin feeling. The names 'Ellasar' and 'Tidal' escape my efforts at analysis, and 'Chedorlaomer' would seem to be a corruption, so only speculation is possible. One suggestion is that is means 'Kedar the Red', a name with fetal significance. The name 'Elam' derives from *älam*, meaning 'concealed' which, together with the name 'Chedorlaomer' may thus signify 'the concealed red one'.[103]
Genesis 14:2 That these made war with Bera king of Sodom, and with Birsha, king of Gomorrah ...	The name 'Bera' yields no etymological links, but the Hebrew outline may offer a remote link with the word *baraq*, meaning 'lightning'. The name Sodom in Hebrew is Cedôm, meaning 'to scorch' or 'to burn'. The name 'Birsha' is alleged to derive from a word which means 'wickedness', but there is also a root word *resheph* which has the meaning 'lightning' or 'heat'. 'Gomorrah' means 'a ruined heap'.
Genesis 14:3 Shinab king of Admah, Shemeber king of Zeboiim, and the king of Bela, which is Zoar.	The name 'Shinab' is alleged to mean 'father has turned', being derived from the word *ab* = 'father' and the word *shanâ* = 'to alter'. The name Admah is closely linked etymologically to the word 'Adam', and thus with the fetal skin feeling. The name 'Shemeber' seems to mean something akin to 'illustrious', while the name of his kingdom, Zeboiim, appears to be connected with the idea of speckles or stripes upon the skin. The name 'Bela' appears to derive from the root *bâla*, meaning 'to make away with' and 'to destroy by swallowing'. The name 'Zoar' is alleged to come from *tso'ar*, signifying 'to be brought low'.

There seems to be a significant difference between the names in Genesis 14:1 and Genesis 14:2, namely that in the former all the indications are directly nuclear and fetal, while in the latter all these indications are linked with destruction. Thus Amraphel of Shinar suggests a symbolic effort to refer to an immortal, plus the idea of pointedness. Arioch means 'a lion', with all its fetal associations, while Chedorlaomer of Elam has the possible meaning of 'the red and concealed one'. All these are plausibly fetal insofar as they yield any kind of consistent meaning. Contrast this with Bera of Sodom, which seems to suggest 'the Shining One who was burned', Birsha of Gomorrah, which could signify 'the Shining One who was brought to a ruined heap', and Shinab of Admah, associated with 'the father feeling of the red skin which became reversed'. The last four names, Shemeber, Zeboiim, Bela and Zoar, show a different manner of division, the first two being possible representations of the fetal skin feeling (illustriousness and speckled skin), while the last two both signify a sense of destruction.

It seems that the first two verses of Genesis Fourteen may be roughly interpreted as symbolizing a struggle between the state of being nuclear and the state of being brought low and destroyed. This is a large part of the feelings of the fetus for the placenta, felt partly to be a destroying monster. That these several kings should be represented both as warring and also as all 'joined together' in the vale of Siddim, which is the salt sea,[104] appears significant in this light, for the placenta could be symbolically represented by a salt sea (a pool of blood), in a 'flat place', this last being a fair translation of the word 'Siddim', from the Hebrew *saday*, meaning 'to spread out like a flat field'. Apparently there is no etymological link in Hebrew between the names Sodom and Siddim, though the transliterations into English are suggestively alike. But the two do come into association through the fact that it was into slime pits of Siddim that the king of Sodom fell.

The whole of Chapter Fourteen of the Book of Genesis goes on in a similar vein, but for the present purpose of analyzing the tale of Lot, enough has been written here to show that there are strong uterine undertones to the whole story. This symbolic content does not require that the historical elements be entirely excluded: myth and history are not necessarily mutually exclusive, for myth can easily be made of history by means of a little conversion. Just as some external events provide ready-made situations for a dream context [299-308], so do some historical situations provide similar conditions for the growth of myth. Mythical elements are not necessarily disproven by the simple demonstration that the main story in which they are found is generally historical. Similarly, many a myth which has lost all historical links, may nonetheless have grown from certain basic historical conditions. Thus, for instance, we have no cause to doubt the historical existence of that Thebes which Alexander overthrew, but we are not compelled for that reason to believe that it is history that informs the tale of Oedipus.

CHAPTER SIX

The Testimony of Thebes

The mythology of Thebes leads us back into a definite cosmic atmosphere through the mists of which we can dimly see the Sun and the Moon mating through the flesh of a bull and a cow, and a sky-god mating with an earth-goddess.[105]

sun and moon

sky god — blastocyst
earth goddess — endometrium

sky god mating ō earth goddess — implantation

These are perceptible in the legend of the founding of Thebes by Kadmos, and by the myths which surround that builder. Kadmos was a son of the Phoenician Agenor and Telephassa, the mother's name meaning 'the far-shining one' and thought to signify the Moon. There is evidence of Kadmos's solar nature in the etymology of his name, in the Hebrew word *gadmown,* which refers to the East, and is related to *gaduwm,* which signifies 'a pristine hero'. This 'hero from the East' combination may also refer to the rising Sun. The myth tells that Zeus fell in love with Europa, sister of Kadmos, and in order to possess the maiden he turned himself into a gentle bull. When he had lulled her fear of him, he swam with her on his back to Crete, where she became the mother of Minos. A. B. Cook shows that in ancient times Zeus was sometimes portrayed as a bull and his partner as a cow, a theriomorphic representation of the Sun as male and the Moon as female. It has already been shown that the fetal nuclear feeling is male in character [175] and that the placenta is sensed as primarily female.

172 *Mythology of the Prenatal Life*

```
Agenor
Telphassa  ⟩
                 Kadmos
    Zeus (bull) → Europa
                    ↓
                  Minos

    Sun          moon
    Agenor      Telephassa
—▸ ⌠Zeus ⌡       ↓
                Europa
    Kadmos       ↓
                heifer
    bull         cow
```

Agenor, incensed at the abduction of his daughter by Zeus, sent his sons to find Europa. Kadmos set forth, accompanied by his mother Telephassa. This mother and son pair is a doubling of the symbolism of the Moon and Sun. Zeus in the form of a bull mating with Europa, and Kadmos fleeing with Telephassa, appear to be two forms of the same basic symbolism. This view is supported by the fact that after Telephassa died, Kadmos was directed to forget all about Europa and look instead for a heifer with the sign of the Moon on her flanks. In this medley of symbolism we can see that Kadmos = Zeus, and Europa = heifer. The coalescing of the primal figures shows their inherent nature. Thus Kadmos is the symbol of the Shining One whose concern is the possession of the uterine placental sphere represented by the 'virgin cow'.

Already we can see not only the cosmic background of the mythology of Thebes, but also how it reaches out to link with the wider mythological field: the bull which carried Europa to Crete and bore Minos (thus giving rise to the legend of the Minotaur in the Labyrinth) was linked in ancient thought with the bull which Herakles was ordered to catch. Indeed, according to Acusilaus, these two bulls were actually one and the same creature.

The Theban mythology quickly assumes a manifestly uterine character when Kadmos journeys to Delphoi to ask what he shall do to retrieve his lost sister. For we have already seen that Delphoi is the city of the womb, the name deriving from delph, which is Greek for the uterus. Here in this 'womb-town', Apollo (the fetal nuclear feeling) slew the Python (the umbilical cord), which naturally is accorded its monument in the shape of the *omphalos* (the navel). This city of Delphoi sends its influence through large reaches of Greek mythology, always playing the part of the mysterious uterine impulses and memories that are lost in the depths of the feelings, but which unwittingly direct much of our external action. Thus it was at Delphoi that Kadmos was directed by Apollo to give up looking for Europa, and to concentrate instead upon the finding of a special heifer which he must then follow until she lay down, and there build a city. The heifer is, of course, none other than

[Handwritten annotation: Founding of cities = 'implantation' site]

Europa herself, and the city to be founded where she lay down will inevitably be another 'womb city'. This part of the story of Thebes reaches out to touch upon the whole vast tale of Ilium (Troy), for Ilos founded Troy at the spot where a dappled cow lay down to rest – like Kadmos, he did it at the command of Apollo.

Intent upon carrying out the commands of Apollo, Kadmos set forth in his quest for the special heifer. He found it at Phokis, in the herds of Pelagon. Some say that the heifer was white, but others say that on her flanks was set a white circle like the orb of the Moon. In this symbolism we may see the undertow of uterine meaning, namely that the Shining One from the East (the Sun = fetal nucleus) unites again with the Moon (placenta) wherever on this Earth the city of the womb is occupied. The image of Io may be seen in this Phokian heifer, the heifer of Zeus, through which we may discern a connection between the Theban mythology and the vast mythology of Prometheus.

Kadmos followed the heifer faithfully and thus came to the fount of Dirke, where the beast at last lay down. According to Jane Harrison, the fount of Dirke has powerful uterine associations. Writing of the mythology of the 'blazing child' or the 'child in the fire', she tells us that there was an ancient Bacchic rite of 'bathing in Dirke' which, so it seemed to her, might almost be regarded as a symbolic 'quenching of 'the burning child'.[106] This rite she links with the old Christian rite of plunging a burning brand into the waters of the font before using them for the baptism of the child. We have met this 'burning child' several times in the course of the preceding pages, and we know that it represents the fetal skin feeling, with its sense of light or fire upon the body surfaces. We can only regard it as natural, therefore, that the heifer, symbol of the womb, should come to this fount of Dirke with its manifest uterine associations. It is by such associations that myths are formed, for they constitute the peculiar logic of the feelings. By bringing the heifer to the waters of Dirke, the myth not only emphasizes the uterine nature of both, but it links the mythology of Thebes, if obliquely, to the myth of Demeter who laid Demophoön in the fire, and to that of Isis, who also sought to burn away a child's mortality.

Once the heifer had marked the building site by lying down, Kadmos decided to sacrifice it to Athena, and to that end he sent men to fetch lustral water from the nearby well of Ares. But the great snake, a son of Ares, which guarded the well, rose up and slew the men, whereupon Kadmos went to the well and slew the snake. Athena directed him to sow its teeth in the earth, which he did, whereupon armed men rose up from the soil like plants. Ares, at first wrathful at the slaying of his snake, was eventually appeased by Zeus to the extent of giving his daughter Harmonia to Kadmos, as his wife.

This part of the story takes us deep into the human feelings of umbilical aggression and counter-thrust. Ares, the god of destruction, symbolizes the sheer aggressive thrust of the umbilical arteries. Although there can be found no authority for presuming to identify Ares with Aries yet, apart from any accidental similarity of the names, they are allied through their associations: both have connotations of aggression, and both are linked with the planet Mars in ancient thought. Certainly Ares has a good claim to be considered fetal, and therefore we can understand the directing presence of Athena at his well, for she has already been identified as a markedly placental goddess. The two were indeed closely linked together in the ancient Greek mind. Wherever we find the symbol of the fetus we tend also to find a representation of the placenta, and vice versa, while the existence of both alerts us to look for the umbilical image. Certainly we find that umbilical image in the snake of Ares, dynamically expressed in the back and forth thrusts between it and Kadmon and his men. A similar back-and-forth sense is conveyed by the thrusting of the snake's teeth down into the earth followed by the back-thrust of the armed men. This story of the sowing of the snake's teeth and the crop of armed men or heads (a tale told not only of Kadmos but also of Jason) belongs to the later postnatal state, when the child seems to thrust something down into the earth and get it back in the form of the up-thrust to the head [119-122].

Mythologically, the story of the snake of Ares takes us far afield. The snake that guards a well is in no way peculiar to Thebes: a similar situation existed, for instance, in the garden of the Hesperides, where a great snake guarded not only the famous tree on which the golden apples grew, but also the well at its foot. Thus one might say that the snake-slaying Kadmon at the well of Ares is essentially the same as the snake-slaying Herakles in the garden of the Hesperides. The sowing of the snake's teeth and the resultant crop of armed men links directly with the quest of Jason, for he found the Golden Fleece hanging on a tree guarded by a great snake, and he slew it, sowing its teeth and reaping a crop of armed heads. The link with Jason emphasizes the uterine content of the total mythological background, since Jason was taught in a cave (uterus) by Cheiron the centaur (placenta) and was recognized by Pelias because he had lost a shoe when he crossed the river. This loss of a shoe can be seen to have direct umbilical significance as soon as we know that the legs feel to be umbilical and the feet placental [109-110].

The marriage of Kadmos to Harmonia repeats the basic uterine theme in fresh terms. The female relation of the male fetal representative is invariably a representation of the placenta, be she sister, mother, daughter, wife or any combination of them. Therefore when Ares gives his daughter to Kadmos, it is simply a fresh interweaving of the basic terms. Kadmos set forth with Telephassa, his mother, to find Europa his sister, but he lost both and found the Moon-heifer instead and, when he sacrificed her, then he got Harmonia. The equation may be stated thus: Telephassa = Europa = heifer = Harmonia = placenta = Moon. In relation to them all Kadmos, whom we have seen as plausibly solar and hence fetal, plays the fetal role, and we are not surprised that it involves a snake, and that much of the sequence is directed from womb-town (Delphoi) by the Snake-woman (Pythia). The fetal-placental nature of this primal Theban pair is supported by the fact that at their wedding Kadmos gives Harmonia a wondrous necklace specially made by Hephaestus, the god of fire, whom we have already seen to be markedly fetal. The umbilical character of this necklace is implied in its background – it was forged by the god of fire and presented by a fetal to a placental figure, and was destined to play so fatal a role in the ultimate destruction of Thebes. For indeed, at the root of our feelings lies the memory that the umbilical cord brings not only marriage but destruction. Pausanias asserts that the bridal chambers of both Harmonia and Semele were to be found upon the Acropolis of Thebes,[107] and a little later I shall show how this supports her placental status.

The final incident in the lives of Kadmos and Harmonia serves to heighten their uterine nature: both were turned into snakes when they departed from Thebes. Jane Harrison seeks to explain this by conjecturing that this merely signifies that:

Kadmos who is a snake-slayer is also himself a snake ... Kadmos is turned into a snake because he was a Snake-man, the snake-man, head and king of a Snake-group.[108]

The shallowness of this explanation is typical of all efforts to explain mythology without the key that lies in the depths of our own feelings. Kadmos and Harmonia are turned to snakes in the myth because indeed they represent *the* snake in the umbilical coils of which our very selfhood is first evoked.

There is a legend of the building of Thebes which warrants our attention, namely that its architects were the twins Zethos and Amphion. These twins have about them a familiar aura, which already we have sensed in the myth of Esau and Jacob:

Zethos the stern hunter and herdsman, Amphion the milder and more civilized musician.[109]

In short, Zethos and Amphion represent the uterine organism, fetus and placenta, and their role as co-architects of Thebes contains, to my mind, an echo of the assertions made by me that the fetus gains its first geometric sense – its first sense of architectonics! – in its vascular relationship to the placenta [36-40].

Zethos = tropho blast

Amphion = embryo

This is supported somewhat by Kerényi[110] who states that ancient towns were built to the same ideal plan in accordance with which man 'knows',

Mythology of the Prenatal Life 177

mythologically speaking, that his own totality is organized. Kerényi, knowing nothing of the material in *The Nature of the Self*, was compelled to use the word 'mythologically' where I would be able to employ the more concrete term 'umbilically'. Kerényi draws upon Plutarch and Ovid to describe the ancient Roman method of founding a city. The focus of the city was a circular pit where a sacrifice was made, and from which focus a large circle was ploughed to mark the boundaries. He quotes from Frobenius the following related information concerning the building of a West African city:

> A bull was led three times around the city. He was then brought into the place marked off, together with three cows. After covering three of them he was sacrificed. His member was buried in the middle of the new city and a phallic altar erected alongside a sacrificial pit.[111]

Here we have a very powerful uterine symbolism when viewed in the light of this book, for the bull is, as I have amply shown, a prime fetal symbol, and one cannot help seeing the 'thrice-used penis' as an excellent if grisly symbol of the umbilical cord, by means of which the 'fetal bull' may be said to 'copulate' with the placental 'cow'. The bull's penis at the center of the city is thus in essence closely related, through its umbilical symbolism, with the snake of Ares slain at the point where Thebes was to be built. It seems to me very pointed, in the terms of this book, that a symbol of the umbilical cord (whether serpent, or its *omphalos*, or the bull-penis and its phallic stone) should lie at the center of a city that is built 'to the same plan as that to which man's own nature is organized'.

blastocyst → embryo → fetus

Zeus → bull

chorionic villi = teeth → armed men

These elements of 'umbilical geometry' [35-38] are clearly evident in the primal structure of the city of Rome. At the ideal center of the city stands the Forum, and there was situated a brick structure called the Umbilicus Romae, meaning simply 'the navel of Rome',

178 *Mythology of the Prenatal Life*

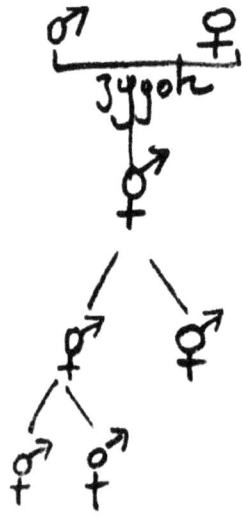

which clearly has the same significance as the *omphalos* at Delphoi. The name and the central location point to a literal uterine interpretation of this 'navel', for here also at the *Umbilicus Romae* we have a direct association with the ubiquitous twins who, under other names, represent the fetus and the placenta. In ancient Rome this presence of the universal twins was acknowledged by the legend that the umbilicus in the Forum was the tomb of Romulus, legendary Founder of Rome, with whom is intimately associated the name of his twin Remus. There are two legends of Romulus, which illustrate how inexorably the dreamlike processes of feeling-association operate to clothe a fetal figure in appropriate symbolism. One of these states that Romulus was torn to pieces by the Senators of the city, a tale which plainly echoes the sense that the fetal skin feeling is 'torn to pieces' by the placenta, as illustrated in the stories of Joseph, Osiris,

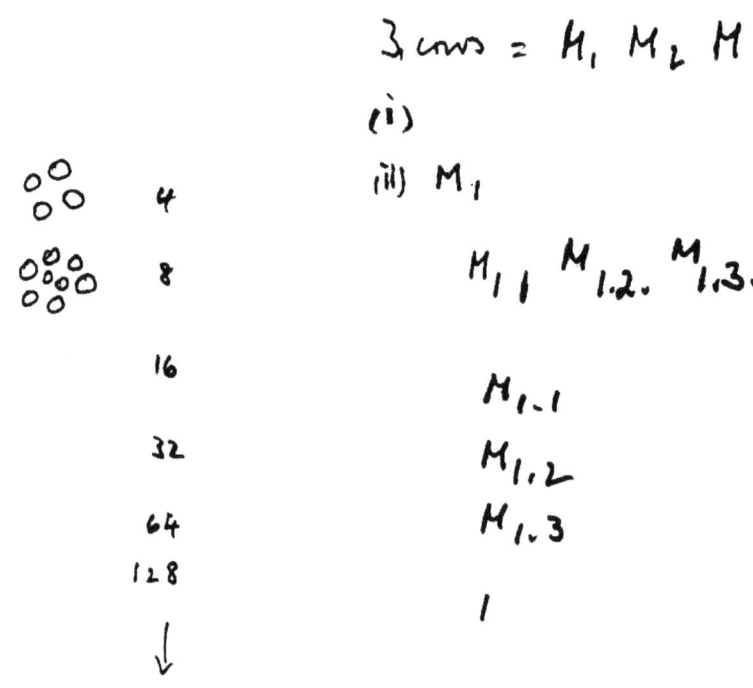

Dionysus and others. The second legend of Romulus which shows fetal associations is that which declared him to have disappeared in a thunderstorm. In dreams, the thunderstorm often appears as a symbol for birth, presumably because at birth we first see light flashing in the eyes, hear booming sounds, experience a colder environment and experience the sound of our own gasping and crying, a noise often related in dreams to howling and rushing wind. Therefore it is symbolically natural to ascribe the 'disappearance of the fetus' at birth as a disappearance during a thunderstorm. A large brass struck in Rome in 23 A.D. is shown by A. B. Cook on p. 441 of Vol. 2 of his *magnum opus*, and which I roughly produce here.

This diagram shows the heads of Romulus and Remus emerging from horns set on each side of a *caduceus*. I have already shown that a *caduceus* is a formalized representation of the umbilical cord, so that the situation of the Roman twins in this umbilical locus could hardly speak more plainly of their uterine nature.

The myth of the founding of Thebes by Zethos and Amphion links the city to Thebes in Egypt, said to have been founded by the Egyptian twins Set and Horus, whom we have already seen to represent the fetus and the placenta. The names Zethos and Set reverse the fetal-placental symbolism, since Set is a symbol of the destroying placenta, while Zethos is the symbol of the fetus. The ruling principle of such associations is obviously not historical, as we understand it, but is the urge to make collectivized representations of that personal history which is the core of the self. The ancient city was not a spiritually barren wilderness of straight streets created by modern men who have, in this special sense, lost their umbilical cords, but a living entity created to that universal design which is first felt in the cord.

We may now understand, in the light of the uterine associations embedded in the ancient towns, why the city of Thebes – its site indirectly given from womb-town (Delphoi) – should be built on the spot where the white heifer lay down, where the snake of Ares was slain, and where Kadmos married Harmonia. Here were born four daughters, of whom I propose to note only one, Semele, mother of Dionysus. The ever-roving eye of Zeus fell upon this maiden, and upon her likewise fell the inevitable jealous hatred of Hera. The goddess visited the maiden in disguise and persuaded her to demand that Zeus should appear to her in his full glory, as he did to her, Hera, his wife. Despite the god's entreaties, the girl persisted in her demands, whereupon Zeus came with his lightning bolts and burned her up, snatching from the blaze their child, Dionysus. The earthly maiden is manifestly the humanized version of the earth which Zeus penetrates with his lightning (and rain!) to bring forth the fruits which Dionysus, lord of the vine, no doubt originally represented. For on the Acropolis at Thebes stood the temple, open to the sky through which Zeus hurled his bolts and fructified the maiden. One might see this as a formalized representation of that constant 'marriage' between the sky-god and the maternal earth, a marriage which the Greeks felt so holy that they protected from the human foot all places where lightning had struck, calling them by the significant name of *enhlusion*, which means 'places of coming'.[112] Such a place was the bridal chamber of Semele upon the Acropolis at Thebes.

Thus Thebes, founded by directions from womb-town (Delphoi) and by a Moon-heifer's guidance, was herself a womb to the lord Zeus, with a vaginal temple open to the sky into which his seminal bolt might fall, creating therein the 'blazing child' – the fetal skin feeling. That Semele did in fact represent the earth as mother is supported by H. J. Rose, who tells us that the name Semele is a modification of the name of the Phrygian earth-goddess Zemelo. This story of the lightning thrust of Zeus into the chamber of Semele also contains symbolic references to the fact that the human skull eventually assumes much of the lost feeling for the mother's womb [141] and also receives a certain down-thrust of energy from the sky [164-169]. This overlay of memories is reproduced both in dreams and in myths [311-312], and the cephalic elements plainly evident in the myth of Zeus and Semele are a reflection of the uterine ones.

Indeed, through the myth of Zeus and Semele the story of Thebes is given an entirely fresh inward link with the whole mystery of the uterine life, and by this particular portion of the tale it is linked with the myth of Dionysus, that great Traveler and Umbilical Hero. Through Dionysus the Theban mythology is related with the mystery of the divine child who was lured away, torn into pieces, eaten and then restored again. This mythologem extends far and wide, involving not only Dionysus, but Zagreus, Sabazios and in more oblique form, Joseph and Christ. It is linked with the universal rites of initiation wherever these involve, as they widely do, the death of a god or of an animal or of a young man (real or simulated), and of some form of initiatory eating and resurrection. Moreover, through his birth from the fire, Dionysus links the Theban mythology with that of Demeter, who put the king's son in the fire to burn his mortal nature away, with that of Isis, who also placed a king's son in the fire. In the course of his travels, which concern the cultivation of the vine (umbilical cord) and the invention of wine-making (blood), Dionysus is to be found constantly rending those who oppose him, or causing their nearest and dearest to rend them, so he represents in another form the traveling Herakles, who symbolized the same destruction and restoration in quite other terms.

The link between Dionysus and Herakles is established in yet another way, namely through the telling mythology of Triptolemos, whose name appears to derive from the idea of a 'thrice-ploughed field' – a suggestive umbilical name. Some asserted that Triptolemos was brother of Demophoön whom Demeter burned in the fire, which would directly associate with the Shining One. Others alleged he was the child of Okeanos and Ge. Either way, the story continues with Demeter giving to Triptolemos a chariot-seat of winged snakes by means of which he mounted up into the sky and thus from on high sowed the world with grain. The snake-chariot is markedly umbilical, as we already have seen, but Triptolemos did not always have such a chariot – at other times he was represented in a single-wheeled chariot, which A. B. Cook identifies with the solar wheel and also with the cup on which Herakles journeyed upon Okeanos. A. B. Cook writes of this:

> *I believe it (the wheeled seat of Triptolemos) to have been simply an early expression to denote the sun. Just as Herakles, when he crossed the sea, voyaged in the solar cup lent him by Okeanos or Nereus or Helios himself, so Triptolemos, when he crosses the earth, travels on the solar wheel received at the hands of Demeter.*[113]

182 Mythology of the Prenatal Life

So there we see link between Triptolemos and Herakles. Both are representations of the perpetual movement not only of the cosmos, but of the umbilical blood. This was demonstrated in some detail in the case of Herakles; in the case of Triptolemos it comes out in the fact that his chariot was represented as both solar and as snake-drawn. But there is also a strong link between Triptolemos and Dionysus, for A. B. Cook shows that they were represented in parallel in one era of Greek art, and there can be little doubt that in the feelings of the ancient Greeks there was a link between Herakles, Triptolemos and Dionysus. This presents another fascinating glance at the way in which the mythology of Thebes, by its strong uterine symbology, serves to identify the essential unity within the diversity of all Greek mythology.

Since Thebes is so demonstrably a symbol of the womb, it is not surprising to find that a prime incestuous drama was laid within its walls, namely the story of Oedipus, whose tragedy is demonstrably a representation of the feelings evoked in the umbilical flow. Naturally this drama is closely linked to Delphoi, symbol of the womb in an archetypal sense. It is at Delphoi that Laios first learns that his wife may bear a son who shall slay him and possess his mother, Iokaste. This motif of the son's birth threatening the very existence of the father is common in mythology, and we have noted its umbilical origins [188]. We are also familiar with the protective measures adopted by the father to protect himself: Laios has the child seized at birth, an iron spike run through his ankles before he is hung on a tree to die. However, the child did not die but was rescued, eventually being adopted by foster parents. As Otto Rank long ago pointed out,[114] the hero is frequently of high estate, but is exposed by his wicked parents, rescued and brought up by foster parents who, usually, are either human beings of humble estate or animals. The hero grows to manhood, returns to the scene of his birth and avenges himself upon his wicked parents. The act of exposure of the child no doubt signifies birth, through which the child is seemingly betrayed from his splendor into a barren world, wherefrom he is rescued by the gut, which in turn seems to take him inside it as a surrogate womb [103]. But we must remember that birth and its shocks serve only to sum up what has already been felt to be going on cyclically at the navel [31-32]. Therefore the evident birth symbolism in the myth of the exposed and adopted child should not blind us to the underlying symbolism of the umbilical process at work on another level, in the 'laminations' of primary memory [311].

The child with wounded feet who is hung on a tree makes a very fine symbolic representation of the fetal organism that 'hangs' on the maternal tree by that umbilical cord which is so linked with its feet that the one makes a perfect representation of the other [108]. This is the same child that in other guises was burned in the fire, or who was given some special garment, or who bore a name that linked him with fire, with the Sun or with light. For the fetus cannot entirely distinguish between the blood running in the umbilical arteries and that running in the femoral arteries, in consequence of which there seems to him to be a distinct sense that the placenta is at the feet (or is actually the feet), where it is supplied by the legs as umbilical arteries. Oedipus represents this aspect of the fetal feelings. Other representatives of the fetal state do not emphasize the feet, but some are given not only the symbols of the skin feeling but also of the wounded feet. In this connection I think of Hephaestus, the god of fire who was lamed by his fall from heaven. The same motif may be seen in the myth of Jason, who lost a shoe after he came from the cave of Cheiron. But through the wounded feet of Oedipus the mythology of Thebes goes far beyond Hephaestus and Jason to the Hebrew myth of Esau and Jacob, and their link through the heel. The same theme is to be found in the story of Cinderella, where the wicked sisters cut their feet in order to try to make them fit the golden shoe.

It was, of course, precisely because of these wounded ankles that Oedipus got his name, which means something like 'Swollen-foot' or 'Swell-foot'. Until recently I have assumed that one could press the symbolism of the name no further than a general indication of the umbilicization of the fetal legs, but I am interested to see that P. Kretschmer has suggested that the name Oedipus actually denoted a snake.[115] I have not only seen many dreams in which snakes take the place of legs, or endanger the legs, but have noticed how often young children hesitate when getting into bed for fear of snakes at the bottom where the feet go. I recall vividly my own small boy (who most certainly was never made self-conscious in respect to these matters) coming out from under a mild anaesthetic in the dental chair and saying that his legs felt to be all twisted and twined together. This inevitably reminds one of the facts that the most primitive of the Greek gods and heroes were often shown as having two snake-coils precisely where their legs might normally be expected. In this light it would not be surprising if the name Oedipus had some relationship with the idea of snake-legs.

Oedipus followed the normal procedure of the hero, as stated by Otto Rank.[116] Upon reaching maturity he went back unwittingly to his natal city. On the way there he encountered his father Laios at a point where three roads met, and there Oedipus slew him. Here once more the umbilical three makes its appearance, and most appropriately so, for it is in the flow of blood in the triple vessels of the cord that the father-aspect of the fetal skin feeling is destroyed in order that the new self (as the son) may emerge [187-189]. This immemorial tragedy which takes place upon the triple road links itself inevitably with the mythology of Hecate and all the witches who haunt the crossroads of ancient Europe.

Having unknowingly slain his father, Oedipus moved on to Thebes, where he found a monstrous sphinx besieging the city. This *chimera* will let none in or out of the city, which in consequence is near to despair.[117] Her peculiar interest is in young men, whom she lures to her and enjoys sexually, whereafter she tears them to pieces and eats them unless they can answer her riddle, which until the arrival of Oedipus none had done. The placental nature of this sphinx is readily demonstrable. Her interests in young men establishes her in this role, for what are these young men but the symbols of the male energy, the equivalents of those *Kouretes* who link with the great *Kouros*, the Shining One! That she lechers with and devours these young men represents that agonizing complex of feeling in the human depths between copulation and destruction, for the placenta is both the passionate female and the destroyer [174, 185]. As if this were not enough, this Theban monster was the offspring of that same placental pair (Echidna and Typhon) who begat also the placental monsters whom Herakles mastered, namely Orthros, the hell-hound, Kerberos, the Lernean Hydra and the Nemean Lion. In some degree, the Theban sphinx seems to symbolize the whole uterine organ. She has the body of a lion, which would make her a symbol of the fetal skin feeling. She has the breasts of a woman, which symbolize the feeding role of the placenta. She has the wings of a phoenix, which would possibly symbolize the fact that though she destroys, she also gives newness of life. These symbolic features, added to her general proclivities, make her a multi-determined representative of the uterine process. In addition to all this we have her name, 'sphinx', which means 'the strangler', being derived from the same root as our word 'sphincter'. This title suits the placenta, which though it supplies the fetus with oxygen, never yields enough, so that the fetus always feels slightly 'strangled'. This strangulation would appear to increase as birth draws near, the release from which dread condition is achieved only by the act of breathing, underlying which there is an earlier sense of strangulation or lack of oxygen. I have already shown, in discussing the Gospel mythology, that Judas Iscariot may be suspected of a related etymology.

Through the associations of the sphinx, the mythology of Thebes is related via Typhon with the widespread myth of Osiris, and even with that of Adam; for according to Talmudic tradition Adam possessed a wife, Lilith, before Eve. After a quarrel with Adam, Lilith became a monster who threatened pregnant women, and kidnapped newborn children. The Hebrew name for Lilith is Lilyth, meaning a screech owl or night specter, derived (like the name Delilah) from *layela*, meaning 'night' and associated with a spiral twist. She is a Lamia, cousin of the Empusa, the blood-drinker, and related to that European horror, the Midday Fairy, who seduces young men caught asleep in the midday sun. The young male asleep in the Sun makes a splendid symbol of the fetus and his sense of overall light or fire. It is truly he whom the placenta 'seduces'.

The Riddle of the Sphinx concerns the legs and is given in various forms. This riddle has been the subject of a great deal of conjecture. But the evident placental nature of the sphinx, plus the fact that the fetal legs are so strongly related to the umbilical arteries, makes it pretty clear that the riddle refers to the nature of the link between the fetus and the placenta. It might be said to be poetically true that the fetus does destroy the placental sphinx with every thrust from his umbilical arteries, and that the riddle is merely a symbolic way of stating this fact. It is a vastly different symbolic way of describing the 'riddle' which Herakles solved through his Labors, and which Theseus solved in the Labyrinth. Here again, however, I must warn the reader that this plain umbilical symbolism is overlaid by a clear postnatal experience with other symbolism related to the neck and the skull.

[handwritten margin note: postnatal echo]

This I have described not only in my book *The Nature of the Self* [134-136], but also to some degree (though not then with full understanding) in my book *The Universal Design of the Oedipus Complex*. Here for the moment we must naturally think of the Riddle of the Sphinx only in its plain, primary uterine sense, as involving an understanding of what is going on in that cord that is so closely associated with the legs.

As soon as Oedipus had answered the Riddle of the Sphinx he entered into Thebes, where he took the throne and also took his own mother as his wife. From this incestuous union children were born. This incestuous form of relationship is often found in myths, and I have already shown instances of it in the relationship between Zeus and his wife and daughter, between Osiris and Isis, Abram and Sara, and Isaac with Rebekah. The Oedipus myth, by bringing into a single context the murder of the father by his son, the destruction of the placental sphinx and the entry into the mother, gives vent to the central feeling-complex of the human being. Freud mistook this uterine representation for the postnatal echo of it [176-179 and 311-316].

There was a man in Thebes who knew the whole story of the guilt of Oedipus, namely Teiresias the blind seer. We have already examined the myth of this seer who in his youth slew snakes at the meeting of three roads, the consequence of which was his sex was changed at intervals of seven years. Naturally he knew the story of Oedipus, for it was his own. The slaying of the snakes at the triple crossroads by Teiresias is essentially the same deed as the slaying of Laios by Oedipus at the place where three roads met from Thebes, Daulis and Delphoi. Indeed, in a poetic sense, one might say without stretching the content of the myths, that as Teiresias, by slaying the snakes, changed his own nature (from male to female), so Oedipus by his slaying at the crossroads changed his nature from father to son. Laios and Oedipus are the two aspects of that basic nuclear entity who is both father and son, as the Christian dogma asserts and as the Janus-faced statue of Nemi shows. Teiresias represents the 'blind seer' of the womb, namely the fetus, who in the tick-tock of the blood goes through before birth all the essences of being in such a manner that, after birth, all the external events of space will at once find a focus in the ego – a situation which, no doubt, is a satisfactory explanation of the mysteries of human intuition and genius. Teiresias represents that encapsulated awareness at the root of the self which, though unseeing of the world, sees all.

The change of sex, which Teiresias suffers at the killing of the snakes, is one of the most important pieces of mythology known to me as it touches my discovery of the alternations of configuration caused by the umbilical flow [180-181]. It is also important because it so clearly symbolizes the fact that the umbilical reversals are related to a sevenfold periodicity. This is done by representing Teiresias as becoming female at the end of seven years, and becoming male again after a further seven years. Some myths say that he was made blind at seven, while others assert that his life was prolonged to seven times the normal span, or that it covered seven generations. In these terms alone are we able to link the mythology of Thebes to those of an entirely different racial and geographical origin. As all the myths derive from the common feelings of the uterine life, the underlying context for other associations thus becomes clear: the numerical affinity with the seven years in the story of Joseph and Pharaoh, and the emphasis upon seven given to Apollo, his life and worship. Moreover, it would seem merely absurd to link these sevens and their flavor of mysticism with the intuitive human sense of the musical scale and the color spectrum were it not for the evidence I have offered that the nervous system is conditioned by the umbilical beat to impose this sevenfold schema upon sound and light perceptions.

The myth of the war of the Seven Against Thebes is one that ought to be included here. This story tells of how Adrastos led six other heroes against the city, of how six fell in the attempt, leaving only Adrastos, who escaped upon a fast horse given him by Herakles. Here, clearly, Thebes plays a specifically placental role rather than a generally uterine one. The Seven symbolize the sevenfold beat of the blood in the umbilical cord [37-39], in the cycle of which the elements of attack, death and escape are experienced as the fetal nuclear feelings seem to pierce the placenta, to be destroyed there and yet to be reborn and to 'escape' in that sense which we have already found in the myth of the Flight of Orestes. That the leader of the Seven should escape upon a fast horse supplied by

Herakles helps to confirm the umbilical symbolism, since Herakles symbolizes the fetal nuclear energy which completes the cycle. Further evidence of the umbilical symbolism is given by the story that Kreon, king of Thebes, refused to allow the six slain heroes to be buried, whereupon Adrastos invoked the aid of Theseus, together compelling Kreon to bury the dead. This 'rescue of the dead' (even if only from post mortem disgrace) by Theseus links very closely to the mythology of Herakles, as Chapter Four shows. Indeed, the myth of the Seven Against Thebes could with very little adaptation become a typical Labor of Herakles.

An incident which took place during the march of the Seven against the city, the knowledge of which I am indebted to H. J. Rose,[118] strongly supports the umbilical interpretation which I have given here. The army of Adrastos ran short of water, but the nurse of the local king's son laid her little charge upon the ground and led the Seven to a spring. When they returned, the local serpent had slain the child, for which deed it was dispatched by the Seven, who gave the child a magnificent funeral, naming him Archemoros, meaning 'the Beginner of Death'. If Thebes is the placenta, and the attack of the Seven is a symbol of the umbilical thrust, then it is poetically true that the attackers seek a well, since that is what the placenta (among other things) may be said to be. The death of the child by the snake in these circumstances may be seen as a representation of the fact that the fetal-nuclear sense of self (the *puer aeternus*) is 'slain by the snake in its (the child's) quest for water' (refreshed blood), and that in this way there is generated the primary sense of death – the perpetual sense of death and loss felt in the umbilical cord is the 'beginner of death' for man. It will be found, in fact, that the human fear of death is invariably an unconscious projection of the fear of birth 'forwards' upon future death, and that underlying that birth fear is a still deeper seed that was generated in the perpetual sense of death generated in the placenta. Thus it is true that at the foundation of every human soul there still is a small voice weeping for Archemoros who is the 'beginner of death' for us all.

The umbilical interpretation of the story of the Seven Against Thebes is strengthened by the fact that ten years after the abortive attack noted above, the sons of the original Seven

Heroes marched against the city and destroyed it. The repetition of this foray of Seven Heroes serves to emphasize not only the deliberateness of the numerical element of seven in the myth, but also the repetitive nature of the umbilical experience. To seal the meaning is the fact that it was Teiresias who gave the warning of the impending end of Thebes, and so enabled the populace for the most part to flee. The one who 'sees into the heart of the cosmos' (though outwardly blind) through the umbilical beat and its 'reversal of polarity' (sex) is the one who knows the end from the beginning.

Thus, in brief, does the mythology of Thebes offer itself as a natural tie-post from which to attempt a unification of the whole field of mythology. By this I mean nothing that might interest the scholar of classical mythology *per se*, but rather do I indicate the human content of mythology – a content in respect to which the last-born baby is at least as competent as the more serene scholar. What I have sought to show is that there is only one myth, and that it is not necessary to be eclectic to prove it. One may start literally anywhere and jump upon the carousel at any point. I have chosen the mythology of Thebes because, almost more than any mythology known to me, it is a whole carousel in its own right. I have sought to show that there is but one basic myth, and that it is stated over and over again, in whole and in part, in a riot of almost unending variation. The historical causes of these variations no doubt are fascinating and would fill a hundred tomes, but the examination of them would do nothing to reveal the nature of the central theme. This theme is a uterine one, known to us all, and as much to the individuals of our de-humanized age as to the deeply human age of the Greeks. It is, indeed, the central hope of man's recovery of a new and vital humanity.

APPENDIX I

Notes on the treatment and symbolic representation of the placenta and the umbilical cord by primitive and ancient peoples.

On page 331 of her book *Prolegomena to the Study of Greek Religion*, Jane Harrison offers us a sketch of an interesting altar that was found at Lesbos. It is reproduced roughly here because it shows so clearly the signs of its umbilical symbolism.

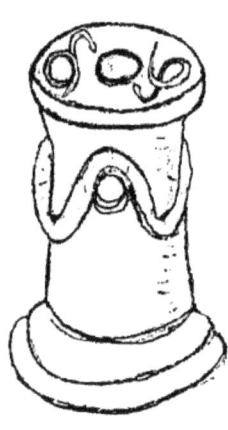

The hole at the center of the altar was for the pouring of libations. That is to say, wine was poured into the central hole by those who attended at the sacred place. On each side of this hole there is the image of a snake, and each is so coiled as to create the appearance of a couple of smaller holes. Harrison wrote of this altar that those who had made it had forgotten that it was erected in honor of a snake, and yet the memory of the snake-hero still clung to it. Very little imagination is needed, in the light of this book, to see that this ancient Lesbian altar makes a representation in stone of the umbilical cord in cross section.

The central hole into which the wine is poured represents the central umbilical vein, while the two snakes represent the snake-like (that is, helically wound) umbilical arteries. The act of pouring the wine into the central hole is a ritualistic representation of the passage of blood through the venous tube, by means of which we all indeed do experience perpetual resurrection and newness of life while *in utero*. Therefore the pouring of the wine as a libation into this altar expresses to the feelings in a most concrete manner that death is at once and inevitably followed by resurrection.

These comments on the Lesbian altar bring to my mind an echo very far from ancient Greece both in culture and in geography. This echo comes from the primitive Australians, who make and revere a

Mythology of the Prenatal Life   191

mysterious configuration which is called a *tjurunga*, which is made on wood or stone by means of formal shapings or markings. In his book *The Eternal Ones of the Dream*, Géza Róheim has the following to say of the *tjurunga*:

> By taking the tjrurunga along on his wanderings the native never gives up the original bond of dual unity which ties the infant to the mother ...[119]

Róheim tells us that in Central Australia, where he had done fieldwork, there is a belief in 'mystic doubles' that is associated with these *tjurunga*. In at least one of these Australian tribes the 'mystic double' or 'spirit double' is associated not with the *tjurunga* at all, but with the placenta. This seems to say very powerfully that the 'mystic double' is the placenta. Informed in this way of the uterine nature of the *tjurunga*, I was extremely impressed when I came upon some pictures which Róheim has printed of these mysterious objects. For there I found that by far the greater number of *tjurunga* designs illustrated by Róheim, which is to say eight out of ten, could be definitely likened to a cross-section of the umbilical cord.

I reproduce here one of the clearest of the Róheim pictures alongside a drawing taken from Arey's *Developmental Anatomy*. The reader will at once see that they are not of the same order, for the one is an actual anatomical drawing, while the other is a projection of an inner feeling-memory of the link between the mother and child before birth.

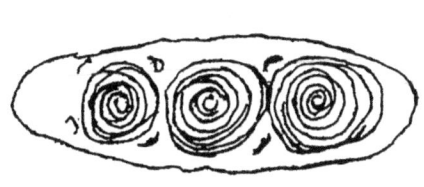 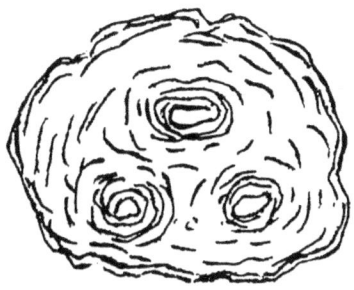

Pictures of a tjurunga taken from Róheim's *Eternal Ones of the Dream*   Umbilical cross-section, Arey

192 *Mythology of the Prenatal Life*

My view of this strange coincidence must be clearly restated if I am to avoid misunderstanding. I am not for one moment suggesting that the *tjurungas* are the fruit of Neolithic anatomical research. They are, I believe, a projection of images in the deep feelings. I must emphasize here that this is not guesswork, as I myself have learned most of my anatomy *first* through seeing bodily organs represented in the dreams of those I was analyzing. When I became fairly confident of my information, I would try to check it up by the requisite study of anatomical books. I have found a very definite subjective knowledge of the body to exist. If this can express itself through the top crust of conscious cerebration laid over our feelings by modern civilization, I can readily believe that the primitive Australians and the ancients of Lesbos would find it infinitely easier to let it do so.

Child's drawing of his pregnant mother

While I was in the very act of writing the above words I received a letter from a young father who wrote to announce that his wife was expecting a new baby. Half-humorously he enclosed a most unflattering drawing which his firstborn, a boy of then six, made of his pregnant Mama. The young father expressed the hope that the boy was not a prophet, and that there would not be triplets. I could not help feeling that the child was superimposing upon his mother's pregnant body dreamlike memories of his own lost umbilical link with her.

The picture, reproduced here, might almost be a primitive *tjurunga*. There are several details about this picture which might be worth comparative study, but the place is not here.

It seems fairly evident that this deep and lingering memory of the uterine life explains why primitive and ancient peoples, as well as the peasant people of more recent times, have often treated the placenta and the umbilical cord with such marked respect. It has, in fact, been quite a widespread custom from most primitive times up to quite recently to treat the cord and the placenta with a reverence akin to that shown by the Central Australian primitives for their *tjurungas*. Even people as civilized as the ancient Egyptians carried before the Pharaoh in ritual procession images believed to represent either his placenta and his umbilical cord or his fetal self.

In Chapter Three I showed that J. G. Frazer, in dealing with the imagery of the Golden Bough, was really dealing with the symbolism of the umbilical cord. Although at no time does Frazer relate the following to his main theme, he adduces a number of instances of the reverent treatment accorded to the afterbirth. He prefaces his major summary of these practices with words that may appear significant in the light of this book:

> ... the fortunes of the individual for good or evil throughout life are often supposed to be bound up with [the navel-string, and the afterbirth, including the placenta] so that if his navel-string or afterbirth is preserved and properly treated, he will be prosperous ...[120]

> The precious object is called the 'twin' of the king, as if it were his double; and the ghost of the royal afterbirth is believed to be attached to it. Enclosed in a pot, which is wrapt in bark cloths, the navel-string is kept in a temple specially built for it near the king's enclosure, and a great minister of state acts as its guardian and priest. Every new moon, at evening, he carries it in state, wrapped in bark cloths, to the king, who takes it in his hands, examines it, and returns it to the minister.[121]

Here we see not only a certain reflection of the *tjurungas* of the ancient Australian people, but also of those beliefs which relate the placenta to the Moon. Is not this 'king's enclosure' an earlier version of the Forum where the brick umbilicus was built, and where a mysterious 'twin' was said to be buried?

The customs of this uterine order reported by Frazer were apparently widespread when the material he drew from was collected. How much of this ancient behaviour has fallen into desuetude with the encroachment of the industrial civilizations I would not even try to estimate. However, I will try to summarize below the general nature of the customs as reported in *The Golden Bough*:

The umbilical cord is sacramentally buried in a secret place, perhaps near a tree or with a sapling planted over its 'grave'. It may be buried directly in the earth itself or in a carefully prepared 'coffin' made in the form of a plot or basket. It may be hung on a tree, being either fastened to the tree or some special place. The umbilical cord may be kept for the child until he is old enough to use it as a plaything. Or it may be placed in a shell and used as a charm. In similar fashion, the placenta may be buried with great secrecy, in which case it may be thought that part of the child's spirit stays with the placenta for later possible reincarnation. It may be buried in a flower-strewn 'grave' above which lights are carefully maintained, or placed in a jar and given a ceremonious 'burial' at sea. It may be put into a coconut shell and kept until the child has grown big and strong, or hung upon a cooking pot or one used for storing food. It is sometimes known as the child's companion.

It is an interesting commentary upon the 'schizophrenic' condition of the modern mind that in the very act of priding itself upon its superior intellect, compared to that of primitive peoples, it could, in the person of J. G. Frazer, collect and consider all these external instances of the care of the uterine objects, and yet never relate it to the mythology derived from them, which in turn originates in the deep uterine feelings common to everyone who has been born.

APPENDIX II
The Uterine Symbolism of the Zodiac

In Chapter Four, I stated that those who insisted upon a purely astronomical interpretation of the Labors of Herakles, or upon an astrological interpretation, or upon any mixture of the two, would find themselves unwittingly led to further evidence of the umbilical involvement because the twelve signs of the Zodiac are themselves closely related to the umbilical cycle. Here, I shall attempt to show that in these famous twelve signs, or divisions of the solar cycle, may be seen a projection of the umbilical cycle upon the cosmic round.[122]

The twelve signs are, as is widely known, divided into four groups of three signs each, relating to the four elements – Fire, Earth, Air and Water. These in turn can be seen to have a relationship with different organic functions in the fetus. The three Fire Signs represent three states of the fetal nuclear energy; the three Water Signs contain considerable placental references; the three Air Signs represent the linkage between the blood and the nervous system; the three Earth Signs represent the functions of the head and the muscular system. I make no claim that I understand fully the nature of these twelve signs, or that we now know them as once did the ancient peoples who created them. But anyone who carefully considers the internal evidence will likely be deeply impressed by what is offered, not merely in support of my general uterine concepts, but even in certain respects as an amplification of them.

The Fire Signs appear to represent the electrical element of the uterine organism as well as the nuclear feeling of the fetus, which seems to be related to light, or lightning, and to fire, as both dreams and myths testify. One might perhaps hypothesize that there is some inner identification between the electrical forces of external lightning and those of the internal fetal blood. In this connection I would like to mention an ancient belief that amber was associated both with electricity and also with the Sun, the Shining One. I quote the following from A. B. Cook:

> Nikias (of Mallos?) definitely explained amber as the juice or sweat of solar rays. Moreover, its Greek name élektron is akin to eléktor, a poetic title of the sun ...[123]

The link between amber and the Sun resides in that mythopoetic faculty which we have seen demonstrated in these pages: there may be an intuition that amber, which yields the faint sign of electricity, is somehow related to that Shining One in the skies, whose energy either symbolizes or in some way is related to the 'electronic' effects in the fetal blood. However, there is no doubt that the fetus feels himself to be the Shining Nuclear one, symbolically related to the Sun itself, and that his nuclear shining energy is generated or evoked both in his heart and on his skin. All this has been discovered through years of patient dream analysis, where the myths confirm and universalize this connection, as we have seen.

The 'ruler' of Leo, the Lion of the zodiac, is the Sun. We are now able to understand with some sympathy what is meant by this: the lion and his shining skin represent not only the solar energies (the energies peculiar to the Sun, the nuclear focus of the solar system), but also the skin of the fetus itself. Each one of us before birth wore this 'shining lion skin', a fact which we have seen represented again and again in the myths, where the solar-fetal hero is either clad in a lion skin or in some way related to a lion. Moreover, those born under the sign of the Lion are traditionally supposed to experience some accentuation in regard to their hearts. Just as all the signs of the zodiac are associated with one or other body part, Leo is said to 'rule' the heart. My discoveries in dream analysis enable us to understand that this assertion may not be nonsense, since I have good reason to believe that the fetal heart may be the actual source of the electrical energies which activate the fetal skin and the umbilical blood in configurational terms [22]. All this coincidence between the facts uncovered by me and the traditional lore of astrology seems too consistent to be merely accidental. But there is still another item which lends its weight to the present discussion, and this is the fact that my own conclusions about the origins of the human ego are matched by the astrological tradition. For I was driven to the conclusion that the nuclear feeling evoked upon the fetal skin [23] is actually the source of the human sense of self [15, 19]. The tradition of astrology is that those born under the sign of Leo have a certain accentuation of the ego, and thus of the search for true self-hood.

The first of the three Fire Signs is that of Aries, the Ram. I cannot pretend that I would have seen in this sign any particular significance had I not been already intrigued with the numerous points of coincidence between the fetal skin feeling and the sign of Leo. This conviction naturally led me to ask whether a similar coincidence might be discoverable between the rest of the zodiac signs and my general concepts. I was intrigued by the fact that in some ancient lore there are signs of a relationship between the solar god and the ram.[124] Thus, for example, in ancient Egypt, the ram-headed Sun-god, Khnemu-Ra was often depicted as wearing the solar disc. It was the Ram with Golden Fleece that carried Phrixus safe to the land of Colchis, where there reigned a child of the Sun. This story has highly umbilical elements, for the carrying of a child through death (the sister fell into water and was drowned!) to the Son of the Sun is manifestly an allusion to the umbilical journey of the fetal nuclear affect. Such symbolical devices caused me to wonder why a Ram should be related to the Shining One in this direct fashion. I asked myself whether this creature, with its twin coiled horns and its tremendous thrusting power, might not make an excellent symbol of the sense of thrust which the nuclear energy of the fetus develops through the beat of blood in its two twisted umbilical arteries. As we have seen, the umbilical cord is retrospectively felt by the human male as a sort of two-way penis, which is to say that the elements of feeling aroused by the postnatal penis acquire, assume, attract or remobilize those feelings earlier evoked in the thrust of the cord [177-178].

In this sense the umbilical thrust is a phallic thrust, and I observed that the ancient peoples regarded the ram as essentially a priapic animal, ancient representations of the penis being sometimes shown with a ram's head. Another aspect of the ram's symbolical use was its use as the ornament for a fountain-jet. This also has a possible link with my discoveries, since the umbilical arteries are felt to be the excretory fountain, thrusting forth liquid. This idea is heightened by the superstitions reported by A. B. Cook concerning a spring which still gushes out of a marble ram's head in a monastery on Mount Hymettos. This spring is apparently still believed, as of ancient time, to aid conception, pregnancy and delivery. The association of a ram's-head fountain with such matters seems unlikely until we understand that the umbilical arterial flow evokes the primary feelings not only of piercing the female [174], but also of causing that female to conceive and to bear a new self [186].

The Sign of Aries is the first sign of the zodiac, and is traditionally said to be ruled by the planet Mars, the veritable god of war. Indeed, all the thrusting and piercing proclivities of the human being do indeed seem to stem back in feeling to the first sense of the fetal thrust through the umbilical arteries into the placenta. All these things, taken together, seemed to point to the reasonableness of my assumption that if the Lion is the symbol of the fetal nuclear skin feeling, then the Ram is the symbol of the dynamic aspect of that same skin feeling as it thrusts down the double, twisted road of the umbilical arteries which, like the coiled horns of the ram, are associated with the forward and aggressive thrust of the self. For the traditional qualities assigned to those born under the sign of the Ram are those of the soldier and the pioneer, thrusting out into the world, to pierce and to open up.

The third of the Fire Signs is Sagittarius, the Centaur Archer. The reader will recall my mentioning of the fact that the centaur and, indeed, the horse generally, was a universal symbol of the placenta in ancient times. The centaur that shoots a single arrow, offering a likely symbol of the umbilical venous flow that enters the fetal navel and gives it the sense of being pierced by the placenta [21]. The single, straight shaft of Sagittarius thus stands in contrast to the two-coiled horns of the ram as the single straight umbilical vein stands in contrast to the twin coiled arteries.

The three Water Signs are Cancer the Crab, Scorpio the Scorpion which, so it is said, was once called the Eagle,[125] and Pisces, the Two Fishes going in opposing directions. I began by assuming that if the Fire Signs of the zodiac are fetal and nuclear in character, then the Water signs might be placental and peripheral. Cancer is the traditional sign of the Mother. The 'ruler' of Cancer is the Moon, which is traditionally a placental symbol, as we have seen. For the consort of the Shining One, the Solar Hero, is frequently the lunar female, the symbology of which is frequently found in a context so studded with uterine elements as to leave little room for doubt as to the meaning of this strange projection of human qualities upon the heavenly bodies. But the sign of Cancer is not only the Full Moon. It is also the crescent Moon, and if we look at the crescent Moon shining on the dim orb of the lunar body, it makes a perfect sectional picture of the placenta clinging to the internal surface of the uterus – like a crab, perhaps! The typical character of a person born under the sign of Cancer is said to be that which we associate with the ideal mother. The woman is the homemaker, the good cook, interested in the work of providing a home and nourishment for her family. It is said that even the man born under this sign may be far more motherly in his attitude to home and children than many people born under less maternal influences. Here, I hope the reader understands fully that I am not taking any side for or against this traditional knowledge. I am merely stating the traditional facts as I have been able to grasp and laying them side by side with my own discoveries as amplified by the myths, and am pointing out the unmistakable coincidences.

The second of the Water Signs of the zodiac is Scorpio, whose symbol is the Scorpion, but once was the Eagle.[126] We certainly have seen the eagle in a placental light in the course of the earlier chapters of this book. Zeus, the Bright One, not only wore the skin of a ram, which links him with the umbilical arterial thrust, but his familiar was the Eagle. I suggest that this Eagle of Zeus is the representative of the placenta, and that when Zeus set the bird to peck at the liver of Prometheus, he was simply providing another symbolic representation of the placenta thrusting in to the fetal body. It will be understood, of course, that when I speak of the fetus thrusting blood through the umbilical arteries, or the placenta responding in similar vein, I am not supposing that the actual physical circulation is a thrust of any real proportions. What I am speaking of is the fetal sense of the umbilical circulation as evoked (presumably) in the electrolytic functions of the blood. To revert to the sign of Scorpio, one can see that if the symbol of the placenta is a crab that clings to the side of the womb, then a scorpion makes a rough poetic representation of 'a crab that stings'. For the fetus feels that he is repeatedly and viciously pricked by the placenta, as a result of which he swells up and expands like a hand, which the scorpion has stung [21].

The third of the Water Signs is that of Pisces, traditionally associated with the feet, and thus demonstrating the link between this sign and the placenta through the involvement of the feet. We have seen previously that the human feet acquire a distinct placental sense, for the reason that the fetal legs are felt as umbilical arteries [108], in which context the fetal feet are confused with the placenta. Also, those born under the sign of Pisces are adept at weaving associations into poetic forms and fantasies, and I have wondered whether this might have any connection with the fact that the hemispheres of the brain are felt to be not only placental in character [142] but also to be the feet [160]. Can these strange associations, linking the brain with the feet and the maternal body, have any part in determining this traditional attribution?

We come now to the Air Signs of Gemini, Libra and Aquarius. These signs seem to represent the linkage between the circulatory elements of the fetus and the nervous system. If the primary elements of mind are evoked in the umbilical cord, where there are no nerves, and if they are related to an electrical function in the blood, then it is only natural that one should look for some means whereby the transformation is made from the blood to the nervous system. The latter we know to be a prime vehicle of the conscious mind, and such a transformer system is indicated, I think, in the Air Signs of the zodiac and their traditional effects upon the human body. These three signs perhaps represent the manner in which the elements of consciousness in the blood are transferred into the nervous system.

Let us consider Aquarius first, the final Air Sign, because it traditionally 'rules' the circulation, and so appears relevant to our present theme, since we are concerned with the possibility of a linkage between something in the circulation of blood and the nerves. The symbol of Aquarius is two wavy lines, which might signify a periodic flow of some kind of energy. There is little of relevance I can discover about Aquarius in relationship to this concept except, perhaps, that the idea that a consciousness 'in the blood' would contrast with the sharp ideation of the conscious waking mind. It is this sharp, rational type of mental action, which characterizes the Geminian, who stands next on our list.

The first of the Air Signs is that of Gemini, the Twins. This sign is traditionally believed to rule the lungs and the nervous system. The person born under this sign is said to possess keen mental action. The lungs do not connect directly to this intellectual function, but the two hemispheres of the brain do present a symbolic reference to the two lungs. However, the relationship is not of an ordinary neural or biochemic order so much as of an association of feeling. As explained in *The Nature of the Self*, the opening of the lungs at birth causes the brain to dilate as a result of a change in blood pressure, whereafter a continuous sympathetic rhythm persists throughout life between the relatively large expansion and contraction of the lungs and the miniscule response of the brain. This is a possible explanation for the association of the lungs with the act of conscious thought. This duality of the Twins may also be related to the division of the nervous system as a consequence of the bilateral symmetry of the human body, from which the basic fetal-placental division eventually comes [153-155].

Let us accept for the moment the idea that in some way Aquarius represents the flow of consciousness in the electrical beat of the blood, and that Gemini represents consciousness in the brain. Then the sign of Libra may be seen to represent the transformer by means of which the consciousness in the blood, represented by Aquarius, is carried over into the sharp, neural consciousness represented by Gemini. The first thing that inevitably strikes us is that Libra is the sign of balance, and its symbol is the Scales. Between what do they hold the balance? Is it between the blood and nerves? The only hint of an answer that I have been able to trace in support of this idea is that Libra traditionally 'rules' the kidneys, as Leo 'rules' the heart.

Now, the kidneys themselves are indeed much concerned with the circulation of the blood, for they take the blood and filter from it the urea, which the liver has manufactured from the dangerous uric acid. But this by itself does not seem to have any possible direct mental function. On the other hand, the adrenal glands which are anatomically (but not histologically) directly related to the kidneys have a profound relationship both to the blood and to the nervous system. These organs certainly show many suggestive features when examined in the light of the present context.

In the first place, we may note a close link between the adrenals and the brain. This reveals itself in the fact that when a baby is born without a brain, then the adrenal cortex also is lacking or is very small.[127] But the adrenals are also very much concerned with the blood, for they have the richest supply of all organs of the body – six times its own weight of blood passes through each gland every minute. Thus, on the one hand, the adrenals are closely related to the brain in a manner unknown, and to the blood in a very obvious manner. This does not by itself support the idea of any linkage in the adrenals between blood and nerve, but another very important aspect of the glands most certainly does so. The core (medulla) of each adrenal gland is a huge nerve-end which, instead of transmitting neural impulses to another nerve, discharges a chemical substance into the blood. This chemical substance is the familiar adrenalin, which is chemically very like to sympathin, which forms part of the chemical bridge between nerves at the synapses.

In this information there is no hint of the transfer of impulses from the blood to the nerves, but only the reverse, namely from the nerves, through the adrenal medulla and its chemical action to the blood and thus to the sympathetic nervous system. But the *principle* is there, and there seems no reason why the reverse process cannot take place. In assessing this possibility it should be remembered that what has been written above is largely concerned with the postnatal adrenals, and in that connection it should be marked that the prenatal adrenals tell quite another story. For whereas in the postnatal body the adrenals are relatively insignificant physically, they are proportionately rather large in the prenatal body. Hoskins, from whom all the above information has been taken, says:

That they [the adrenals] play some highly important role in the prenatal stage of existence is suggested by their precocious formation. Instead of progressing gradually as do most parts of the growing body, the adrenals develop with extreme rapidity so that in the third month of fetal life they are the most prominent structures inside the body cavity.[128]

It looks as if the so-called Air Signs of the zodiac may represent the projection of a deep internal knowledge of the bodily processes such as one finds in dreams. It may well be that the adrenals were roughly represented in ancient times by the kidneys, since there is no reason to suppose that internal knowledge was always correctly linked with external fact, any more than modern anatomy automatically leads its practitioners to a recognition of the configurational use of the organs. In the fetal body, the flow of blood and its elements of consciousness may perhaps be transferred into the nervous system through the action of the adrenal glands.

Lastly, let us turn the three Earth Signs of the zodiac, namely Taurus, Virgo and Capricorn, which may be usefully grouped together and related to Figure Seven of *The Nature of the Self* [147], and also to some extent to Figure Eight [148]. These figures depict in outline my discovery that the neural energy, charged with fetal nuclear undertones, is felt to thrust up through the neck into the head, which is felt to be the mother's womb, exciting there a response in the form of a muscular action. It is a fact that Taurus is alleged to 'rule' the neck, while those born under the sign of Capricorn traditionally exhibit great muscular drive, their delight being in action, work and achievement. Seen in the light of this, Taurus and Capricorn fit into the present context very neatly, for they represent the 'up-thrust' into the skull through the neck, marked in Figure Seven [14], and the efferent thrusts marked 'E' in the same. In that context Virgo becomes both the representative of the skull and of the cortex of the brain, being the peripheral element of the head – the 'virgin womb' which has in a sense 'conceived' without the sexual act and bears the sense of self therein [143]. It is traditionally said that the individual born under the sign of Virgo is inclined to pay overmuch attention to detail, and this might be said perhaps to equate with the idea that Virgo is specially related to the cerebral cortex, which is generally supposed to be the great neural filing cabinet in which details of past experience are stored.

The reader is not asked to declare himself for or against astrology. Certainly I have no interest in what it has become today for the vast majority of men and women. However, I can say that an impartial examination of the facts adduced in this chapter must lead to the conclusion that there is an extraordinary coincidence between some of the things I have uncovered through dream analysis, and various elements of the zodiac. I trust the reader will agree that I have good reason for saying that it is not safe for anyone to dismiss the Twelve Signs of the Zodiac as mere representations of the divisions of the solar cycle, and to assume that the Twelve Labors of Herakles are therefore almost inevitably of a similar order. The reader may also agree that in the light of this chapter, the reverse is just as natural, namely that the Twelve Labors of Herakles represent something about the link between the solar and the umbilical cycles which has become projected upon the heavens. In a word, the zodiac is neither entirely in the umbilical blood nor in the solar cycle, but rather in the resonance between the one and the other.

Implied in the idea of the zodiac is, of course, some relationship between the human being and the solar system. It so happened that as I was in the process of completing this chapter I read an article in *Life Magazine*[129] to the effect that the august Radio Corporation of America has discovered a close relationship between the planetary positions and the electric shield (ionosphere) which surrounds the earth. *Life Magazine* states that John H. Nelson, who was responsible for this discovery, did not at the time have any knowledge of astrological facts, but that after his findings were published he found they coincided remarkably closely with certain traditional knowledge. Thus he found that what astrologers call 'beneficent' aspects of planetary positions had already been independently shown to coincide with a quiescent condition of the ionosphere, while on the other hand 'maleficent' aspects coincided with ionospheric disturbance.

If it can be substantiated that there is a definite electrical correlation between the earth's upper regions and the positions of the planets, then it will be obvious that my discovery of the electrolytic response of the umbilical circulation to the cosmos will be offered a very concrete hypothesis. For if the whole solar system is a sensitive electrical instrument, then its movements may register in the little flow of ionized particles in the umbilical blood [24]. This would take the form of a pattern of relationship between the Sun as a cosmic nucleus and the planets as its peripheral response, a configuration which would reflect the Master Plan of Creation, which governs all things [77]. Whatever the ultimate outcome of this new attitude to the planetary positions, it seems certain that ancient peoples did have a very keen sense of the configurational relationship between the umbilical flow and the cosmos, as I hope this book has endeavored to demonstrate.

N.B. The above discussion of the zodiacal symbolism is tentative and incomplete for the simple reason that it deals only with the prenatal significance of the signs. But the signs also appear to have a relationship to the postnatal evolution of the human affect or libido.

APPENDIX III

The author's original Foreword and Introduction

THIS MIMEOGRAPHED VOLUME DEMONSTRATES THAT DISCOVERY IN THE FIELD OF PATHOANALYSIS UNIFIES THE WHOLE FIELD OF MYTHOLOGY.

THIS UNIFICATION OF MYTHOLOGY CONCLUSIVELY JUSTIFIES THE NEW CONCEPT OF MIND FIRST STATED IN "THE NATURE OF THE SELF" BY FRANCIS J. MOTT

MYTHOLOGY OF THE PRENATAL LIFE
by
FRANCIS J. MOTT

A CONTRIBUTION FROM THE FIELD OF PATHOANALYSIS

Registered at Stationer's Hall, London and in the Library of Congress, Washington, D.C.

Published in England
by
The Integration Publishing Company
© 1960 by Francis J. Mott

MYTHOLOGY OF THE PRENATAL LIFE
by
FRANCIS J. MOTT

FOREWORD

In addition to obvious purposes, this book will also serve to establish priority in the use of the term PATHOANALYSIS as the title of my psychological work. When I began this work I first adopted the title of 'psychosynthesis' as a descriptive label, but had to abandon it in the face of another claim. I hastily replaced it by the word, biosynthesis', a choice which I came quickly to regret because of its biochemical associations. I trust that those already familiar with my earlier works will kindly substitute the word PATHOANALYSIS wherever they find the word 'biosynthesis'.

IMPORTANT NOTE

I am not a mythologist, therefore this book must not be judged by those criteria which would properly apply to an academic work on that subject. Also, I am a pioneer in the field of precise dream analysis, and I must make it clear that my methods of research differ in certain vital aspects from any others in that field. For this reason my conclusions should not be assumed to be but variants of modern psychological ideas.

I see the myths as symbolic expressions, now clear, now dim, of the same subjective facts that I have found. I claim in fact to have uncovered the generative root of mythology. This being so, I can find internal evidence for the meaning of myths where historical evidence is not merely lacking, but impossible. Further, where historical reasons for the coalescence of gods and heroes are lacking, or where new associations or the acquisition of new attributes affront their historical origins, I can often understand the basis upon which such developments were made by the dreamlike associative processes of the ancient mind. For this reason, from a field entirely distinct from that of mythology, I can offer some light upon the puzzles which confront the mythologist, as for instance the reason why Artemis became associated with Apollo.

FOREWORD

This monograph cannot be understood apart from my book 'The Nature of the Self', and it must therefore be presumed that the reader has an intimate knowledge of my book or that he is prepared to read it in conjunction with this present work.

The inseparability of the two works can best be explained by means of a little history. Some fifteen year ago I began to analyze dreams on a new basis, and within the space of two years I came upon a basic fact of the mind's nature - a fact which I could find stated nowhere in the writings of modern psychologists. Treating this fact as a first stepping stone, I proceeded by means of hypothesis and observational proof to uncover an entirely new picture of the origins and nature of the mind. The observational proof was obtained through the precise analysis of dreams, from which I was able to build up a sort of mosaic picture of the evolution of the individual mind. What I mean by this may be understood by reading my book 'The Nature of the Self'.

From quite an early period of my work I began to observe suggestive coincidences between my 'mosaic picture' and certain symbolic elements in the myths.

My reading of the writings of Freud and Jung had, of course, made me aware that others had claimed to see a relation between the content of dreams and that of myths, but what I saw there was unlike anything I had ever seen stated in the context of modern thought. My findings convinced me that the symbolic content of dreams and myths tells the same story, namely the story of the evolution of the individual human mind. The dream offers us fragments of the memory of that process buried deep in the individual. The myth offers us larger fragments of the same memory - fragments which have been given collective form and projected into the social arena in order (presumably) to give collective expression to feelings struggling in each individual mind.

At first I gratefully accepted the testimony of the myths as a simple confirmation of the correctness of my own interpretations, and as evidence that what I had discovered was not relevant to a particular section of mankind, but is relevant to all mankind both now and in the long past of the race. But after a time I began to use myths also as a source of new hypotheses by means of which I could alert myself to new possibilities that could be uncovered by strict dream analysis. The success of that new method meant that I had established a two-way working link between the dream and the myth.

When I planned my book 'The Nature of the Self' I worked on the assumption that I should be able to present my facts and their mythological support in a single volume; but I soon realized that this would mean the production of an enormous volume which would lay a great burden not only upon the reader's time and attention, but also upon his pocket. I realized also that what to me seemed nothing less than complete proof of my discoveries might appear to the reader as an unbearable complication I therefore decided to state the facts first without the mythology, and this was done in 'The Nature of the Self'

This separation of the two elements in my work, while it certainly solved one set of problems, at the same time gave rise to another set. I found that when in due course I came to publish a book on mythology I should be compelled either to repeat a great deal of 'The Nature of the Self' or else insist that the two books be read together. Since the book on mythology would inevitably be an expensive book in its own right, it seemed to be an unhappy prospect that I would have to insist that, in order for it to be understood, the reader must also at the same time purchase and read another quite complex and expensive book, namely 'The Nature of the Self' aforementioned.

I have solved the problem as best I can by dividing the work on mythology into two parts, namely this present part which deals only with the myths of the prenatal life, and another volume, to be produced later, which will deal with the myths of birth and the postnatal life. I have also helped the solution of the problem by producing this first part of my mythological book by means of a duplicator or mimeograph. In short, this present work offers an interpretation of a large portion of mythology which is related to Chapters One, Two, Three and Five of 'The Nature of the Self'. In order to link the mythological material with the facts which they represent, I have placed page references throughout this present work by means of which the reader may easily establish his own connections between the two works. Whenever the reader comes upon a number in brackets in the following pages, he will know that he is being given the page or pages of 'The Nature of the Self' to which the mythology is alleged to have relevance.

At this juncture I would ask the reader, and especially any mythologist or classical scholar who reads this work, to give close attention to the preceding 'Important Note'. Failure to understand my exact position *vis á vis* mythology could ruin my whole case in the eyes of those into whose special fields I may seem to be presumptuously intruding. I have had the aforesaid note specially printed and separated from this Foreword in order that nobody may have a reasonable excuse for missing it.

I have kept the price of this monograph to the lowest possible figure having regard to the relatively few copies which are likely to be called for within a reasonable time. In this way I think I shall avoid adding too much to the reader's financial burden.

The repetitions, mistakes and crudities will, I hope, be forgiven. It is not possible to make large scale changes on a stencil as can be done with printers' galley proofs. I look forward to the day when the demand for this work may be such as to warrant a full scale revision for its reproduction in print.

Finally, though I have referred only to mythology in this foreword, I should make it clear that I have included *märchen* as well and also even primitive legends and other material not commonly included under the head of mythology proper.

APPENDIX IV

Jacob's Ladder

Outline of the Discovery of a Concrete Energy Link Between the Human Head and the Sky

First published by
THE INTEGRATION PUBLISHING COMPANY
Copyright © 1955 by Francis J. Mott

By the use of precise methods of analysis, I have probed beneath the surface of the human mind and feelings. What I discovered there is not only new and startling, but also old and familiar. This sounds at first like an insoluble paradox, but it is easily resolved when we realize that the modern mind sees things quite differently from the ancient mind. Even the minds of our recent forebears, like those of rural peoples, differ from the sharp, logical minds of our time. Therefore, older living people may have an understanding of these ideas in a way that has lost its significance for us. Our ancestors expressed things in symbolic terms different from the language we would use, and in seeking to equate them we discover what is both new, yet also familiar.

In this essay, I propose to briefly outline one particular aspect of my rediscoveries: *the fact that there is a stream of subtle energy circulating between the human head and the sky, and also a stream of subtle energy circulating between the human trunk and the earth.* These circulations of energy are today mostly unknown to the adult mind, but they are evidently known in early childhood. In the depths of our minds we nurture a memory of them – we are still in some way conscious of them, or of their potentiality. These circulations are an integral part of our deeper selves, and no doubt are vital mechanisms of what has been called the soul. They represent, in effect, aspects of the anatomy of the soul, or so I judge them to be.

The reason we know nothing of these deeper functions of the soul is presumably because we have come in practice, if not in theory and philosophical speculation, to identify ourselves with the complex sensations, reactions and social semantics which fill the waking consciousness. Yet everything points to the possibility that the very self that senses, reacts and semanticizes is also the product of the very circulations outlined in this essay. This self, the product of processes now become unconscious in the normal adult, makes thought possible but is not itself composed of thinking elements, or anything normally associated with mind and thinking. It seems that the human being feels himself involved in a struggle between two antithetical forces, one of which acts downward upon the human head, while the other acts upward from the earth upon the trunk. Here we see the very same thing that our forebears sought to identify when they spoke of God being 'up in the sky', the Devil being 'under the earth', and of a war going on between God and Devil over the soul of man.

The Origins of the Human Energy Pattern

These two circulations, between the human head and the sky and also between the human trunk and the earth, though antithetical in their subjective influence upon the human character, appear to be of the same order.[130] They are also obedient to the same pattern. Each affects the other, and both show signs of a common origin, namely *in the pattern of the blood flow in the umbilical cord*. Both are 'haunted' by the organic memories of this umbilical flow. It seems that the basic energy of the human soul is generated or evoked in the umbilical cord, and that the pattern of the flow of blood in the cord somehow sets the pattern of all bodily energy.

The human umbilical cord is normally composed of *three* blood vessels; a more or less straight vein which carries the refreshed fetal blood from the placenta to the fetus, and two arteries helically twisted around the vein, which carry the vitiated fetal blood from the fetus to the placenta, for purification and refreshment. This fetal blood flows in a closed circuit, having no direct contact with the maternal blood. It takes what it needs from the mother's blood through the thin placental tissues, and in the same manner surrenders the fetal waste to the mother's blood for excretion by her. In addition to the biological facts concerning umbilical circulation, we find that this fetal-placental circulation may be the agent for the generation or evocation of a subtler form of energy which persists after birth by transferring itself to other organs. This in turn imposes its pattern upon every flow of matter and physical energy into and out from the human body. Thus, the pattern of the umbilical flow (a single inflow opposed by two helical outflows) persists in every activity of the born organism.

Since the placenta and umbilical cord were evolved ages ago by the first placental mammals, their purpose being the feeding and detoxification of the embryo, one may assume that organs created for one purpose have had another superimposed upon them. Indeed, this is common in the evolution of the animal organism. Thus, for instance, the tongue was originally a digestive organ, but has also become an organ of speech. The evidence of dream analysis, confirmed by mythology, shows a metaphysical function superimposed upon the umbilical circulation. This is as distinct from its original purpose as the tongue's role in speech is distinct from its original digestive role. The mechanism whereby this metaphysical umbilical function has evolved is unknown to me at present. It cannot be a neural energy, since the umbilical cord is not innervated save for a few millimeters beyond the navel. It is difficult to see how the nervous system could register the helical twist in the cord, and yet this is the aspect of the energy pattern which persists most impressively in the behaviour patterns of the postnatal organism. It seems to follow that the blood itself must in some way register the pattern of its flow back and forth along the cord, though how it does this I cannot at present conceive. One thing is certain: no normal human being ever loses this umbilical energy or the pattern associated with it. Physically, the placenta and the umbilical cord are temporary fetal appendages, expendable after birth. However, the energy and the pattern of feeling to which they refer are never lost. However, as they transfer after birth into a variety of surrogate forms, we all feel to have the lost placenta and umbilical cord inside us.

The postnatal organism must accommodate the functions formerly administered by the placenta and the cord: breathing, eating and excreting. However, the placenta and the cord originally took over already-existing functions, adapting them for the shut-in life of the womb. Although breathing, eating and excreting all evolved before the uterus, their psychic involvement with the placenta and the cord does not represent merely an adaptation of pre-existing functions. It is something entirely new, and did not exist prior to the evolution of the uterine organs, appearing only after these had already been established for untold millennia. Indeed, perhaps it is uniquely in the human uterus that this metaphysical energy first evolved, and that this evolution, in turn, distinguishes man from the other placental mammals. Thus, the human organism has become involved in the evocation and perpetuation of a metaphysical energy, and that familiar organs of the body all have a dual function, namely their original biological function plus the evocation and perpetuation of this mysterious fluid pattern.

In modern times, both physiological and psychological authority has become vested in the medical profession, but the doctor's familiarity with the biological functions of the organs tends to inhibit him from looking more deeply into their psychological functions. However, the simpler minds of old knew, intuited or suspected that the placenta and the umbilical cord had a mysterious value which transcended their physical function. This is clear from the importance attached to the preservation and even the sanctification of placental and umbilical organs. These practices are exemplified by the highly sophisticated Egyptian civilization, which paid great respect to the uterine organs. The placenta and umbilical cord of the Pharaoh were reproduced in wax, to be carried before the king in a ritual procession. However, I suspect that the preservation of the physical tissues is due to a misconception. *Rather, it is the energy patterns originally associated with the tissues that are important.*

In order to gain insight into the significance of the placenta and the cord, we must revise the commonly held idea that these organs are mere appendages to the fetus. This may be true enough from a purely biological standpoint, but it is not true as regards the metaphysical aspect under consideration. For in this aspect the fetus, cord and placenta appear to be integral parts of a single vascular organism acting as the generator or evocator of a mysterious energy, so that the postnatal body assumes the energy functions previously carried out by the placenta and the cord. Lacking this integrity, the normal human being cannot develop.

The metaphysical elements generated by this integral uterine unit are concerned with problems concerning giving and taking, and the balance between them: *solidity versus hollowness*. Thus, when the fetus sends blood into the placenta, there is aroused the sense that the fetus is solid, thrusting and penetrative, while the placenta is accordingly hollow and receptive. Conversely, when the fetus receives blood from the placenta, there is aroused the sense that the placenta is solid, thrusting and penetrative, while now it is the fetus that is hollow and receptive. Further, this basic sense of solidity versus hollowness appears to be the basis for the development of human sexual feeling, or becomes powerfully invested in that feeling. The element of solidity and penetrativeness becomes the foundation upon which male sexual feeling evolves, while the element of hollowness is the basis of female feeling. In this sense, one is able to consider the uterine life as basically sexual, or perhaps presexual or even 'ur-sexual'.[131]

A complex of feelings seems to be evoked at the umbilical cord (or in association with it), and this in turns seems to be the nucleus around which our later feelings develop.[132] This complex appears to be composed of the following elements:

1. The flow of blood into the fetal body from the placenta evokes in the fetus the sense of hollowness, and hence of incipient 'femaleness'. Thus, the sense of replenishment and renewal is associated with the feeling of being invaded.

2. The flow of blood away from the fetal body to the placenta evokes in the fetus a sense of solidity, and hence of incipient 'maleness' or the power to invade. However, with this outflow there also goes a sense of loss and depletion.

It is important to outline these ambivalent feelings here, because we meet them wherever the umbilical pattern is evoked by postnatal circulations of energy. Wherever we find an inflow into the body we also find that deep unconscious fears of invasion (of being 'made female') are evoked, and these stem from, and echo back to, umbilical elements. Equally, wherever we find an outflow from the body, we find deep unconscious fears of loss allied with the exultant feeling of possessing the essentially male power to penetrate.

These elements appear frequently in dream analysis, although it is not possible here to adduce extensive dream material in evidence. However, as an example from mythology, we refer to the Egyptian myth already mentioned. Osiris and Isis were represented as brother-and-sister twins who copulated while yet in the womb of their Mother Nut, the Sky Goddess. The myth of Adam and Eve tells the same story. Adam is a symbol of the fetus, Eve is a symbol of the placenta; the serpent feeds Eve the fruit of the Free of Life, and Eve in turn offers it to Adam, a neat symbolic statement of physiological fact. The Tree symbolizes the umbilical vein, and the Serpent symbolizes the umbilical arteries. The Bible thus expresses a literal truth when it asserts that the combination of serpent and tree results in the first appearance of sexual knowledge. That the tree is related to the 'knowledge of good and evil' expresses well the simple fact that the feelings associated with the cord are ambivalent, conjoining the 'good feeling' of feeding with the 'evil feeling' of being invaded, and the 'good' of thrusting with the 'evil' of depletion.

To sum up: the fetus and the placenta, linked by the umbilical cord, constitute a closed energy circuit having a polarity that after birth, and later in life, becomes incorporated into the sexual feelings. Fetus, placenta and cord are thus a single original organism, insofar as these energies are concerned. One might say that, like Adam and Eve, they are the primary and universal 'man and wife' lurking in our individual and biological past, as distinct from our historical past.[133]

Birth and its Sequelae

In the light of the foregoing, we see that birth is much more than a cutting away of appendages which are no longer needed – it cuts an organism in half, so to speak. And insofar as that organism is ur-sexual, birth severs the 'male' from the 'female'. The motivation behind the emotional devices of infancy is *the need to restore the lost half of the self*. Indeed, the migration of physical energy through the body is a succession of approximations which are attempting restoration of the lost energy pattern. This idea of the desperate search for the lost uterine twin is eloquently expressed in the story of the long search by Isis for Osiris, mentioned above.

While we can but speculate as to why the spiritual life of man should be dependent upon the pattern of the umbilical flow, we can see the cord as the veritable stalk through which we were drawn from potentiality into actuality. Indeed, every single atom in our newborn body reached its appointed place only after a journey via the blood circulating through the umbilical cord, the narrow bridge that led the prenatal elements over into the external world, working outwards into self-expression. As the apple, dropped by its broken stalk from the tree, is no longer determined from within by the formative forces of the tree and its inheritance, so we also are dropped from the mother's womb, our umbilical stalk broken, bereft of the formative forces and thus progressively surrendered to the external determinism of the spatial world. We long for that lost link.

Both in dreams and in mythology, this is shown to have concrete expression in the depths of our feelings: *the idea that the umbilical cord is the source of our being, and the link with the formative forces.* Consider the explicit symbolism of the Pythian Temple of Apollo at ancient Delphi: the temple stood where Apollo slew the fabulous Python, shortly after his birth. Without doubt, the Python represents the umbilical cord, since the beast's grave was marked with a stone that was plainly called the *omphalos,* which means 'navel'.[134] This same stone was also called the 'Treasury'. Seeing the symbolic significance of this, we at once understand the reason why the ancient Greeks looked to the Pythoness, the oracle sitting on her tripod in the temple, for the indications of the formative forces at work shaping their lives. For in this light, the navel is the source of wisdom, and the Treasury is where destiny is stored and dispensed. Here is the remnant of the lost stalk (the slain Python) through which we are unfolded into outward being, as an apple on a tree.

The Circulation Between the Earth and the Human Trunk

After a number of accommodations within the body, the original umbilical circulation is felt to establish itself between the human trunk and the earth: *the earth becomes the placenta.* This appears to take place early in an infant's life. Metaphysical as this circulation is in its significance, this link between the trunk and the earth is implemented in a very physical way, by the urinary and fecal excretions. At a precise but unknown moment in the life of an infant, the metaphysical elements that originated in the dual outflow through the umbilical arteries become superimposed upon his excretions. So in the developing infant, the combined flow of urine and feces becomes, in effect, the successor to the umbilical arterial blood flowing from fetus to placenta. At the same time, a mysterious thrust is felt to rise up from the earth, between the legs, and to impinge upon the lower parts of the body, awakening the fear of invasion. This up-thrust from the earth parallels the in-thrust of the umbilical vein to the fetus from the placenta. *The lost placenta is now rediscovered in the earth,* as the fecal and urinary excretions permit the rediscovery of the ambivalent feelings originating in the umbilical arteries – all that once was felt in the umbilical flow now is reanimated.

I cannot explain the back-thrust from the earth, but I venture here an hypothesis which seems to accord well with such facts as I can muster. I suggest that the operation of the rectal and urethral organs somehow *alters the relation of the organism to currents operative from the earth.* We know that such currents exist, as demonstrated in the art of dowsing. The infant's experience of his anal and urethral excretions immediately evokes the sense of a counter-thrust back from the earth, upwards into his body. It is only in this way that the energy pattern can attach itself to the nervous system. In other words, the umbilical pattern does not appear at first to influence the nervous system by direct association within the body. The energy must first be thrust out of the body and down into the earth, whereafter it rises again from the earth, and only then can it affect the nervous system. This is symbolized in the famous story of 'The Devil With the Three Golden Hairs'. Here, the young man is permitted to marry the princess only after he has been down into the depths of hell, where he learns the deep (umbilical) secrets of the well that gives wine, the tree that bears golden fruit and the ferryman who ever rows back and forth. The wine-giving well is the symbol of the umbilical vein; the gold-fruited tree is symbol of the excretory (golden) arteries; and the ferryman represents the back-and-forth flow of the blood. The story of Jesus raising Lazarus from the dead expresses the same symbolism.

It appears that the correct accommodation of the earth's up-thrust is of profound importance. The little boy ought not to suffer the penetration of his anus by this energy, while the little girl must properly exclude it from both rectum and vagina. I make this assertion on the strength of observations which show the harmful physical and mental effects of such inadvertent penetration. The correct accommodation of this uprising energy from the earth appears to be in the nervous system and in the skeleton, especially in the spine, where the up-thrust seems to be related to the upright posture. The normal infant of both sexes first senses its relation with 'Mother Earth' in the form of a *meta-umbilical flow* in which the urinary and fecal excretions act the role originated by the umbilical arteries, while the mysterious back-thrust from the earth carries out the role originated by the umbilical vein. Upon this two-way flow between the trunk and the earth are superimposed the feelings which originated in the umbilical cord. Thus it is that the infant fears the acts of urinary and fecal excretion, because they appear to deplete and drain away his vital energies. However, the infant also loves these outward thrusts because they evoke in him the sense of a male penetrative power. Similarly, the infant fears the up-thrust from the earth just as he once feared the blood pulsing into his fetal body from the placenta. And just as the fetal-placental relations through the cord were felt in ur-sexual terms, so now the earth, through the agency of its up-thrust, becomes the penetrating 'male' seeking to enter the anus or the vagina of the infant, or both. Here we are reminded of Freud's perhaps over-concrete reporting of childhood fears and fantasy of rape by Father, either anal or vaginal.

The pattern of connection between the earth and the trunk changes for the normal boy, while remaining unchanged in the normal girl. This change occurs when the small boy's penis overmasters its urinary aspect, by the assertion of the erection. When this is achieved, the boy suddenly loses the pattern of two-down-into-the-earth-and-one-back. Now only the fecal excretions function as the one-down, and opposed to this single down-thrust there are now felt to be two up-thrusts from the earth, one of which is taken up the spine and the other up the penis. Dreams reveal that this sudden splitting of the unitary feeling of the up-thrust results in some bizarre misconceptions, the spine being mistaken in the deep unconscious for the penis, and vice versa. In other words, the body changes its response to the earth currents.

This earth-trunk circulation plays a vital role in the mechanism of repression, and in the relationship of the individual with his unconscious depths. Indeed, the notion of 'unconscious depths' may be more concrete than we have commonly been led to suppose, since the dynamism of the unconscious is related to the earth itself, while the process of repression is related to the act of excretion. Dreams readily illustrate how the original human contact with the unconscious is through the excretory acts. There lies in all of us a deeply rooted confusion as to our vertical direction, so that part of us feels upside down, with our head in the ground and in relation with something deep in the earth.

It is necessary always to bear in mind that underlying the earth-trunk link is a reflection of the older umbilical-placental link. In fact, it appears that *the earth itself is the organ of the unconscious, but only as the successor of the placenta.* It is the placenta which first acts the role of the unconscious agent, and this it does through the content of the maternal blood. I slowly realized this through many dreams telling me of the existence of a primary communication of feeling by the mother to her unborn child through the umbilical cord. Indeed, our simpler ancestors believed that a mother could affect her unborn child if her emotions were sufficiently aroused.

Some very positive dream material (and equally positive association material) led me to suspect that a patient's mother had actually conveyed to him a quite specific idea while he was still *in utero*. The idea was quite a simple one, but charged with much emotion. It was to the effect that my patient's mother had engaged in copulation while pregnant with him, and this had conveyed the specific fear that the thrust of her husband's penis into her vagina was endangering her baby. My patient's dreams reflected this experience not in terms of any direct fetal fear of the father (for this would be manifestly impossible), but in terms of an identification of the placenta with father, and an identification of the umbilical vein with the father's penis. In other words, the mother conveyed to her fetus a fear-laden impression of the male thrust into her vagina. However, having no cognizance of such external organs or events, the fetus translated what he received into his own organic feeling terms, namely that he too was being 'entered and made hollow' by a vascular thrust from a 'twin' (the placenta) with whom he shared the mother's body. In other words, the fetal feeling may be summed up thus: 'I am mother, and the placenta is father. The placental father is thrusting something into my navel that may harm me'.

When I first detected this dynamic I was sceptical, but continued to bear it in mind. As time went on, I recognized the same element in an increasing number of cases, until at length I was compelled to recognize that the fetus does indeed form a primary identification between the 'umbilical copulation' going on between himself and the placenta, and the ordinary sexual act going on between his parents while he is *in utero*. Evidence mounted to suggest that it was upon this 'carrier wave' of configurational identities that the mother conveyed a fear to her fetus. It was not merely a general atmosphere of fear released in the fetus by a hormone (such as adrenalin), seeping into its circulation from the mother's blood. The dreams were not merely recording a dim fetal memory of a purely biochemical or generalized reaction. On the contrary, the fetus actually received from its mother a rudimentary concept strong enough to enable it to identify its own internal experiences in terms of outside events of which the fetus could have had no knowledge.

As soon as I became fairly certain that the fetus could receive specific information through the umbilical cord, I asked myself what the limit of such communication could be, as a completely new mechanism of inheritance was implied. Whereas oviparous creatures are limited to the inheritance they can get from the genes and, in the case of the higher creatures, the short space of life with their mother, mammals seemed to have a new kind of link resulting in a more malleable and more expansive inheritance. But I will suggest that *the umbilical cord might be the mechanism of inheritance as well as of fetal ingestion and egestion*. There are strong observable indications that we receive, as fetal organisms, a level of inheritance through the umbilical cord that lies like a stratum between the lower level of gene inheritance and the higher level of postnatal learned behaviour and education. *The placenta, in the light of this idea, may be a transformer of organic knowledge as well as a biochemical transformer.* The mother's blood is the repository, in some unknown manner, of organic memory, as are the genes on a far deeper organic level. Thus the mother is not aware of what she is handing on to her fetus, any more than she is conscious of the

Mythology of the Prenatal Life   221

biochemical processes operating in her uterus. However, any deep emotional experience can, it appears, touch the upper surface of this organic memory, and then be transferred to the fetus through the umbilical cord. In other words, the ability of the mother to convey an impression to her fetus (as in the example mentioned) is but a superficial and occasional activity, which slightly disturbs what is otherwise a deep, consistent and entirely unconscious process.

What is true of the placenta is true also, I believe, of the earth. The earth, like the mother's blood, carries within it a deep mnemonic record. In part, this record appears to be created by living individuals in the manner already suggested, namely by the fact that the psychological process called repression is related to (or is the subjective aspect of) the physiological processes of excretion. We excrete into the earth what is rejected from consciousness, and also what we have not been able to bring into consciousness. The earth record may thus be said to be fed or charged, in some mysterious manner, with the product of human excretion. This, however, is not the whole story, for on a still deeper level, more remote from consciousness, the same thing is true of both the human dead, and also, specifically, human bones. Possibly, these are in some respects one and the same thing, since it may be the bones of the dead which carry down into the earth the mnemonic elements associated with them. Certainly it is true that *in dreams there is a definite relationship between these three outwardly distinct items, namely human excrementa, the bones and the dead.* It seems the feces are felt as dead things that are rejected from the body. But as the bones themselves are felt to be moulded out of excrementa, there is a three-way link between the dead, the bones and the feces – these associations are frequently in evidence in dream analysis.

The process of bone formation in the body seems to be in some way linked in the deep feelings with the production of excrementa. One might say that it feels to be a sort of centripetal excretion – an excretion inwards. Whether this has any physiological basis I cannot say, but I am sure that this connection is felt by us all, as an entirely unconscious feeling. Thus it would appear that two forms of excretion are at work in relationship to psychological repression: one an immediate process, namely that of fecal excretion, and the other a delayed process, namely that of the consignment to the earth of the bones of the dead. The indications are that both these forms of excretion somehow carry mnemonic elements down into the earth, where they build up a certain level of inheritance. It is perhaps not so much that deep organic memories are stored in this way, but rather that the more superficial levels are thus created, to do with local, racial and national endowments. These earthy memories are reactivated, as it were, by the up-thrust from the earth into the human body in the manner already indicated. That is, they seek to enter the infant's anus or vagina, but must be properly steered into the spine and the nervous system and, in the case of the boy (after a certain epoch), up the penis.

The so-called 'unconscious' is not a mere schema of consciousness, nor any airy or purely personal condition of mind. It is the subjective aspect of our relationship firstly to the blood through the umbilical cord, the placenta and thus the mother's blood, and secondly through the relationship outlined above between the human trunk and the earth. This concrete view of the unconscious is not without its reflection in ancient thought and practice. One is reminded, for instance, of the ancient Greeks, who revered the tombs of their dead as repositories of wisdom. It is noteworthy that the gods of the earth, the *chthonioi*, with whom the dead were closely related, were often identified with snakes. By such imagery, the Greeks were trying to give collective, everyday expression to the deep feeling that the umbilical cord (the universal snake) was somehow involved with the relationship of man to the earth, to the dead and to the mystical powers hidden therein. One is reminded, too, of the Greek legend of Cadmus sowing the Dragon's Teeth, which was immediately followed by the up-thrust from the earth of a host of armed male heads.[135] This legend is more readily comprehensible when we recall that to the Greeks the dragon was not lizard like, as in the Chinese culture, but was simply a serpent, which is a prime symbol of the umbilical cord.

Note also the Greek belief that it was Hermes with his *kerykeion* (the snake-wound staff) who could raise the dead; as the god of reincarnation, he attended upon Pandora-Anesidora when she rose up from the earth. That the spirits of the dead are often shown as winged images, called *keres*, fluttering like little germs or butterflies, underlines the earth-sky link which we are exploring. This ancient Greek imagery seems to represent what is also indicated by modern dreams, namely that we thrust psychological elements down into the earth, to be restored to us again (in degree only) by the circulation of the meta-umbilical (snakelike) energy between our bodies and the earth.

Folklore about the mandrake plant provides another repository of symbolism. The mandrake has roots that frequently assume a suggestively human shape, sometimes uncannily so. It was believed that this plant was generated in the ground from the excretions of men on the gallows; that it represented the dead buried in the earth and awaiting the Resurrection; that it possessed aphrodisiacal properties, and that it could be safely pulled up only by lashing it to a dog. Thus we see that in ancient folklore the dead in the earth are linked with human excretions, a fact which is emphasized by the detail about the dog, a universal anal symbol. That the mandrake was regarded as an aphrodisiac may be related to the fact that the up-thrust from the earth becomes strongly associated with the up-thrust of the erect penis. Hermes, who raised the dead with his snake-wound staff, was also worshipped as a phallic *herm*, or boundary marker.

We may see in these old myths, legends and superstitions an indication that something thrust down into the earth is doomed to remain there, or at best to engage in a dreary circulation, unless it is brought into contact with a transforming and revivifying agency acting downwards from the sky. These myths reveal something which the ancients dimly knew, which modern man has forgotten, and which the man of the future must know by new means, giving rise eventually to a technique for his conscious evolution.

The Circulation of Energy Between the Head and the Sky

At a certain epoch in the life of the child, the brain appears to be acted upon by a mysterious energy that has its source somewhere in the atmosphere above its head. This appears to be a dynamic energy which sets up a circulation running between the brain and the 'sky'. Just as the human trunk reacts to the earth currents by imposing upon them the pattern of the umbilical flow, so does the human brain react in a similar manner. The circulation between the human head and the sky feels to be threefold in character, reanimating on a new level the old reactions first evoked in the umbilical cord. What is more, *this 'head-sky' circulation seems to take on the feelings earlier experienced as between the trunk and the earth.* It is this last modification which appears to determine the difference between the mental character of normal men and women.

The woman, having achieved and maintained two excretory thrusts into the earth, and having experienced a single back-thrust, carries this same pattern into her 'head-sky' circulation. Thus, she senses a dual up-thrust from her head to the sky, and senses a single counterthrust from the same source. In the normal man this pattern is exactly reversed. The man, having experienced a single excretory thrust into the earth, and having sensed a dual back-thrust from the earth, now senses the same pattern in his 'head-sky' circulation, namely a single up-thrust and a dual down-thrust.

Here, the suggestion is neither that there is a physical reality in these circulation patterns, nor that there is any actual difference in the circulation of energy to the male and female heads. Rather, it is supposed that *the organism imposes the original biological pattern on the energy circulation.* Likewise, the circulation itself would seem to be not psychical in character, but physical or near-physical. It evokes certain subjective phenomena by its operation upon the human head, and renders them possible. The 'head-sky' circulation need not be considered as more 'spiritual' than the circulation of the umbilical blood. It may be the product of atmospheric, electrical, magnetic or gravitational currents, or associated with cosmic rays or their secondary beta radiation, but its physicality is not in question.

However, *just as the placenta and the earth are repositories of past experience and knowledge, so the 'sky' represents the source from which all that past was originally derived.* As an analogy, if we liken the content of the placental and earth circulations to the accumulated pre-existing body of literature, the content of the 'head-sky' circulation would represent the inspiration of the contemporary poet. The former is done and static, and can but be repeated over and over again, supplemented with endless commentary while becoming the instrument of human egotism and comfort. But the latter is a spring of endless newness and creation, able not only to add to the store of the known and the once-done, but also to change and modify the old ways – to adapt them to new ends, to expunge them when they have ceased to be fruitful and have instead become static, or even degenerate.

This wellspring of creativity should not be necessarily identified with the source of ordinary artistic, literary or scientific endeavour which leaves man himself essentially unchanged. On the contrary, the creative influence of the 'head-sky' circulation bears primarily, even uniquely, upon the man himself and upon his moral and spiritual nature. It enlivens the soul, and opens up a new pathway for life itself.

The gradual establishment of the 'head-sky' circulation releases the pent-up forces which, first evoked in the umbilical cord and then modified in the earth-trunk circulation, must later satisfy their inherent need for thrust and counterthrust. For this is what the basic nature of man demands: the power to thrust out and the power to take back, or receive. This is the nature of the umbilical dynamism, by which I mean not the simple back-and-forth passage of the fetal blood through the cord, but rather the configurational energy that is thereby evoked. This energy and its accompanying pattern manifest in the unique overtones that imbue all our human physical behaviours, preventing us from being mere animal organisms. Eating and excreting, and later, sexual activity, normal and perverted, are no longer for us mere animal functions, but become subservient to the energies of the umbilical pattern. Even the rounds of commerce, theoretically concerned with the winning of bread, become caught up in the aggressive back-and-forth struggle of individuals, firms and nations. In the drive to sport, to war and the hunting of defenceless animals, this same demand is found. Even the processes of thought, which the logicians and the grammarians so coldly analyse, may be employed not to achieve precision nor to unravel truth, but simply to penetrate the ego of another, and thus to reanimate the original umbilical thrill of being solid (that is, 'male') enough to invade the placenta with blood, to make it hollow (that is, 'female'). The tongue is not only an organ of speech superimposed upon a digestive organ, it is also an organ of aggressive penetration, a 'penis'.

All these thrusts and counterthrusts are released as the head regains its link with the 'sky'. For who would willingly weaken the power to make this link, losing its treasures by employing the essential energy at a lower level? No doubt it is just such considerations which have provoked exhortations to personal righteousness, involving not only the cessation of trying to penetrate and thereby reduce our fellowmen, but also the modification of our aggressive drives, whether military, economic, sexual or alimentary.

Note that I speak not of gaining but of *regaining* this 'head-sky' circulation. In the past, presumably during the days of childhood, we have all experienced this, but it becomes lost to us. The memory is generally swallowed up in amnesia, but in a few cases, a dim memory has been preserved. I myself have been privileged to see this in the few children it has been my good fortune to be able to observe with some constancy. I have noted the little signs – of a fear of the sky or of birds – going hand in hand with a fear of the earth, and a curiosity as to what lay under the earth. I have noted that in many adults, as soon as the analysis of dreams has uncovered these forgotten experiences, a partial return of memory takes place. Descriptions of the event are given, frequently accompanied by such detail as to preclude the possibility of deliberate or unwitting invention and deceit. I myself had most certainly forgotten my own experiences of this order until they were brought to light through dream analysis. Then incidents not previously understood came back to me – I was even able to describe where they took place, and who was with me at the time. For instance, I recalled a small companion asking me what was the matter with me, then turning away and saying to another small boy: 'Come on, let's go, he's got one of his quiet fits on again'. I recall quite definitely a feeling above my head as if the sky were boiling. I did not dare to look up, but got the impression that a small patch of ringed cloud was forming, and that through this' hole in the sky' the angel Gabriel was about to appear blowing his trumpet – in a word, the dreaded Last Day was at hand. The patch of boiling sky was part of a theological stereotype imposed on me by my early Church of England training. I was conscious then of being all too unready for the Last Trump, and rejected it with all my strength. The apparent success with which my puny efforts postponed the Day of Judgment encouraged me to resist this experience when it recurred, and this resistance gradually inhibited it altogether, so that it was forgotten until I was over thirty years of age. It appears to me now as a tragedy that the very religious stereotype which presumably had as its intent the preparation of the individual for just such an event, should be so misrepresented as to leave him with no emotion but horror, and so cause him to resist in fear the very thing it should have prepared him to receive.

J. G. Frazer tells us that Jacob's Ladder is widely represented in various forms through imagery of heavenly ladders, vines and creepers.[136] In these myths, mankind is depicted as having been one time in active communication with gods in the sky, either by means of a ladder between earth and heaven, or by means of a magical tree or vine which grew between them. This heavenly link becomes lost, and much lamented, through some error on the part of human beings. It is my belief that this legendary past refers not to a lost epoch in the historical life of collective mankind, but rather to *the lost epoch of each individual going through these childhood experiences.* 'Human error' can indeed be fostered by priestly ignorance and theological stereotype, resulting in the loss of this link. The magical and mysterious figures of the mythic past do not necessarily belong to any historical epoch, but rather to the infant past within each one of us, now become legend, swallowed up in the amnesia that cuts off the conscious waking mind from its own depths.

In the light of what I have written, we can see the classical Christian picture of the Crucifixion as precisely a religious stereotype of the real experience of the 'head-sky' link.[137] In this picture, three crosses are raised upon Golgotha or Calvary, the central cross holding the divine figure destined to rise up to union with the Father, while the two crosses either side hold robbers doomed to descend into hell. This pattern of 'one-up-and-two-down' is the perfect representation of the original umbilical pattern. And the fact that it is set upon Golgotha or Calvary heightens its significance and power, for both these names, in Hebrew and in Latin, refer to the skull.

This picture is the symbolic representation of the 'head-sky' circulation of the normal man. But the woman's circulation also has its place in the gospels. In the Gospel of Luke, we are told that one of the thieves abruptly turned repentant, and because of his change of heart was told that he should that day rise up with Christ.[138] By this means, the classical picture is changed. No longer is there one cross holding the uprising Christ, and two crosses laden with down-going robbers. Now there are two crosses holding uprising figures, leaving only one robber to go down. In this way, the picture of the woman's 'head-sky' circulation is presented.

Whether accepted or rejected, the power of these images over the human emotions must not be discounted. Neither should we pretend that 'after all' it is the literal teachings of Jesus which really matter, thus ignoring the most vital part of Christianity, namely its power to reach the deep unconscious by means of symbolism charged with emotion. The 'teachings of Jesus', even supposing we know them, are not enough should they merely incline us to a static sentimentality. What is needed is a conscious and deliberate effort to understand man's unconscious spiritual nature, so that it may be precisely known and deliberately cultured. The Christian picture of the crucifixion should neither be believed as literal history, nor rejected as untrue. Nor should it be lamely temporized as a 'truth of another order', with the implication that this 'other order' is too mysterious to be exactly understood. *The 'other order' of this Christian mystery is the unconscious depths in which lives the memory of our lost link with the 'sky'.* No myth, no legend, no religious stereotype can restore that link. They can but hide the reality and impel us to a superstitious acceptance or to an intellectual rejection, both equally false.

Why is it that the 'head-sky' circulation appears to have ceased in the majority of humankind? The answer seems to be that *it is inhibited by the false associations loaded upon it by the circumstances of its original evocation, and its subsequent transformations through the body after birth.* Thus, the thrust upwards from the head bears all the guilt of the umbilical thrusts, and the sense of disgust associated with bodily excretions; the down-thrust from the sky bears all the fears of invasion evoked long ago in the womb when the blood thrust inwards through the cord. Similarly, the downward thrust from the sky bears the impress of the thrust upwards from the earth – as once we feared the raping up-thrust from the earth between our infant legs, so now we fear the down-thrust from above. The spiritual sustenance from the heavenly Father, so to say, has become poisoned by our fear of his determination to 'hollow us out' and to 'make us female'.

Evidence from dreams reveals that the normal man's head is 'female' in feeling, and thus is associated with placental rather than with fetal feelings. The man's head emits a single up-thrust to the sky and receives back two counterthrusts, just as the placenta emits blood through a single vessel and receives it back through two. The reverse is true of the woman's head, which takes on more of the fetal elements, since she is 'male' at the head. Her head feels to give two up-thrusts to the 'sky' and to receive back a single down-thrust, just as the fetal body *in utero* emits blood to the placenta through one vessel and receives it back through two. However, for simplicity, no distinction need be made between the head feelings of the man and those of the woman, in relation to the sky, although these do differ, as shown. The most important feature, for all humans, male or female, is that the primal prenatal experience of the umbilical circulations, as described, is recapitulated, matured and fulfilled after birth in the gradual establishment of the link to both sky and earth.

BIBLIOGRAPHY

Arey, Leslie Brainerd,
Developmental Anatomy, W. B. Saunders and Co., Philadelphia, 1935.

Cook, Arthur B.,
Zeus: A Study in Ancient Religion, Vol. 1, Zeus: God of the Bright Sky, Cambridge University Press, UK, 1914.
Zeus: A Study in Ancient Religion, Vol. 2, Zeus: God of the Dark Sky (Thunder and Lightning) Parts I and II, Cambridge University Press, UK, 1925.

Frazer, James George,
The Golden Bough, A Study in Magic and Religion: The Magic Art and the Evolution of Kings, Vol. 1, Macmillan & Co., London, 1920.
The Golden Bough, A Study in Magic and Religion: Adonis, Attis, Osiris (Part II), Vol. 6, Macmillan & Co., London, 1914.
Folk-lore in The Old Testament: Studies in Comparative Religion, Legend and Law, Macmillan & Co., London, 1919.

Freud, Sigmund,
Totem and Taboo: Resemblances Between the Psychic Lives of Savages and Neurotics, Routledge & Sons Ltd, London, 1919.

Guerber, H. A.,
Myths of the Norsemen: From the Eddas and Sagas, Harrap & Co. Ltd, London, 1908.

Harrison, Jane E.,
Themis: A Study of the Social Origins of Greek Religion, Cambridge University Press, UK, 1912.
Prolegomena to the Study of Greek Religion, Cambridge University Press, UK, 1903.

Hoskins, R. G.,
The Tides of Life: The Endocrine Glands in Bodily Adjustment, Kegan Paul, Trench Trubner & Co., London, 1933.

Jones, Ernest,
   Essays in Applied Psycho-Analysis, Vol. II: Essays in Folklore, Anthropology and Religion, Hogarth Press Ltd, London, 1951.

Jung, C. G.,
   Psychology of the Unconscious, Moffat, Yard & Co., New York, 1916.

Jung, C. G. and Kerényi, Carl,
   Essays on a Science of Mythology: The Myth of the Divine Child and the Mysteries of Eleusis, transl. R. F. C. Hull, Pantheon Books, New York, 1949.

Mott, Francis J.,
   The Nature of the Self, Starwalker Press, UK, 2012.
   The Meaning of the Zodiac, A. A. Beauchamp, Boston, 1941.
   The Universal Design of the Oedipus Complex, David McKay, Philadelphia, 1950.

Rank, Otto,
   The Myth of the Birth of the Hero, Journal of Nervous and Mental Disease Publishing Company, New York, 1914.

Róheim, Géza,
   War, Crime and the Covenant, Medical Journal Press, Monticello, New York, 1945.
   The Eternal Ones of the Dream, International Universities Press, New York, 1945.

Rose, Herbert Jennings,
   A Handbook of Greek Mythology, Methuen and Co. Ltd, London, 1928.

Smith, Sir William,
   A Dictionary of the Bible, John Murray, London, 1863.
   Dictionary of Greek and Roman Biography and Mythology, John Murray, London, 1849.

Strong, James,
   Exhaustive Concordance of the Bible, New York, 1890.

Virgil,
   The Aeneid of Virgil, transl. E. Fairfax-Taylor, J. M. Dent & Sons Ltd, London, 1915.

PERMISSIONS

The following publishers, agents or individuals have kindly granted permission to reproduce quotes from copyrighted material.

Cambridge University Press:
   A. B. Cook,
   Zeus: A Study in Ancient Religion, Vol. 1, Zeus: God of the Bright Sky, UK, 1914.
   Zeus: A Study in Ancient Religion, Vol. 2, Zeus God of the Dark Sky (Thunder and Lightning), Part 1, UK, 1925.

The Master and Fellows of Trinity College Cambridge:
   J. G. Frazer,
   The Golden Bough, A Study in Magic and Religion: The Magic Art and the Evolution of Kings, Vol. 1, Macmillan & Co., London, 1920.
   The Golden Bough, A Study in Magic and Religion: Adonis, Attis, Osiris (Part II), Vol. 6, Macmillan & Co., London, 1914.

Princeton University Press:
   C. G. Jung,
   Psychology of the Unconscious, ©1992 Princeton University Press. Reprinted by permission of Princeton University Press, for worldwide rights excluding the Commonwealth.

   C. Kerényi and C. G. Jung,
   Essays on a Science of Mythology: The Myth of the Divine Child and the Mysteries of Eleusis, transl. R. F. C. Hull, © 1963 Bollingen, renewed 1991. Reprinted by permission of Princeton University Press for North American rights.

Random House:
   Ernest Jones,
   Essays in Applied Psycho-Analysis, Vol. II: Essays in Folklore, Anthropology and Religion, The Hogarth Press Ltd, London,

1951. Reprinted by permission of The Random House Group Limited, for worldwide rights excluding the US.

Routledge:

H. J. Rose,
A Handbook of Greek Mythology, Methuen & Co. Ltd, London, 1928.

Sigmund Freud,
Totem and Taboo: Resemblances Between the Psychic Lives of Savages and Neurotics, Routledge & Sons Ltd, London, 1919.

C. G. Jung,
Psychology of the Unconscious, Moffat, Yard & Co., New York, 1916, for Commonwealth rights.

C. Kerényi and C. G. Jung,
Essays on a Science of Mythology: The Myth of the Divine Child and the Mysteries of Eleusis, transl. R. F. C. Hull, Pantheon Books, New York, 1949, for worldwide rights excluding North America.

The Estate of the late R. D. Laing

All annotations, shown in facsimile handwriting, are from a copy of the original monograph of this work which is in the R. D. Laing Archives of the Special Collections in Glasgow University Library.

Every effort was made to contact the publishers or copyright holders of the following works. Where no reply was forthcoming, permission is assumed according to the terms of our request:

Géza Róheim,
The Eternal Ones of the Dream, International Universities Press, New York, 1945.
War, Crime and the Covenant, Medical Journal Press, Monticello, New York, 1945.

Ernest Jones,
Essays in Applied Psycho-Analysis, Vol. II: Essays in Folklore, Anthropology and Religion, for US rights. Published by The Hogarth Press Ltd, London, 1951.

R. G. Hoskins,
The Tides of Life: The Endocrine Glands in Bodily Adjustment,
Kegan Paul, Trench Trubner & Co., London, 1933.

Acknowledgment is given to the following authors and translators whose work is understood to be in the public domain:

Jane E. Harrison,
Themis: A Study of the Social Origins of Greek Religion,
Cambridge University Press, UK, 1912.
Prolegomena to the Study of Greek Religion, Cambridge University Press, UK, 1903.

Virgil (transl. E. Fairfax-Taylor),
The Aeneid of Virgil, J. M. Dent & Sons Ltd, London, 1915.

All reasonable effort has been made to trace the copyright holders of the quoted material in this book. However, if any credits have been inadvertently omitted, the publisher, on being informed, will endeavour to incorporate any necessary amendments in future editions.

Notes

1. Harrison, Jane E.: *Themis: A Study of the Social Origins of Greek Religion*, p. 7-8.
2. Cook, Arthur B.: *Zeus: A Study in Ancient Religion*, Vol. 1, p. 1.
3. Harrison, *op. cit.*, pp. 11, 12.
4. *Ibid.*, p. 22.
5. *Ibid.*, p. 18-19.
6. *Ibid.*, p. 517.
7. Our word 'hour' comes from the same root as the name *Horai*.
8. These references may be found in Matthew 26:27-29, Mark 14:25, and Luke 22:20.
9. Smith, Sir William: *A Dictionary of the Bible*.
10. Acts I:18.
11. See John 13:29 for mention of the money bag as a source of food.
12. Harrison, *op. cit.*, p. 7.
13. Genesis 37:33.
14. Genesis 49:3-4.
15. Genesis 40:9-11.
16. Genesis 40:16-17.
17. Genesis 41:17-24.
18. Genesis 46:2-4.
19. Matthew 12:40.
20. Strong, James: *Exhaustive Concordance of the Bible*.
21. Jones, Ernest: *Essays in Applied Psycho-Analysis*, Vol. 2, p. 336.
22. Quoted in Jung, C. G.: *Psychology of the Unconscious*, p. 238.
23. Editor's note: Lanugo is a fine downy hair often classified as fur. It grows on the fetus, but is normally shed by about week of gestation. Therefore it is not uncommon for premature babies to be born with vestigial lanugo. Re-growth of lanugo in adult life may be a symptom of *anorexia nervosa,* an interesting consideration in the light of the material in this book.
24. Jung, *op. cit.*, p. 237.

25. Jones, *op. cit.*, p. 268.
26. Editor's note: Matthew 12:40. This quote is not in the original text, but was included because it refers to the symbolic associations under discussion.
27. Genesis 8:7.
28. Róheim, Géza: *War, Crime and the Covenant*.
29. Róheim, Géza: *The Eternal Ones of the Dream*, p. 196.
30. *Ibid.*, p. 193.
31. Editor's note: The Milky Way is the visible trace of the galaxy which we inhabit, being thus the placental counterpart to the nuclear 'fetus' of our solar system.
32. Frazer, J. G.: *The Golden Bough, A Study in Magic and Religion: Adonis, Attis, Osiris* (Part II), Vol. 6, p. 156.
33. See Strong's *Exhaustive Concordance of the Bible*, from which most of my Hebrew etymology is taken.
34. Judges 16:21.
35. Judges 16:23-24.
36. See Appendix A of *The Nature of the Self*, since this symbolism is of the same order as that mentioned in the last paragraph of that appendix.
37. Judges 14:14.
38. Genesis 25:25.
39. Genesis 25:30.
40. It is my theory that legend is simply history 'softened up' either by the passage of time or by deliberate intent, so that it can become the plastic material for the making of myth. In other words, the unconscious is always seeking to make its own story out of the story of external history.
41. Editor's note: Arthur Bernard Cook (1868-1952) was a British classics scholar, specialising in archaeology and the history of religions. He was a 'disciple' of J. G Frazer.
42. Editor's note: The source of this quote is not listed in Mott's original manuscript, and could not be found. However, Karl Otfried Müller (1797-1840) was a German scholar and admirer of the ancient Greek culture of Sparta. He is sometimes credited with introducing the modern study of Greek mythology as depicting the interaction between individuals and their specific historical context, rather than the traditional religious view. So this quote describes the power of a mythical apotheosis that would affect even such a sceptic.
43. Genesis 3:22-23.

44. Genesis 1:27.
45. Freud, Sigmund: *Totem and Taboo: Resemblances Between the Psychic Lives of Savages and Neurotics*, p. 236.
46. Rose, H. J.: *A Handbook of Greek Mythology*.
47. It is a fact that in dreams the navel is frequently regarded as a wound and as snakebite. If the umbilical cord can be symbolized by a snake, it is almost inevitable that the wound 'left by the cord' should be regarded as a snake bite.
48. Editor's note: The epithet 'Dithyrambos' refers mainly to the Dionysian rites in which wild music was played. However, the epithet *dimētōr* does refer to his title 'twice-born'. When Semele, pregnant with Dionysus, was consumed in the fire of Zeus, the baby was rescued and sewn into the thigh of Zeus, from whence he was 'born again'.
49. Editor's note: Károly (Karl, Carl) Kerényi (1897-1973) was a Hungarian philologist who collaborated with C. G. Jung, and whose work has had a profound influence on the psychological interpretation of myth.
50. Jung, C. G. and Kerényi, C: *Essays on a Science of Mythology: The Myth of the Divine Child and the Mysteries of Eleusis*, p. 156-157.
51. Harrison, Jane E.: *Prolegomena to the Study of Greek Religion*, p. 288.
52. Cook, *op. cit.*, p. 229-231.
53. Jung and Kerényi, *op. cit.*, p. 179.
54. Editor's note: Hainuwele is a 'coconut girl' from the folklore of the island of Seram, in the Maluku Islands, Indonesia. See Wikipedia for a fascinating amplification of this story, which richly reflects many nuances of Mott's uterine symbolism.
55. Jung and Kerényi, *op. cit.*, p. 183.
56. Smith, Sir William: *Dictionary of Greek and Roman Biography and Mythology*.
57. Jung and Kerényi, *op. cit.*, p. 185.
58. *Ibid.*, p. 186.
59. Rose, *op. cit.*
60. *Ibid.*
61. Virgil: *The Aeneid of Virgil*, p. 150.
62. *Ibid.*, p. 152.
63. Harrison, *Themis*, *op cit.*, p. 91.
64. Guerber, H. A.: *Myths of the Norsemen: From the Eddas and Sagas*.
65. Frazer, J. G.: *The Golden Bough: A Study in Magic and Religion*, Vol. 1, p. vii.

66. *Ibid.*, p. 12.
67. *Ibid.*, p. 20, author's italics.
68. *Ibid.*, p. 30.
69. Harrison, *Themis, op. cit.*, p. 34.
70. Modern man may suppose that he is beyond this kind of thing if he is 'normal', and that he may safely leave such projections to the psychotic, the neurotic and the odd. But he is even more driven by compulsions than the ancient peoples because, through being ignored and thus unimplemented, the pressures in the psyche are free to become perverted at their leisure!
71. Harrison, *Prolegomena, op. cit.*, p. 232 ff.
72. *Ibid.*, p. 236.
73. Frazer, *op. cit.*, Vol. 1, p. vii.
74. Jung, *Psychology of the Unconscious, op. cit.*, p. 231.
75. Smith, *Dictionary of Greek and Roman Biography, op. cit.*
76. Editor's note: Alternative motivation for the Labours exists in other sources. See Seneca's *Hercules Furens Part II* for a description of how the curse of Hera prompted Hercules to slay his own family, which crime was followed by the expiatory activity of performing the Labours.
77. Rose, *op. cit.*
78. Harrison, *Prolegomena, op. cit.*, p. 435.
79. Cook, *op. cit.*, p. 394.
80. *Ibid.*, p. 230.
81. Cook, *ibid.*, p. 490. As Cook puts it: *'From Knossos to Hampton Court may be a far cry; but ... in the chain connecting them hardly a link is missing.'* By this he referred to the fact that the maze at Hampton Court, in common with all mazes, is a direct derivative of the fabled labyrinth.
82. Cook, *op. cit.*, Vol. 2, p. 539-540.
83. Cook, *op. cit.*, Vol. 1, p. 490.
84. *Ibid.*, p. 409-410.
85. Editor's note: A variant of this story states that Prometheus was released when Cheiron the centaur changed places with him. This refers again to the prenatal symbolism of the horse.
86. Harrison, *Themis, op. cit.*, p. 14.
87. Rose, *op. cit.*
88. Rose, *op. cit.*

89. Editor's note: The original manuscript used the word *rhabdos*. The word *caduceus* was substituted here as *rhabdos* refers to the stick used in athletic training, while *caduceus* has connotations linking its function with the healing arts.
90. Cook, *op. cit.*, Vol. 2, p. 481-482.
91. *Ibid.* p. 481.
92. Genesis 2:9-12.
93. Genesis 2:11.
94. Strong, *op. cit.*
95. Cook, *op. cit.*, Vol. 2, p. 481.
96. Jones, *op. cit.*, p. 22-23.
97. *Ibid.*, p. 98.
98. *Ibid.*, p. 46.
99. *Ibid.*, p. 78.
100. See Chapter One and my analysis of the Hymn to Zeus Diktaios.
101. Harrison, *Themis, op. cit.*, p. 194.
102. Jones, *op. cit.*, p. 29.
103. Editor's notes:
    i) 'Ellasar' may be synonymous with 'Alassa', now in Cyprus, where a Bronze Age palace was destroyed by sea-faring raiders, c. 1200 BCE.
    ii) The name 'Chedorlaomer' comes from the Hebrew words meaning 'sheaves of corn', and the name is also associated with familiar components from the Elamite language such as *kudur*, the word for 'servant'. (Wikipedia). Thus, fetal and placental elements can be seen to be combined in this name.
    iii) 'Tidal' is the name of a king involved in the battle of the Vale of Siddim, already mentioned in this chapter in connection with the story of Lot's wife.
104. Genesis 14:3.
105. Cook, *op. cit.*, Vol. 1, p. 543 ff.
106. Harrison, *Themis, op. cit.*, p. 34.
107. Editor's note: This must be assumed to be the Pausinias who is given significant lines in Plato's Symposium (385-380 BCE).
108. Harrison, *Themis, op. cit.*, p. 434.
109. Cook, *op. cit.*, Vol. 2, Part I, p. 445.
110. Jung and Kerényi, *op. cit.*, p. 14.
111. *Ibid.*, p. 24.

240 *Mythology of the Prenatal Life*

112. Editor's note: Grateful thanks to Dr. Dorian Gieseler Greenbaum, whose research yielded the following information. This etymology is footnoted to *Greek Religion*, by Walter Burkert, 1985, p. 198, and suggests that the name of the Elysian Fields, the post-mortem abode of those who had been heroic and virtuous in life, is derived from this word. In the German language journal *Glotta* (*Glotta* 39, 1960-61, pp. 208-213), Burkert wrote an article on the etymology of 'Elysion' (Greek, *Hlusion*). Burkert's argument is that Elysium (*Hlusion pedion*) is related to the Greek word *enhlusios*, and is not from a foreign name or word. *Enhlusion* is the place of impact where the lightning bolt struck. Burkert argues that this can be connected to *eleusomai* (the future tense of the verb *erchomai*, 'come', and the noun *eishlusion* is an entrance or entrance fee) which is perhaps where 'places of coming' came from. See also *'Reading' Greek Death: To the End of the Classical Period*, by Christiane Sourvinou-Inwood, OUP, 1995, p. 49, which demonstrates that Burkert's etymology has been accepted.

113. Cook, *op. cit.*, Vol. 1, p. 225.

114. Rank, Otto: *The Myth of the Birth of the Hero*.

115. Cook, *op. cit.*, Vol. 2, Part II, p. 1152-1153.

116. Rank, *op, cit.*

117. Editor's note: Although the word *chimera* has other and more specific meanings, in this context it refers to a monstrous creature comprising several different animals.

118. Rose, *op. cit.*

119. Róheim, *The Eternal Ones of the Dream*, p. 238.

120. Frazer, *op. cit.*, Vol. 1, p. 182.

121. Frazer, *op. cit.*, Vol. 6, p. 147.

122. Editor's note: The astrologically educated reader will doubtless have many more associations than described in this Appendix, which the author himself describes as incomplete.

123. Cook, *op. cit.*, Vol. 2, Part I, p. 498-499.

124. Editor's note: In astrological tradition, the Sun (ruler of the sign of Leo) is said to be 'exalted' in the sign of Aries.

125. Editor's note: The following story may clarify this connection. The Scorpion was asked by Gaia, the earth goddess, to slay the giant Orion, the hunter, who had threatened to slay all the beasts on earth. After this battle, both were immortalized by Zeus in constellations of the same name, located on opposite sides of the night sky, so eternally 'chasing' each other. The eagle is indeed associated with Zeus, and his role in the immortalizing of the Scorpion is perhaps the only allusion which makes sense of the author's inclusion of this symbolism.

126. See note 125, above.

127. This quotation and much of the material concerning the adrenal glands is taken from *The Tides of Life: The Endocrine Glands in Bodily Adjustment* by R. G. Hoskins, PhD., M.D.

128. *Ibid.*, p. 28.

129. Darrach, Henry B.: 'Up Horoscope!' *Life Magazine*, February 22, 1960.

130. Here, I employ the word 'sky' in a deliberately loose manner, since at present I am unable to describe the situation more precisely.

131. Editor's note: The prefix 'ur' derives from Old High German, and means 'proto' or 'primitive'. See http://en.wiktionary.org/wiki/ur-

132. The word 'feelings' is used in a loose sense, since we usually tend to think of feelings as either neural or emotional. Whatever they may be, I am certain they form around the original umbilical element, even though the cord has no neural equipment.

133. Editor's note: See this present volume for numerous examples of the author's detailed interpretation of Biblical symbolism in the light of this material.

134. See Harrison, *Themis: op. cit.*, pp. 291 and 295 and associated passages.

135. Editor's note: See the work of Lloyd de Mause and others on the website www.psychohistory.com for unique material which explores historical and political processes as reflecting projected and displaced perinatal and prenatal affect.

136. Frazer, J. G.: *Folklore in The Old Testament: Studies in Comparative Religion, Legend and Law.*

137. The phrase 'classical Christian picture' is used here in order to separate the priest-made religious stereotype from any possible historical substrate derived from the death of a Hebrew Prophet by crucifixion by the Romans at the instigation of the Sanhedrin.

138. Luke 23: 39-43.

www.ingramcontent.com/pod-product-compliance
Lightning Source LLC
Chambersburg PA
CBHW070557100426
42744CB00006B/312